surprised by sound

surprised

by sound

RHYME'S
INNER
WORKINGS

Roi Tartakovsky

LOUISIANA STATE UNIVERSITY PRESS
BATON ROUGE

Published by Louisiana State University Press
www.lsupress.org

Designer: Barbara Neely Bourgoyne
Typeface: Calluna

Library of Congress Cataloging-in-Publication Data
Names: Tartakovsky, Roi, author.
Title: Surprised by sound : rhyme's inner workings / Roi Tartakovsky.
Description: Baton Rouge : Louisiana State University Press, 2021. | Includes
    bibliographical references and index.
Identifiers: LCCN 2020039207 (print) | LCCN 2020039208 (ebook) | ISBN 978-0-
    8071-7475-3 (cloth) | ISBN 978-0-8071-7542-2 (pdf) | ISBN 978-0-8071-7543-9 (epub)
Subjects: LCSH: Rhyme. | Poetics. | Sound in literature.
Classification: LCC PN1059.R5 T37 2021 (print) | LCC PN1059.R5 (ebook) |
    DDC 808.1—dc23
LC record available at https://lccn.loc.gov/2020039207
LC ebook record available at https://lccn.loc.gov/2020039208

For Dara

contents

acknowledgments

This book would not have come to light if it were not for a great many people whom I am fortunate to have in my life both intellectually and personally. The project had its beginnings in my doctoral dissertation on poetry and rhyme, completed at Tel Aviv University under the generous spirit and guidance of Karen Alkalay-Gut, who has taught me so much of what I know about poetry. The interrelations between poetry and psychoanalysis, so crucial to my own thinking, were shown to me by Shirley Zisser, whom I am proud to call my teacher. Early on, I attended a graduate seminar taught by Reuven Tsur, whose impact on, and support of, this research is immeasurable. Throughout the years, Hana Wirth-Nesher has offered superb advice and direction. I am also grateful for the kind help of Noam Reisner, chair of the Department of English and American Studies. Many a time, I benefited from consultations (and even commiseration) with colleagues and friends, chief among them Milette Shamir, Yeshayahu Shen, Nir Evron, and Maya Klein. Finally, I am appreciative of the dedicated help of Hen Pinnes, my research assistant.

Outside of Tel Aviv University, I am thankful to Margaret Freeman, who made significant suggestions on an earlier version of the manuscript. Crucial to the development of my work, Perry Meisel has consistently encouraged me to articulate better and to finish articulating when the time came. The manuscript has been vastly improved by Haun Saussy, who inspired me to think of rhyme more comparatively. I owe much gratitude, also, to David Caplan, Marjorie Perloff, and Charles Bernstein for numerous chats (in person and in writing) about rhyme and related topics. I had the opportunity to present some of my ideas at the International Conference on Literature and Psychology (University of Belgrade, 2007), the "Recent Trends in Comparative Literature: Sound, Sight, and Text" colloquium (University of Maryland, 2013), the Louisville Conference for Literature and Culture since 1900 (University of Louisville, 2015), and the "New Poetries—New Poetics? Cultural and Aesthetic Transformations in American Poetry" workshop (Konstanz University, 2020). I wish to thank the organizers and participants at these events for their thought-provoking questions and comments. And, almost last but not least, James W. Long, and the entire staff at Louisiana State University Press, have been a pleasure to work with. I could not ask for a more positive first book experience.

Above all, before all and after all, I am indebted to Dara Barnat, partner in crime and life, who has enabled this work in more ways than I can say.

Thanks to the following publications that previously published some of the material included in this book:

A very early version of the section "Psychoanalyzing Rhyme: *Nachträglichkeit,*" from chapter 5, appeared as "Rhyme and Nachträglichkeit," in *Psychoanalytic Encounters: Interdisciplinary Papers in Applied Psychoanalysis,* ed. Aleksandar Dimitrijevic, Elizabeth Fox, and Murray Schwartz (Belgrade: Belgrade University, 2009), 41–49.

An early version of sections from chapters 3 and 4 appeared in "Towards a Theory of Sporadic Rhyming," *Language and Literature* 23 (2014), 101–17.

Thanks to the following publications that have kindly allowed me to include all or portions of certain works:

"Oh No" republished with permission of University of California Press, from *The Collected Poems of Robert Creeley: 1945–1975.* Copyright © 1982; permission conveyed through Copyright Clearance Center, Inc.

"Morning at the Window" and excerpt from "The Love Song of J. Alfred Prufrock" from *Collected Poems 1909–1962* by T. S. Eliot. Copyright © 1936 by Houghton Mifflin Harcourt Publishing Company, renewed 1980 by Thomas Stearns Eliot. Reprinted by permission of Houghton Mifflin Harcourt Publishing Company. Reprinted by permission of Faber and Faber Ltd. All rights reserved.

"Pertinax" by Robert Frost from the book *The Poetry of Robert Frost* edited by Edward Connery Lathem. Copyright © 1969 by Henry Holt and Company. Copyright © 1936 by Robert Frost, copyright © 1964 by Lesley Frost Ballantine. Reprinted by permission of Henry Holt and Company. All rights reserved.

"The Rose Family" by Robert Frost from the book *The Poetry of Robert Frost* edited by Edward Connery Lathem. Copyright © 1928, 1969 by Henry Holt and Company. Copyright © 1956 by Robert Frost. Reprinted by permission of Henry Holt and Company. All rights reserved.

"Firstborn" by Louise Glück (*The First Five Books of Poems*, 2007) is reprinted here by kind permission of Carcanet Press Limited, Manchester, UK.

"Firstborn" from *The First Four Books Of Poems* by Louise Glück. Copyright © 1968, 1971, 1972, 1973, 1974, 1975, 1976, 1977, 1978, 1979, 1980, 1985, 1995 by Louise Glück. Used by permission of HarperCollins Publishers.

Excerpt from Lyn Hejinian, *The Cell.* Copyright © 1992 by Lyn Hejinian. Used by permission of the author.

"Peace for Awhile" from *Poems 1934–1969* © 1970 by David Ignatow. Published by Wesleyan University Press and reprinted with permission.

"The Death of the Ball Turret Gunner" from *The Complete Poems* by Randall Jarrell. Copyright © 1969, renewed 1997 by Mary von S. Jarrell. Reprinted by permission of Farrar, Straus and Giroux. Reprinted by permission of Faber and Faber Ltd.

"On the Death of Friends in Childhood" from *Collected Poems* by Donald Justice, copyright © 2004 by Donald Justice. Used by permission of Alfred A. Knopf, an imprint of the Knopf Doubleday Publishing Group, a division of Penguin Random House LLC. Used by kind permission of Carcanet Press Limited, Manchester, UK. All rights reserved.

John Logan, "Two Brothers: Two Saltimbanques," from *Collected Poems*. Copyright © 1989 by The John Logan Literary Estate, Inc. Reprinted with the permission of The Permissions Company, LLC on behalf of BOA Editions, Ltd. boaeditions.org.

Excerpt from "Jinglejangle" is reprinted from *Sleeping with the Dictionary* by Harryette Mullen, copyright © 2002 by The Regents of the University of California. Reprinted by permission of University of California Press.

"The Dust Storm, or I've Got Texas in My Lungs" by Ogden Nash from *The Private Dining Room*. Copyright © 1953 by Ogden Nash. Reprinted by permission of Curtis Brown, Ltd. Reprinted by permission of Welbeck Non-Fiction Limited (previously Carlton Books Ltd.).

Howard Nemerov, "The Common Wisdom," from *Trying Conclusions: New and Selected Poems 1961–1991*. Copyright © 1991 by The University of Chicago. Reprinted with the permission of the Howard Nemerov Literary Estate.

Excerpts from *For Paul and Other Poems* are reprinted from *Lorine Niedecker: Collected Works,* copyright © 2002 by The Regents of the University of California. Reprinted by Permission of University of California Press.

surprised by sound

Introduction

At Tel Aviv University, each year on Yom HaShoah, Holocaust Remembrance Day, a different Holocaust survivor speaks in front of the university, giving testimony. Members of the university community come together, carefully listening to a very personal story that speaks to a history that is in many respects shared. One year, the survivor recited her devastating story in perfectly and consistently rhymed couplets. Some listeners, so consumed by the narrative, did not consciously register the rhyming—nor, I imagine, would they want to. Such attention to rhyme could be perceived as inappropriate, focusing on a tangential stylistic issue that shrinks in comparison to the enormity of the horrific events described. But others seemed genuinely perplexed by the rhyming, even aghast.

To my ear, and to some others' as well, the testimony that year was chilling not only because of the experiences the survivor described but also because their organization in rhyme seemed to confer upon them an unfitting embellishment, perhaps even a playfulness or lightness. Such is the effect that rhyme may have today, when we hear its line-ending, euphonious chiming or its associations with light verse or doggerel, both at odds with the dark content of the testimony.

Yet there are other ways to think about rhyme. In the seventeenth century, for example, playwright and poet John Dryden was involved in a lively dispute about the desirability of rhyme for the stage and, through Neander, one of the four interlocutors in his "Essay of Dramatic Poesy," argued that rhyme is particularly well suited for tragedies. If comedies imitate common people, tragedies represent noble plots and characters that are "exalted above the level of common converse" and should therefore be rendered in "heroic rhyme," which is "the noblest kind of modern verse" (72). According to this line of thought, using rhyme to discuss atrocities is not disharmonious but quite fitting.

In contemporary times, though, the heroic and dignified connotations of rhyme have almost entirely given way to connotations of the inflated; "artificial" in the good sense has become artificial in the bad sense. And so rhyme, in the context of the autobiographical survival story with its claim for authenticity, becomes especially disturbing, standing in an uneasy and ironic relation to the spirit of the text it occupies.

But there may be another explanation, besides irony, for the chilling effect of rhyme in that case. Precisely because rhyme seems out of place, displayed in a context where it is least expected, it is foregrounded. Its foregrounding offers the listener a particularly acute encounter with rhyme, a kind of hearing rhyme for the first time. As such, the encounter presents the listener with rhyme in a type of pure form, detached from a web of expectations that prepare us for it and from a conventionalized system that absorbs it (say, the prosody of a regularly rhyming poem). Thus, something of the structure of rhyme becomes audible, available to consciousness, or else operates subliminally. The device is laid bare, as it were, and the structure of rhyme speaks with every new rhyme instance, realized in its temporality of back-and-forth and displaying the odd chiming of seemingly unrelated words, the mix of magic and chant, the puncturing of the prosaic sense, the rhythmic thumping at the end of each phrase, the slight shift in pronunciation to ensure rhyme.

This is a study of that kind of rhyme, one that can lead us not only to hear rhyme's familiar operations but also to discover new ones. Though rhyme is something very small (materially), it is also very big (perceptually, conceptually). Part of its force is signaling contradictory positions: light and serious, comic and tragic, and much more, both in between and outside of these polarities. In all cases, rhyme is laden with rich poetic potential to awaken, evoke, suggest, invite, sway, sooth, surprise, startle. A central question in this book is how the structure of rhyme makes it such a source of poetic production and enduring fascination.

My way of getting at the question of how rhyme works is by introducing a distinction between two kinds of rhyme: the more expected, recurring, and foreknown *systematic* rhyme, and its counterpart, which I call *sporadic* rhyme. Though less studied, sporadic rhyme is in fact more varied in manifestation and possibility. As rhyme that is not systematized or expected, sporadic rhyme is any rhyme that appears in a form in which rhyme does not occur normally (as in most English free verse) and also any rhyme that falls outside of the typical end rhymes in poetic forms that do employ rhyme (as the sonnet). Just as the exception to the rule sheds light on the rule, my hypothesis is that sporadic rhyme, as any rhyme that occurs apart from an organizing and regularized rhyme scheme, sheds light on conventional manifestations of rhyme precisely because it is not conventional. Sporadic rhyme is prototypical rhyme.

My definition of sporadic rhyme as rhyme that is nonrecurring, nonsystematic, and not part of the poem's prosody tilts the orientation of the investigation from the historical to the functional. My interest is therefore not to present a history of rhyme, or even of sporadic rhyme, nor to insist on the newness of sporadic rhyme. In fact, as chapter 1 demonstrates, the designation "sporadic rhyme" is emphatically *not* historical, because we encounter sporadic rhyming across different periods of the history of rhyme usage, all the way to contemporary free verse poets. For example, we will see that sporadic rhyme can coexist with systematic rhyme in the same poem, as when Dryden inserts a triplet amid couplets, or when Gerard Manley Hopkins includes internal rhymes in addition to end rhymes that form the rhyme scheme. Moreover, before rhyme ever became systematic in English, it was used sporadically, only gradually making its way into the systematic role that became the norm around Geoffrey Chaucer's time.

This study makes reference to rhyming practices in other languages when relevant, but its topic is rhyming in English-language poetry. Thus, it leaves out alliterative verse and most dialect forms, though it does deal with forms some would consider adjacent to poetry, like rap. English

rhymed, blank, and free verse poetry from 1500 onward is also a subset
of the longer and broader European poetic tradition, with its many influences and transformations. Nonetheless, though tracing these would be
highly interesting, it likewise is outside the scope of the current project.

Studying rhyme within its language and the language's prosody, and
within its literary tradition, is paramount, because rhyme is somewhat
different in different languages. The comparison between English and
French is a case in point. Derek Attridge provides several reasons why the
phonetic and phonological characteristics of the language make French
rhyme "relatively unobtrusive" compared to English rhyme (*Moving Words*
57–62). For example, since stress (accent) in French is not fixed to specific
syllables from the outset, as in English, but occurs with less force and
greater freedom, depending more on the location of the word within
a phrase, the rhythm of the alexandrine of classical French verse tends
to dominate the natural rhythms of the language less than in English's
accentual(-syllabic) verse. In English, rhyme will mark as even more
prominent rhythmic patterns of regularity that are already established
throughout the line, while in French, end rhyme is essential for the perception of the line itself as metrical, "a vital part of the metrical organization" (58–59).

This has significant consequences, as Attridge goes on to show, for the
status of rhyme in the two languages' verse drama, where the relation
between the characters' speech and natural speech is an issue of great
interest. English dramatic verse has been inclined, throughout much of
its history, to drop the rhyme in order to combat the sometimes too-
obtrusive rhythms, whereas in French drama, such blank verse is very
rare. Therefore, my claims in this book, about the enduring power of
rhyme and the category of sporadic rhyme as an index of this enduring
power, are worth exploring in French and other languages as well, but the
precise definition and functioning of sporadic rhyme would need to be
theorized, together with rhyme itself, from within the characteristics of
the language and the subsequent history of its verse forms.

Within English-language poetry, no single poet has exhausted the
virtually illimitable poetic possibilities of sporadic rhyme, and there are
poets who use sporadic rhyme sparingly but quantitatively provide invalu-

able examples of usage. My ultimate focus, therefore, while restricted to English poetry, is not exclusively on any individual poet, poetic school, or historical period. While I recognize the complexities and inevitable shortcomings involved in casting such a wide net of investigation, my hope is that a net less bound by delineations of periodicity is able to capture something recurrent and of value. If the ultimate goal is to gesture toward uncovering the secrets of its enduring power, rhyme should be listened to across historical periods.

Though in principle they are not historically bound, many of the poems I have found most fruitful to discuss are ones that occur after the presumptive loss of the importance of rhyme, with the popularity of forms loosely called free verse. It is no accident that many of the richest poetic examples of sporadic rhyming come from twentieth-century poets who are sensitive to sound and choose to write in the various modes of nonmetrical poetry. One explanation is that sporadic rhyme reaches its maximal markedness when it is the only such rhyme in the poem, and free verse poems are typically devoid of systematic rhyme.

It also is the case that, historically, some of the later poets I discuss are at a unique moment: they are now at a safer distance from the initial modernist revolt against rhyme and meter, a distance that allows them to allow rhyme to reenter poems effectively (and sporadically). Moreover, they have the entire history of rhyme, especially its systematic, dominant forms, behind them. Harryette Mullen, a contemporary poet whose work is informed as much by the Black Arts Movement as by experimental language-centered writing, is a case in point. In an interview, Mullen spoke of the function of rhyme in her 1995 book: "I also wanted to suggest, with *Muse & Drudge*, that rhyme is too powerful a tool to be abandoned to advertising, greeting cards, or even platinum rap recordings. I hoped to reclaim it" (*Cracks* 206).

The desire to reclaim rhyme, the recognition that rhyme is too fundamental to poetry and too rife with possibilities to be forgone or forgotten, is manifested in the tremendously varied usages of rhyme one finds in much contemporary poetry. More often than not, the kind of rhyme found to be resounding is not systematic, traditional end rhyme but sporadic rhyme. A bonus of the focus on sporadic rhyme is therefore that it reveals the ways in which rhyme still resonates in modern and contemporary poetry, for poets of different schools and orientations.

Rhyme, whether sporadic or systematic, is a sonic device of poetry and so it inevitably involves questions of sound, of hearing, and of listening. Recognizing that hearing rhyme is a prerequisite for its poetic operation, chapter 1 addresses some of the difficulties of hearing rhyme today. It also demonstrates the basic distinction between sporadic and systematic rhyme and fleshes out the (a)historical status of the former. Then, and in keeping with the objective of uncovering the mechanisms of rhyme through the prism of sporadic rhyme, the book is organized around a host of attributes or features of rhyme. Each of the four subsequent chapters takes up a pair of seemingly antithetical rhyme attributes as a strategy to frame the prolific and paradoxical nature of rhyme: rigid/pleasurable, organizing/disruptive, accidental/motivated, progressive/regressive.

Chapter 2, which tackles the first pair, rigid/pleasurable, starts with the rudimentary fact that rhyme's first word asks for a complement and limits the options for what that complement can be. This limiting feature of rhyme is the basis for its use in demonstrations of linguistic copiousness, exhibiting creativity and taking back control of the very fetters by which one is bound. The dynamic of linguistic dexterity is used in the chapter as one explanation for the promise rhyme offers to hip-hop, where it reaches unparalleled levels of intricacy. But rhyme also is as pleasurable as it is rigid, at least as far as poets' declarations are concerned; the notion of harmonious rhyme as "sweet" is a complementary metaphor to its fetter-like constraints. Pleasure is the flip side of rigidity: the confined rigidness turns into soothing regularity, everything harmoniously fitting into place. The operation of quite a few sporadically rhymed poems, like ones that employ monorhyme, become intelligible (audible?) once they are understood as operating in the liminal space between the stifling and the pleasurable.

Chapter 3 addresses the antithetical pairing of organizing/disruptive. The organizational is one of the oldest functions of rhyme, grouping the linguistic material into stanzas by creating rhyme schemes. It is the hallmark of systematic rhyme, though a misguided conflation of systematic rhyme with all rhyme has occluded its flip side, namely its potential to disorganize. Sporadic rhyme shows the poetic potential of destabilizing the rhyme-as-organizing paradigm. In an irregular ode, for example, the ever-changing shifts in proximity between rhyming partners facilitate poetic goals such as signaling a shift in a relationship to a given word or creating suspense and differentiation.

Moreover, in poems in which even the fact of end rhyming is not consistent, the rigid and well-delineated structure of rhyme is thrown unexpectedly into the poem and becomes more disruptive (or irruptive) than organizing. When situated strategically in the middle of a line or across two stanzas, rhyme can subversively undercut the integrity of the line or stanza unit. When situated at or close to the end of the poem, sporadic rhyme is able to mark that ending while avoiding the conclusive ring that for some poets resounds too authoritatively.

Chapter 4 is dedicated to the accidental/motivated pair. Rhymes stand out from other words, exhibiting a mysterious sonic fit. Their fit tends to elicit in readers an interpretive desire to uncover rhyme's reason—the reason that two seemingly unrelated words would be rhyming partners. And yet we know that the relationship between rhyming words, except in some exceptional cases, is simply accidental. The duplicity of motivated/ accidental is there in every rhyme, but when a poem contains no more than a few dispersed rhymes (seemingly) randomly presented, the very appearance of the rhyme in the poem partakes of this duplicity. Therefore, in this chapter I look at poems in which sporadic rhyme entices readers to question and interpret the appearance of rhyme, or the semantic implications of rhyme itself. In some cases, rhyme overwhelms its own words and stretches the semantic possibilities of the poem. In others, rhyme collects words together and turns them into a conceptual layer within the text, a layer that achieves distinction and operates vis-à-vis other thematic concerns.

The final pair, explored in chapter 5, is regressive/progressive and suggests a new and admittedly speculative understanding of what rhyme is, based on its temporality. For this, I rely on the fact that rhyme is backwards-oriented: it pulls us back not simply to older traditions of poetry that rhymed systematically, or to our older selves (with the association, now prevalent, between rhyme and children's language games), but literally and phenomenologically back within a text. A recognition of rhyme inevitably presences the past of the text. For the reader, the rhyming situation is one in which a word that is part of the text's past is brought up through its conjunction with a word in the text's present. What is unique about sporadic rhyme is that *any* word in the poem can potentially be part of a rhyme, but we will only find out after the fact, when it is "too late"; the second rhyming partner turns the earlier word into its rhyming partner.

This backwards-looking, regressive temporality appears in many arenas of both everyday life and literature (most notably in narrative), since, as Søren Kierkegaard says, we live forward and understand backwards. Still, rhyme has a special claim to this temporality. And this temporality is not only a matter of cognitive processes; it occupies a central place in Sigmund Freud's theory of the operation of the unconscious, which makes it possible to suggest a definition of rhyme as an *enactment,* or realization in language of a temporal structure of the unconscious. With this, the book puts forth a possible answer to a question that intrigues from the outset: How can rhyme, a materially small linguistic phenomenon turned poetic device, come to do and mean so much?

Finally, within the performativity of poetic language more broadly, I go on to pursue the curious and difficult coupling of rhyme and trauma, motivated by the fact that Freud himself saw trauma as the grain of this larger temporal logic. I underscore the implications of isomorphism between rhyme and trauma and demonstrate how something of the specificity of the structure of trauma, in diluted form, is preserved in rhyme.

I

Hearing and Listening to Rhyme

If negotiating with linguistic constraints and literary conventions comes with the territory of writing poetry, rhyme occupies a great part of that territory. Certainly, in the case of English, it is difficult to overstate the association between rhyme and poetry, or the significance of rhyme to poetry. This association is attested to in rhetoric by rhyme's synecdochic or metonymic substitution for poetry itself. Rhyme-as-poem is a prevalent trope throughout much English-language poetry and is nowhere more evident than in William Shakespeare's ending of Sonnet 17: "You should live twice, in it and in my rhyme."

In practice, rhyme's prevalence is attested to by the overwhelming number of rhymed poems written by generations of poets. Of course, rhyme is not the only sound device, nor the earliest in the history of English poetry. A perfect or full rhyme is, in fact, one of numerous poetic sound devices, including assonance, alliteration, consonance, and many forms of partial rhymes. But it is the more encompassing member among most of these weaker or partial sound relations because full rhyme typically requires a correspondence of both the vowel *and* the following consonant sounds of the last stressed syllable of each word.[1] Assonance was never used systematically in English verse, partial rhyme is best appreciated as a subset of full rhyme, and alliteration, while carrying its own historical connotations of Anglo-Saxon prosody, seems, at least in poetic consciousness, more distant and dimmed today than rhyme.[2] Rhyme, both historically and phonetically, is set up to stand out in the soundscape of the poem or of poetry.

As prevalent as rhyme is (or *was*—a question I will get to momentarily), it is easy to forget that rhyme's entry into English poetry was a gradual process and one that—in spite of scholarly interest—remains somewhat murky. Murkier yet is the larger question of the historical origin of rhyme itself. Henry Lanz details some of the theories and approaches, concluding that though "speculations on the historic origin of rime have been numerous and sometimes highly ingenious," the history ultimately is quite impossible to pinpoint, for "there is no first rime, as there is no first word uttered by man" (106, 131).

One approach to the historical question is to try to trace the route of rhyme from elsewhere into English, with Chinese, Arabic, and old Irish usually included with Latin as potential candidates. Since Latin is of such strong influence on English in this respect, the history of its own relationship with rhyme is particularly relevant. Arthur Melville Clark traces the emergence of rhyme in Latin within the context of relaxing the quantitative prosodic rules that were, from the beginning, "an alien imposition on Latin which had naturally strong accents," as well as the emergence of Christian Latin literature that for various reasons employed rhyme (156–57). In particular, the Christian hymn, which came to rely more and more on rhyme, is widely considered to be a major contributor to the dissemination of rhyme. Michael McKie notes the "seductive power" of the early hymns, and their creators' desire to appeal to the uneducated, and remarks that "the reasons for rhyme's adoption by the Church (its popularity, ease of use, and emotive appeal) in part explain the recurring hostility to rhyme, from the Renaissance onwards, owing to its supposed 'vulgarity'" ("Origins" 824, 831). And M. L. Gasparov tells the story of the emergence of rhyme in medieval Latin verse as, at least in part, a gradual migration of like endings from rhetorical prose, where they had always been used to emphasize parallel syntactic constructions, since these tend to end in identical flexions (97). Hence, what was an ornamental and occasional component of some prose becomes a required and rigid part of verse.

There also is a linguistic, structural explanation of what is accepted as a prerequisite for the deployment of rhyme as a significant device in a given language. William Harmon writes that "proper rhyme is impossible, as a rule, in a synthetic-suffixal language and will not emerge as a stylistic device of any importance until the language has migrated far enough toward being analytic-prefixal to yield a robust stock of important words that either end with a stressed syllable or are simply monosyllabic" (367). Note that Harmon is talking not just about any rhyme but about rhyme that acts as a stylistic device of importance, rhyme that is able to fulfill a prosodic, structural function in verse. With regards to timing, Harmon says, "no Indo-European language reached such a condition before AD 1000" (367). McKie writes that, in English, "only by the time of Chaucer did rhyming approach the exactness of the early modern period," though "Middle English verse from the later thirteenth century onwards was regularly rhymed" ("Origins" 821).[3] Indeed, as a look at any poetry anthology will show, from Geoffrey Chaucer onward, rhyme reigned supreme in English poetry, and one would be hard-pressed to find a major English poet from the fifteenth through the nineteenth centuries who did not employ rhyme.

The employment of rhyme in English verse rests on (or participates in the creation of) the psychological reality of rhyme, or rather *rime*—the part of the syllable that includes the vowel and the subsequent consonant. The three components of a syllable made up of an initial consonant, a vowel, and a final consonant (C-V-C) are experienced as divided or grouped together in a specific way, namely C and V-C (the latter is the rime). When English speakers are given a series of nonword syllables and then asked to repeat them, the errors they tend to make in the repetition reveal the division within the syllable. Thus, speakers will sometimes take the initial C and combine it with the V-C of another nonword, but the V-C unit tends to remain glued together and will only rarely be divided into its parts (Treiman and Danis).

The syllable in English is thus understood to be coded as onset (C) and rime (V-C), and there is now evidence to suggest that this is not the case for all languages. For example, in a series of experiments with speakers of Korean, researchers have found that, for them, possibly because of the

difference in the availability of consonants at the beginning and end of
syllables, a C-V-C syllable is actually experienced as divided into C-V and
C. The rime is therefore "not an integral psychological unit, as far as (real)
native speakers of Korean are concerned," and in this regard the researchers bring up the fact that Korean, like quite a few other languages, does
not have a tradition of poetic rhyme (Yoon and Derwing 229–31).[4]

Syllabic perception, linguistic changes, and literary history all coincide to prime English for rhyme. Of course, this is not to suggest that
rhymeless poems were not being written, some by major poets. John
Milton's strong position against rhyme (specifically the heroic couplet),
expressed in the note attached to the blank verse *Paradise Lost,* is perhaps
the most famous example of antirhyme sentiments in English. I discuss
Milton's position and that of others later, but it is worth noting here that
in spite of his misgivings about rhyme for epic poetry, Milton not only
used rhyme extensively elsewhere but also had to defend his position of
not using rhyme when he made such a choice. Walt Whitman is a marked
American counterexample, but the early resistance to accepting his writing as poetry at all attests to the defining position that rhyme, together
with meter, held throughout a long period of English verse history.

The advent and tremendous expansion of free verse challenged rhyme
in significant ways but, as I hope to show, did not at all eliminate the use
of rhyme. Though it is an issue of heated debate and controversy, implicated in cultural, philosophical, and aesthetic concerns, it is safe to say
that the vast majority of English poets have employed rhyme vastly.

And not just vastly but also *systematically.* At least from Chaucer onward, we find rhyme as a prosodic device in English verse. Rhyme is found
in innumerable poetic forms and genres, where its use is replicated and
often defines the form itself, whether that form was imported from elsewhere, was modified, or was created in English. Reading any number of
Alexander Pope's long works in heroic couplets, one comes quickly to
expect the rhyming pairs at the end of the line. Reading a Shakespearean sonnet, one knows or learns to expect where the rhymes will fall,
the rhyme scheme scheming the logic of the entire sonnet, as is the case
with Petrarchan and Spenserian sonnet forms and their respective rhyme
schemes. The reading of the quatrains of Alfred, Lord Tennyson's *In Me-*

moriam is accompanied by the recurrence of the envelope rhyme /abba/, just as the reading of Edward Fitzgerald's translation of *Rubaiyat,* Omar Khayyam's quatrains, is accompanied by the recurrence of the /aaxa/ scheme. Similarly, the reading of most realizations of what Derek Attridge (*Rhythms of English Poetry*) has called the "underlying four-beat rhythm" (nursery rhymes, ballads, hymns) is accompanied by the recurrence of /aabb/, /abab/, or /xaxa/ schemes.

In each of these cases, and in so many others, rhyme is systematized, appearing at the end of the line and following a discernible, often predictable, often repeated, pattern. Either within the poem or within the genre or poetic form, rhyme recurs and is institutionalized. Already in 1589, George Puttenham is able not only to list different rhyme schemes but also to start assigning differential effects to each of them, one being "vulgar," another "pleasant" (84–91). Rhyme's systematic employment marks one of rhyme's central functions, the schematic or organizational function—in Puttenham's terms, "a band given to every verse in a staffe, so as none fall out alone or uncoupled," like the band provided by a mason to fasten the bricks of a house (89). Even today, thinking about rhyme defaults to its systematic variant or schematic function: "rhyme" generally means end rhyme that one finds forming a discernible gestalt or rhyme scheme.

Returning to the historical narrative, it is no less significant to note that the era of systematization was preceded by an era of sporadic use. Though rhyme's dissemination into English verse in a systematic way is viewed as starting in 1400, McKie notes "the sporadic but slowly increasing use of rhyme in Old English verse over three centuries" ("Origins" 821), and specifically describes how the rhyme in Latin church hymns affected Anglo-Saxon versifiers, who at first used it "for merely ornamental purposes," and then increasingly more, though still occasionally rather than prosodically (829). This occasional use preceded the Norman Conquest, which itself encouraged rhyme because of the linguistic changes it introduced into English.[5]

A similar situation has been described in other languages too. For example, Benjamin Hrushovski (Harshav) shows that systematic rhyme has been in existence in Hebrew verse for more than 1,500 years, but he finds rhymes that lack a structural function as early as in the Bible (722,

738). Rhyme may thus long precede its systematic employment, and the process of its gradual migration into the prosodic system depends on outside influences and the characteristics of the language. When rhyme is outside the prosodic system and occurs sporadically, it does not fulfill an organizational function, and this kind of rhyme is oftentimes seen favorably as benign ornamentation, or negatively as a dangerous distraction to be avoided, two characterizations that resonate in responses to much later manifestations of rhyme as well.

RHYME LOSES (OR LOOSENS) ITS FOOTING?

Before it became systematic and prevalent, rhyme was sporadic. But what about after it became systematic and prevalent? Has rhyme all but disappeared today? Had it disappeared with the advent of modernism?

It is easy to equate modern and contemporary poetry with a rejection of meter and rhyme, but while this is not entirely wrong, it is not exactly correct, either. Certainly the practice of *systematic* rhyme has diminished in tandem with the advent of free verse. But to the systematic stage of rhyme abundance one needs to add the postsystematic one. Contrary to popular belief, free verse and rhyme are not mutually exclusive. Looking at modern European poets of various languages, Gasparov, for one, finds not a unanimous elimination of rhyme but rather "a competition between renewed rhyme and complete rhymelessness" (280). One trend, shared by both English and Russian (but not French and German) poets, is to accept as legitimate more kinds of rhyme based on consonance (English) and assonance (Russian), rather than just full rhyme, with Emily Dickinson's slant rhymes a precedent (Gasparov 279–80).[6] Loosening the phonetic exactitude of rhyme is certainly one avenue open to poets who wish to rely on the power of rhyme while lessening its rigidity, and it has been used by poets as varied as Dickinson and William Butler Yeats, though I am more interested in another possibility: changing not the rhyme but its mode of use; employing full rhymes but in a different way.

A close examination of some of the pronouncements about rhyme around the time that free verse was being debated reveals a nuanced approach. First, without a doubt, one can identify resistance to rhyme, never less ambiguous than in William Carlos Williams's words: "Very early I began to question whether to rhyme and decided: No" (26). In 1917, T. S. Eliot said that "excessive devotion to rhyme has thickened the modern ear" ("Reflections" 188). Ezra Pound, too, in "Affirmations: As for Imagisme," writes that "emotion is an organizer . . . also of audible forms," but he is quick to leave rhyme out: "Emotion also creates patterns of timbre. But one 'discards rhyme,' not because one is incapable of rhyming *neat, fleet, sweet, meet, treat, eat, feet,* but because there are certain emotions or energies which are not to be represented by the over-familiar devices or patterns; just as there are certain 'arrangements of form' that cannot be worked into dados" (354–55).

For Eliot, Pound, and others, systematic rhyme is no longer a viable option because of a desire for newness and a rejection of artificiality, sweetness, overfamiliarity, and mechanical rigidity, which—though inherent in rhyme always—were salient in the ways they understood it to have been used in the past. But unlike Williams, Eliot was unwilling to advocate a simple wholesale rejection of rhyme. Eliot's vision of free verse, so the story goes, was inspired by French vers libre and specifically by Jules Laforgue, whom he was reading as an undergraduate at Harvard. Laforgue, in turn, was inspired by the free verse of Whitman, whom he was translating just as he was developing his vers libre. (In 1886, Laforgue published both his translations of Whitman and his first free verse poems.)[7]

Rhyme is an interesting element in this cross-linguistic influence. While Whitman's *Leaves of Grass* showed an avoidance of rhyme, Laforgue's example showed the possibility of "rhymed free verse," a verse that takes liberties with rhyme (for instance, ignoring the traditional requirement to alternate masculine and feminine rhymes, or rhyming singulars with plurals) but does not necessarily forego rhyme altogether. Rhymes can still come at the end of lines, but rhyme schemes are no longer "the sole source of stanzas"; rather, they are "as much in search of definition as other structural elements" (Scott 176–77, 204–5). Perhaps by way of Laforgue's example, then, Eliot, makes the following assertion: "And this liberation from rhyme might be as well a liberation *of* rhyme. Freed from its exacting task of supporting lame verse, it could be applied with greater effect where it is most needed" ("Reflections" 189).[8]

Eliot thus opens the door not just to rhymes that are more phonetically flexible (partial rhymes) but also to phonetically perfect rhymes that will be dispersed in strategic places within the verse. Donald Wesling adds to this idea and claims that free verse "displays modernity's exposure of the rhyme device in the fullest way" (*Chances of Rhyme* 51). Especially promising for anyone interested in rhyme in its postsystematic stage is Wesling's claim that if we "listen for rhyme and rhyme-related parallelism in much free verse, we will be amazed at the richness and variety of what we hear" (95–96). Naturally—and this is the point of Wesling's historical perspective—rhyme has changed: "In an age like the present, which distrusts teleological effects, rhyme, as affording the ring of authority and conclusiveness, will be felt inappropriate; other, less emphatic types of rhyme will be revived or invented" (129). Rhyme, I contend, has not disappeared, but its mode of employment has changed. Our somewhat impoverished habits of listening to the poem's sound, coupled with this change, have by now rendered rhyme less audible, though not less crucial.

Rhyme's bad rap, the hostility to rhyme which one associates with Pound and Williams and Charles Olson (but which far predates them), has endured well beyond the early days of modernism. In 1972, X. J. Kennedy proclaimed, "To write in meter and rime these days is to give yourself a permanently suspect credit rating" (206). And in 1979, Paul Fussell scrutinized three anthologies of modern poetry, published in the 1960s and 1970s, and found "an attitude toward rhyme as a formal device which can be described only as a programmatic hostility" (150).[9] There is significant resistance to rhyme today, too, and it seems safe to say that by an overwhelming margin, mainstream written contemporary poetry is not rhymed. But, again, this is only true if we take "not rhymed" to mean "not *systematically* rhymed." There are many other formations of rhyme, in use today and also in the past, that can be uncovered if listened to carefully and sympathetically. What falls under the heading of those other formations is what I term *sporadic rhyme.*

SPORADIC RHYME

Sporadic rhyme is any uncharacteristic, unconventional, or unexpected instance of rhyme; any rhyme outside of a discernible rhyme scheme is sporadic. Sporadic rhyme stands out and asks that we notice it.[10] Mani-

festations of sporadic rhyme abound, and this category, defined in contradistinction to systematic rhyme, is paradoxically larger than its more
prevalent counterpart, though considerably less studied. A single rhyme
in an otherwise nonrhyming free verse poem would be an example of
sporadic rhyme, as would any rhyme at all in blank verse. Any inconsistent internal rhyme in any poetic form that has end rhymes as part of its
generic repertoire also would be sporadic rhyme, whether these internal
rhyming words occur within the same line or across lines. Or a poem may
have a few scattered sporadic rhymes, unevenly distributed throughout
it. Finally, a poem can rhyme quite consistently at the end of each of its
lines, but in a way so intricate that it does not form a scheme per se, as in
the tradition of the irregular ode in English or in the style of the French
practitioners of vers libre (most notably Laforgue), whom Eliot imitated.
In all of these examples, rhyme exists outside of a fully systematic rhyme
scheme and is therefore to be considered sporadic.[11]

Sporadic rhyme refers to the mode of rhyme's dissemination in the
text, not to its phonetic qualities, and so there could be both full and partial sporadic rhymes just as there are full and partial systematic rhymes.
Still, sporadic rhyme here almost always means full (exact) rhyme because,
especially if it is the only rhyme in a poem or the only rhyme amid other
partial sound devices, it needs the full force of phonetic exactitude in
order to resound. There is, in that sense, an inverse relation between
the degree of systematicity and the degree of phonetic overlap between
words. A weak overlap (say, nothing more than a similar consonant somewhere in the middle of both words) would only be noticeable if it occurs
regularly. In order to make a single instance stand out, it would need to
be phonetically strong.

There really are no typical examples of sporadic rhyme, since it is rhyme
that by definition is atypical. Theoretically, at least, it is entirely particular
to the poem at hand and is best studied within the context of the poem.
Here is one example from the first stanza of Ruth Stone's poem "Incarna-
tion" (underlining indicates the rhyming I am calling attention to):

Every day a woman stands in her kitchen
and listens to a bird.

It is the voice of her dead husband,
only now he has <u>wings</u> and <u>sings</u>
to another female sitting on a nest. (14)

The stanza, made up of five lines and two sentences, has a single rhyme
in its penultimate line: *wings* : *sings*. The stanza has not internally generated an expectation for that rhyme, nor does that expectation come from
outside the stanza or poem, since there is no familiar poetic form that has
four nonrhyming lines and then an internal rhyme in its fifth line. And
yet, in spite of this lack of preparedness, or perhaps because of it, *wings*
and *sings*, to my ear at least, resonates powerfully. The sonic markedness of rhyme itself, together with its unexpectedness, together with the
proximity between the rhyming words, creates favorable conditions for it
to stand out. Moreover, the rhyming *wings* : *sings* becomes, in this short
stanza, an actualization of the various references to sound (*listens, voice,
singing*); as an irruption of the sonic, rhyme itself takes wing and sings.
Made up of a noun (*wings*) and a verb (*sings*), both of which refer to the
husband-turned-bird, the rhyme itself comes, in these lines, not just to
refer to but also somehow to signal the husband and the bird. As such, the
stanza comes to associate the husband/bird with rhyme itself, creating a
kind of sonic and conceptual overlay against the background of the other,
nonrhyming words.

Ruth Stone's example, as a free verse poet, is emblematic of how sporadic rhyme becomes empirically prominent in twentieth-century poetries. It is exactly when rhyme is no longer taken as part of the definition
of what poetry is that a set of effects, latent in every rhyme, reveal themselves. The investigation of sporadic rhyme in the chapters that follow
encompasses poems by numerous poets in addition to Stone, of various
poetic styles and concerns. Most of the poems analyzed are written by
post-Victorian twentieth-century, or even twenty-first-century, poets,
including Robert Creeley, Robert Frost, T. S. Eliot, W. B. Yeats, Howard
Nemerov, May Swenson, Lyn Hejinian, Sylvia Plath, Louise Glück, Harryette Mullen, Donald Justice, Wallace Stevens, Lorine Niedecker, Theodore Roethke, David Ignatow, Kay Ryan, John Logan, and Randall Jarrell.
Even a cursory look at this list immediately shows that it is host to poets

of vastly different poetic orientations, but that is precisely the point: the use of sporadic rhyme crosses poetic lines.

It is tautological to state that rhyme is indispensable for poets who emphatically work within a rhyming tradition, from the older poets all the way to contemporary New Formalist poets. There also are the special cases in contemporary poetry where systematic rhyme comes to inform whole projects, like Derek Walcott's *Omeros,* a book in terza rima. But many of the poets who do not employ systematically rhyming forms and genres (such as sonnets, ballad stanzas, or couplets) nevertheless employ sporadic rhyme.

American poetry of the past several decades is characterized by a sectarian split between what is roughly considered mainstream and that which is avant-garde, with the avant-garde associated with the writing-centered and the mainstream with poetry that is narrative in nature and relies on, rather than destabilizes, reference. Rhyme is a viable option for both of these camps, and for many outside of these designations. And so sporadic rhyme is employed by poets who are engaged in formal innovation and experimentation, like Hejinian and Mullen, and by poets who belong to the tradition of free verse and who remain attuned to sound, like Swenson or Stone. In some cases, rhyme plays a salient role in the oeuvre of a poet, as with Ryan, Niedecker, or Creeley, and sometimes it peppers a poet's work, as in the cases of Nemerov, Glück, and Reginald Shepherd. Even poets who rhyme systematically employ the unexpected sporadic rhyme, like Yeats, who includes the odd internal rhyme, or Frost, who experiments with monorhyme. Certainly in poets who write poems that are not in closed form in any strict sense but who retain some affiliation with form, we find islands of tremendously effective uses of rhyme, as in Plath or the Robert Lowell of *Life Studies.* This is true in different ways both for poets for whom the sound threatens to take over sense, like Stevens, and for poets whose sense seems more self-evident, like Logan.

SPORADIC RHYME OLD AND NEW

Sporadic rhyme is a way for poets to tap into the extraordinary poetic potential of rhyme without resorting to the old ways of rhyme schemes. It is the rhyme of choice for a significantly varied number of twentieth-century poets—"for *most* American poets now, the only kind we can use," wrote Burt in 2011 (65). But it is crucial to realize that the two types of rhyme, sporadic and systematic, are not fully separable historically. In spite of the fact that it reaches an artistic peak in and after modernism, sporadic rhyme is ultimately not a historical designation. Specifically, sporadic rhyme is not synonymous with modern rhyme; it is also found, sporadically, throughout the systematic periods of rhyme. In a recent essay, Simon Jarvis sings the praises of rhymes that fall outside of what he calls the "*metricization* of rhyme" in dominant rhyme theories. These "fugitive," "buried," "unfixed" rhymes, sometimes inside the line, sometimes even "buried within word-units," would not be recognized as rhymes because they do not serve an organizational, metrical function as traditional, systematic end rhymes do ("Why Rhyme Pleases" 28, 38–39). Curiously, Jarvis finds some of the most compelling rhymes of this kind, which I would call sporadic, in none other than Pope, a master of systematic rhyme.

So while a history of systematic rhyme in English divides fairly neatly into the period before its advent, the period of its flourishing, and the period of its decline, no such division is possible for sporadic rhyme, which was essentially "there" throughout all these periods. Moreover, the two kinds of rhyme, systematic and sporadic, are themselves not completely separate or separable because the degree of rhyme's sporadicity is influenced by the reader's familiarity with the form, when it exists; even the most conventionalized rhyme scheme can appear as a nonce form to the uninitiated reader. And, poets do much to render systematic rhyme sporadic, working creatively with given rhyme schemes, changing them, subverting them, combining them, and inventing new ones. Finally, sporadic rhyme, in some interesting cases, poses the question of the accidental or random—Is this really a rhyme here? Isn't it just an accidental and meaningless quirk of language that the poet let slip?—and destabilizes the very category of rhyme. For all these reasons, "systematic" and "sporadic rhyme" are best seen less as historical designations and more as structural, functional, or pragmatic ones.

Whether used in so-called free verse (the term should always be taken with a grain of salt, given Eliot's point that no verse is ever truly free) or alongside traditional rhyme in closed forms, sporadic rhyme is there to be heard. In fact, part of the appeal of opening up our listening to sporadic rhyme is that it invites readers to recognize, indeed to hear, rhyme in much older poetry as well, a backwards effect that is not unlike the phenomenology of rhyme itself. An example of old sporadic rhyme appears in the first two quatrains of Shakespeare's Sonnet 21:

So is it not with me as with that Muse	A
Stirr'd by a painted beauty to his verse,	B
Who heaven itself for ornament doth use,	A
And every fair with his fair doth rehearse;	B
Making a couplement of proud compare,	C
With sun and moon, with earth and sea's rich gems,	D
With April's first-born flowers, and all things rare	C
That heaven's air in this huge rondure hems.	D (13)

In this sonnet, the speaker separates himself from, and negatively appraises, a poet prone to ornamental and excessive comparisons. As in almost all his sonnets, Shakespeare ends each line with a rhyme to create the characteristic scheme of /abab cdcd/. This alternating form of the quatrain, /xyxy/, is a fairly simple one, and it recurs both within each sonnet (three times) and across sonnets. As systematic end rhyme, it structurally divides the eight lines above into two groups of four: /abab/ and then /cdcd/. The two groups are distinct but thematically linked, both by repetition and by continuity. The first group, or quatrain, criticizes that other poet, who uses even "heaven itself" for ornament in his verse. The second quatrain continues the tone of the first, bemoaning the "couplements" the rival poet makes, as in comparing the beloved to the sun and moon as well as other "things rare." In that sense, the two C-rhyme words, *compare : rare,* are significant not just for their structural role at the end of lines but also semantically. The items used in the *compare* are *rare,* the speaker seems to say, and that is what makes the comparison *proud,* faulty, over the top.

And yet an attentive ear may pick up on other rhymes that Shakespeare adds to those semantically and organizationally important ones: *fair* (at the end of the first quatrain) and *air* (at the end of the second). Here are the lines again, this time with the sporadic rhymes underlined:

So is it not with me as with that Muse
Stirr'd by a painted beauty to his verse,
Who heaven itself for ornament doth use,
And every <u>fair</u> with his <u>fair</u> doth rehearse;
Making a couplement of proud <u>compare</u>,
With sun and moon, with earth and sea's rich gems,
With April's first-born flowers, and all things <u>rare</u>
That heaven's <u>air</u> in this huge rondure hems.

These rhymes are a kind of unexpected bonus beyond the conventionally positioned ones, and they lend extra embellishment or ornamentation to the lines. As sporadic rhymes, they interact in a complicated way with their systematic counterparts. *Fair* precedes the pair *compare* : *rare,* and *air* succeeds it. The placement of these additional rhyming words counters the neat division into two quatrains, since it introduces rhyming *between* the two.[12] It also is the case that when the reader first encounters *fair,* it is not yet known that the word will become the first in a long series of rhyming words—*fair* : *fair* : *compare* : *rare* : *air*—a succession that retrospectively forms a semantic unit as well. The words on both ends of this succession add, perhaps, a hint of irony, suggesting that "every fair" (beautiful or fine characteristic) is nothing but *air.*

Two thematic elements in the lines seem to have an affiliation with rhyme itself: the mention of ornament (rhyme is often said to be euphonious or ornamental, especially, as here, when it exceeds its designated allotment) and references to rehearsing, coupling, and comparing (all forms of repetition, which rhyme sonically and literally embodies). In Stone's poem, the sonic markedness of rhyme invites the reader to engage in the very act of listening that the lines describe ("Every day a woman stands in her kitchen / and listens to a bird").

In both poems, rhyme thus signifies on at least two levels: the level of the specific rhyming words and the level of rhyme itself in a symbolic capacity. In other words, in both cases, the very presence of rhyme, if we hear it, grants hermeneutic dividends. Stone's and Shakespeare's sporadic rhymes therefore differ in many respects but also share functional similarities. Moreover, Stone benefits from her rhyme being the only such rhyme in the lines and from the fact that there is no expectation or requirement for rhyme. Shakespeare benefits from the fact that his sporadic rhymes appear in a place in the sonnet where one does not expect rhyme, as well as from an interaction between those rhymes and the words that *are* a part of the rhyme scheme. The mere fact of including structurally uncalled-for rhymes creates sonic and semantic excess around the rhyming words, making them resonant and inviting an interpretation thereof.

THE ROOT OF RHYME?

Sporadic rhyme serves poetry both old and new, and it is the kind of rhyme that proves more enduring than systematic rhyme. Today, rhyme endures not just in popular song lyrics but also in poetry, though its most exemplary usages have shifted away from traditional forms where it serves a schematic or organizational function. These nontraditional manifestations of rhyme, which I am calling sporadic, are uniquely situated to expose some key features of all rhymes, traditional and nontraditional alike, and there are significant gains in listening to them. What are those key features and what is their status? Does it make sense to speak of an unchanging "essence" of rhyme, or of any poetic form?

In this regard, David Caplan writes of "poetic form's ability to claim contradictory political meanings," and showcases the innovative uses contemporary poets have put traditional forms like the sonnet and the sestina. Going beyond the common distinction between the rival camps of traditional and avant-garde (or post-avant), whereby the traditional is associated with political conservatism and avant-garde with its opposite, Caplan calls for literary criticism to "stay alert to each form's elasticity, vigilant to the uses that verse technique makes of each context and occasion" (*Questions of Possibility* 14). I would like to heed this call, recognizing that rhyme is nothing if not elastic, and has been used to signal myriad contradictory aspects (for example, both teleology and its exact opposite, randomness). Still, I would not subscribe to the notion that rhyme is a kind of empty form. In fact, the various ways in which rhyme has been used reveal certain inherent features that constrain and direct its use.[13]

But inherent features are tricky to articulate and are especially suspect in a critical age that is (rightly) weary and wary of any attempt to essentialize or universalize anything, be it human subjects or poetic forms. In an excellent recent essay on rhyme in that spirit, Gerard Cohen-Vrignaud shows how rhyme's political and cultural connotations shift with changing historical circumstances. As the essay moves throughout the centuries, with a particularly illuminating delve into Romanticism, the writer finds contradictions in what rhyme comes to connote, "crude and working class" but also "over-civilized and aristocratic," rough but also refined, native but also foreign: "These irreconcilable views can be explained, I have argued, by the class perspective from which they emanated. At first, bourgeois 'seriousness' defined itself as wholesome progress against the decadent affectations of blue-blooded elegance and absolutist fawning. Later, a sense of middle-class superiority was opposed to the 'Cockney' predilection for rhyme deemed fit only for the nursery, a distinction that made mature taste synonymous with the appreciation of poetic depth over 'momentary amusement'" (1008).

Reading economic or class positions, as well as political and religious leanings, into the poet's choices of rhyme is far-reaching in its implications. But the attempt to offer an "antiessentialist" account of rhyme leads Cohen-Vrignaud to take an additional step: "Of course, forms have no inherent politics. Meter, for instance, is neither conservative nor liberal: it just is. But the socio-cultural baggage that weighs upon formal gestures can be as binding a meaning as any 'internal' qualities" (988).

Illuminating are the quotes around "internal," which would seem either to cast doubt on the possibility of identifying any such internal qualities or to disparage a tradition of so doing, evoking the ghost of critical schools like New Criticism and structuralism. Rather than reject the notion of internal qualities, I would put the point slightly differently: it is in fact the internal qualities or characteristics of rhyme that create complicated potentialities for different, even contradictory, sociocultural and poetic appropriations.

Relegating rhyme, or any poetic device, to the class sympathies and ideological affiliations of its practitioner tends to underplay the ways in which the device functions within a given poem. Such a critical stance also will have difficulty accounting for the different ways that a single poet uses the device. My sense is that it is actually within the poem that the most fundamental features of rhyme reveal themselves, and often reveal themselves *as contradictory*. And sporadic rhyme, because it is rhyme stripped of much conventionality of usage, defamiliarizes rhyme, allowing readers an exceptional opportunity to hear rhyme again and to ask what it is.

So what is the root of rhyme that has kept it alive, though flexible and changing? What does one recognize, activate, respond to when one encounters rhyme? I aim to show that rhyme's enduring value for readers and writers across different poetic traditions can be accessed by tapping into its paradoxical nature. Rather than a specific or stable "thing," I understand rhyme as a manifestation in language of a host of dynamics. Through a series of seemingly antithetical pairings—rigid/pleasurable, organizing/disruptive, accidental/motivated, and finally regressive/progressive—I highlight how rhyme works as a dynamic and how it is able to do work that is at once poetic and psychic.

Moreover, rhyme doesn't just exhibit each of the terms that make up a pair. In fact, it traverses the distinction within each pair, and sporadic rhyme tends to do this more than systematic rhyme. So, to take the first pair as an example, rhyme plays out both rigidity and pleasure. Indeed, one can argue that it is pleasurable *because* it is rigid. The ongoing fascination with rhyme arises precisely because it pits the two aspects against each other: at times the rigid features of rhyme are foregrounded, at others the pleasurable, and rhyme always, in some sense, mixes the two.

The same is true for the other pairings. For instance, rhyme is endlessly intriguing because it is at the same time accidental (occurs in language randomly) *and* motivated (harnessed for poetic means), and one is never sure which is which in a given instance of sporadic rhyme. Rhyme therefore has the potential to thematize this very question of randomness or literariness. Such is also the case in the sphere of time: rhyme's temporal arrow, realized in the reader's encounter with it, constantly goes both forward and backwards, but sporadic rhyme exclusively anchors the reader in the past, taking one back to an earlier part of the text, where a rhyming partner is now found(ed), retrospectively.

THE CHALLENGE OF HEARING RHYME TODAY

"Rhyme—so marked a literary feature that it can be a synonym for poetry itself—is the epitome of literariness through sound," writes John Creaser (454). Like poetry, its metonymic synonym, rhyme needs to be listened to if it is to fulfill its role as a stand-in for poetry. And yet our current time seems to show a diminished attention to soundscapes in poetry, and perhaps even a diminished capacity for such attention. "To judge from contemporary critical vocabularies," wrote Adalaide Morris in 1997, in the introduction to a collection of essays that seeks to remedy the dearth of attention to sound, "most readers have a tin ear for sound in texts" (2).

The reasons for this are numerous, from disciplinary trends to philosophical biases, from real to real-because-imagined causes, and I can only sketch out a few. Certainly, the general dominance in literary studies of prose fiction is both a symptom of and a contributor to this diminishment, with many important critical orientations, like postcolonial studies, finding examples more readily in prose than in poetry, or even treating poetry as if it were prose.[14] But even among readers of poetry the inclination to discuss sound and rhyme is impoverished.

The dominant way in which poetry is approached bespeaks of this impoverishment. In 2006, the MLA Presidential Forum was dedicated to "The Sound of Poetry/The Poetry of Sound." Marjorie Perloff, who, together with Craig Dworkin, initiated and headed the forum, bemoaned the state of attention to sound in poetry, claiming that "the discourse on poetry today, largely fixated as it is on what a given poem or set of poems ostensibly 'says,' regards the sound structure . . . as little more than a peripheral issue, a kind of sideline" ("Sound of Poetry" 750). If we go to poetry primarily for what it says, then the *how* of what it says is pushed aside, and sound, the most literal of hows, is pushed to the side of the side.

On a very large scale, one can think of inattention to sound as related to what Susan Stewart identifies as an impoverishment of "entire spheres of sense experience . . . for many first-world people." Many are now missing "a tacit knowledge of tools and forms of dancing or of carrying infants," Stewart writes, and she notes "the disappearance of ways of living with animals or cultivating plant life, along with the smell and feel and sounds and even tastes that accompanied such practices; the sound of wind in uninhabited spaces; the weight of ripe things not yet harvested" (*Poetry* 332). And if all senses are locked in an (imagined?) past when we were more in tune with them, the issue is particularly acute with regards to hearing and to the story of its receding in tandem with modernity or modernism.

Highlighting the ways in which sound reproduction and related technologies (like the telephone, radio, and phonograph, but also headphones and stethoscopes) are central to modernity, Jonathan Sterne's *Audible Past* attempts to counter the narrative that "in becoming modern, Western culture moved away from a culture of hearing to a culture of seeing" (3), though that narrative, associated with Walter Ong, still holds tremendous sway. In an equally broad fashion, the privileging of sight over sound in Western philosophy or discourse—as seen, for example, in the very term *Enlightenment* and in the inescapability of visual metaphors (see this very sentence!)—adds another layer to the problem. The link between sight and knowledge is an old one, even if one can imagine, with R. Murray Schafer, earlier days of prophets and epics when, prior to the invention of the printing press, important information and the word of God were heard, not seen (101-2).[15]

On the other hand, anyone wishing to write about sound these days is immediately met with Derrida's logocentrism (as it pertains to speech and sound) as a deterrent. This fear of committing what David Nowell Smith (*On Voice in Poetry*) has recently called "the cardinal sin of 'phonocentrism'" persists in spite of the fact that rhyme can be subvocalized and discussed, as Derrida himself does, without evincing the primacy of speech.[16] Finally, one may sense another, adjacent cardinal sin that attention to sound risks committing, that of audism.[17]

It is no small irony that at the same time that many readers pay sound in poetry little concerted attention, there is a pull to pay more attention to sound in general, perhaps a backlash against the diminishment of senses that Stewart bemoans. The burgeoning field of sound studies, a younger sister to visual studies, is working to expand our understanding of sound to include such topics as urban noise and acoustic ecology, film sound and sound art, the politics of listening, and psychoacoustics. The body of work that is collectively produced or collected under the banner of sound studies has been doing much to elevate sound in the hierarchy of senses, where sight typically reigns supreme (at least in the West), but—alas—it seems less interested in poetry, that site of unparalleled attention to verbal sound.[18]

Closer to home, recent times and technology have occasioned attention to the actual performance of poetry, and therefore enhanced listening. The popularity of poetry slams and the exposure to spoken word poetry (for example on HBO's *Def Poetry Jam* in the mid-2000s),[19] as well as the lively world of archives of poetry recordings available on the Web,[20] attest to the fact that growing numbers of people are now literally listening to poetry. The rising popularity of podcasts is fortuitous in this regard. The podcast *PoemTalk,* which typically features a discussion by three guests and host Al Filreis, incorporates a recording of the poet reading the poem under discussion, and quite often part of the ensuing discussion involves references to, if not an interpretation of, the performance.[21] Therefore, in some sense there are many opportunities to learn to rehear sound, even specifically the sounds in/of poetry. Nonetheless, there is a difference between interpreting the voice of the poet performing a poem and attuning to sound schemes in that poem, and interpretation does not necessarily lead to attunement.

This inattention to poetic sounds is especially troubling because sound schemes are of tremendous importance in poetry, notwithstanding fluctuations in the understanding of poetry and its forms or our inclination to listen to it. Born of an old relationship between poetry and orality, or a "prelapsarian marriage of music and poetry" (Hollander, *Vision and Resonance* 14), sound's special status is everywhere apparent. From theorizations about the roots of the lyric in infants' babbles or archaic sound-rich spells and charms, to ongoing debates about the relationship between sound and sense; from the fear that musicality take over poetic sense, to the practices of homophonic translation and Dadaist sound poetry that artistically flaunt the results of succumbing to this fear; from the hundreds of years of prosodic treatises about the rhythms and sounds of words, lines, and entire poems, to cognitive poetics' positing of a "poetic mode" of language perception in which acoustic information reaches consciousness—poetic practice and theory alike again and again bear out what T. V. F. Brogan says toward the end of his discussion of poetic sound: "Not to attend to sound in poetry is therefore not to understand poetry at all" (1179).[22] Too much is lost when the rich sounds of poems are muted, and no sound device is more evocative and resounding than rhyme.

The countermeasure to the muting of sounds, of rhymes, is an insistence on close listening, but listening and hearing are both always contextual, an insight that sound studies foregrounds, thanks to its cultural studies bent. Jonathan Sterne writes in the introduction to the pioneering *Sound Studies Reader* about the relation between perspective and epistemology: "Depending on the positioning of hearers, a space may be totally different. If you hear the same sound in two different spaces, you may not even recognize it as the same sound. Hearing requires positionality" (4).

Hearing requires positionality also in the radical sense that one may not be in a position to hear something or, positively put, that one needs to be in a certain position to hear. After all, what we hear in a poem is intimately linked to the set of expectations that we bring to the poem. Even the very definition of rhyme, of what linguistic material is registered or acknowledged or *heard* as rhyme, fluctuates among languages, among eras (think of the "legitimacy" of slant rhyme, or changes in pronunciation), or among modes of dissemination within the poem (sporadic or systematic). Something like *be* : *he* is a legitimate rhyme in English but not in Russian or medieval Hebrew poetry, which would demand the participation of the preceding consonant (Scherr 193), and even in English the pair would likely be received as rhyme only if it appears emphatically at the end of proximate lines rather than randomly in a piece of prose.

Context can be crucial, too. As I am writing this (September 2, 2018), a CNN headline appears on the TV screen: "Trump Expected to Stump in 7 States in September." Since we are hardly primed to expect the rhyme there, it could very well be that we would not notice it, unless subjectively prone to enthusiastic and zealous listening. A poetic context primes readers, at least some readers, to listen attentively, a mode of heightened listening that would be deemed unhelpful or even inappropriate in other situations.

On the most fundamental level, one cannot simply say that rhyme is "there," and so a strictly statistical approach that seeks to tabulate the rhyming in different periods of literary history would inevitably fall short. Listening to rhyme is a multidimensional effort that shows the intertwining of the historical and phenomenological. Eliot describes the entrance of a new work of art into an existing tradition as a bidirectional process in which the new makes all previous works adjust and change: "The past should be altered by the present as much as the present is directed by the past" ("Tradition and the Individual Talent" 15). A new work of art is not just compared to the old and seen in its light but also causes past work to be seen differently, as it brings forward things that would not have been noticed at the time. In that sense, rather than free verse causing rhyme to sink into oblivion, its advent potentially *heightens* our awareness of rhyme. Reading a modern poem devoid of systematic rhyme brings to the fore the rhyming in poems of the past, which in turn brings to the fore the nonrhyming of the current poem, which, in its turn, creates a favorable context for picking up on the (sporadic) rhyming that *is* there in the poem.

So we are caught in a curious situation. Sound is crucial to the inner workings of a poem but, for many, our habits of listening at this moment are stacked up against hearing it, at least in most poetry (unlike in jingles or ads or Dr. Seuss). On the upside, though, sporadic rhyme, present as a potential in so many poetries, is an ideal candidate to bring about and reward close listening, especially when it appears in an otherwise nonrhyming poem. Finding it where we least expect it—say, in a free verse modern poem—is both risky and rewarding. From the attentive reader's side, it can shake up habitual modes of listening and attune (or retune) us to other sounds. From the poet's side, it offers more possibilities than its systematic partner. From the critic's side, it offers a glimpse into some fundamental aspects of all types of rhyme. Rhyme is a trigger to listening. Be warned.

2

Rigid and Pleasurable

Rhyme's Imprisoning Allure

TYRANT RHYME

In this chapter, I develop a model of rhyme as a complex of rigidity and pleasure. Rigidity is, by definition, part of any rhyme: rhyme requires at least two words, and when the first one is given, there are more, or less, strict limitations for the soon-to-come second word. This *soon-to-comeness* is a particularly strong feature of systematic rhyme, rhyme that creates a discernible rhyme scheme. There, the systematization often engenders an expectation for the rhyme, expectation that is a recognition in advance of the rigidity. I speak of a *discernible* rhyme scheme, since the discerning of a rhyme scheme, or gestalt, is the very activation of this rigidity; the rhyme scheme supplies a rhyming environment that actualizes the rigidity. As we shall see in the second part of this chapter, this limiting feature of rhyme is the basis for its use in demonstrations of particular linguistic copiousness, always part of the work of poets, and more recently achieving new heights with rap lyrics and performance.

Pleasure is as much a part of every rhyme as rigidity, the sonic *delight* of poetry's old twin objectives: to teach and to delight. We may think of rhyme as a kind of verbal candy, and a synesthetic reference to rhyme as "sweet" is not uncommon.[1] When we think of rhyme as pure, sweet sound, we are close to its long-recognized euphonious function. John Hollander characterizes this as "the chime of rhyme considered as an accompaniment of pure sound to the sense of the text" (*Vision and Resonance* 121), though a poem does not necessarily subordinate sound to sense.[2]

Pleasure goes with rigidity, but it is also its flip side: the confined rigidness turns into soothing regularity, with everything harmoniously fitting into place. As a dynamic, rhyme is constantly playing out this complex of rigidity and pleasure, with the envelope pushed this way or that. At times, the inevitability of rhyme is embraced, and at others it is creatively combated. At times, the soothing element is used as a distraction, and at others it is put in jeopardy. The complex itself works as a generative force, holding both writers and readers in fascination with rhyme and producing unlimited poetic outpouring. To the extent that rhyme is a test case for an interaction between reader and text—or more to the point, reader and language—rhyme is a strategy of encountering rigidity and pleasure: dancing around rigidity, curbing and systematizing pleasure. In fact, systematic end rhyme systematizes and thus *regulates* the pleasure in rhyme by putting it into a scheme, setting a place for the points of pleasure, creating expectations for them, and then (potentially) fulfilling these.

To start at the beginning, the single most important aspect of rhyme that is played out in its familiar functioning in oral and print-based poetry is its inherent rigidity. David Rubin, in a study of oral traditions, explains that rhyme is prevalent in some of these traditions because it aids memory (70). Rubin posits that "when a sound repeats, the first occurrence of the sound limits the choices for the second occurrence and provides a strong cue for it," and therefore rhyme offers an advantage in oral traditions in which the performer's memory is crucial (75). This is the so-called mnemonic function of rhyme; rhyme's memorability depends on narrowing options and, by extension, creating a sense of predictability or even inevitability. Predictability is apparent whenever rhyme is involved, but a few linguistic or poetic phenomena exploit it more clearly than others. It is never more apparent than in the famous "Sweet Violets" folk songs, in which the text takes the hearer's expectations in the predictable rhyming direction, only to supply different words in their place:

There once was a farmer who took a young miss
In back of the barn where he gave her a . . .
Lecture on horses and chickens and eggs,
And told her that she had such beautiful . . .
Manners that suited a girl of her charms,
A girl that he wanted to take in his . . .
Washing and ironing and then, if she did,
They could get married and raise lots of . . .[3]

"Sweet Violets" appears simple enough, but its smooth functioning requires three conditions: first, hearers must be cued that this is a rhyming situation (the creation of an expectation for a rhyme); then they need to be provided with a word with a fairly obvious rhyming partner; and finally, hearers must be denied that rhyming partner, thus leaving it to them to supply one. In this case, the cuing of the rhyming situation is provided indirectly, via the nursery rhyme style and four-beat rhythm of the text. The obvious rhyming partner (the word that is implied and suppressed) is assured due to the fairly simple semantics of the lines. The fact that the rhyming word is at the end of the couplet, or that in performance there is often a pause before the word, enhances this cue. (Note that each even line is missing the fourth beat, which would fall precisely on the missing rhyming word.)

That the implied rhyme words, those words the lyrics raise in the hearer without actually realizing them textually, are more daring than the words supplied at the beginning of the following line (*kiss* instead of *lecture*, *legs* instead of *manners*) is part of the purpose. The technique of "Sweet Violets" is to transfer responsibility to the hearer and, accordingly, to alleviate the responsibility of the text. The text is able to indirectly evoke, via a rhyming mechanism, a word that it does not wish to utter, and thus the word is brought up but not stated explicitly—an implied rhyme. Hearers are given an active role, and their linguistic competence works against them.

Being able to say and *not* say something at the same time can be useful in many contexts. When Barbara Bush referenced Geraldine Ferraro (a political adversary of Bush's husband, George H. W. Bush), she said: "I can't say it, but it rhymes with *rich.*" She later clarified that she had meant *witch* (Anderson 603). This real-world example works just like "Sweet Violets." We are cued to the rhyming situation with the mention of rhyme, and then we are given the rhyming word while its obvious partner is withheld. Bush's later clarification that the word intended was *witch* rather than the obvious *bitch* tries, albeit feebly, to push responsibility more aggressively onto the hearer, not unlike the work of the mischievously naive implied author of "Sweet Violets," as if each were saying, "It was you who thought of that word all by yourselves, not me."

This rudimentary but important quality of rhyme is that it asks for a complement and limits the options for what that complement can be. Certainly, the same mechanism can be put to more favorable uses, too. The poet and critic John Ciardi makes use of this quality in a book of poems written for his first-grade daughter. The book's objective is to get the child to learn to read unfamiliar words using the fact that they rhyme with words she already knows how to read. Rhyme thus leads the child to fill in the inevitable new word, and she recognizes in writing the implied rhyme that she knows to be there. The advantage that rhyme has in facilitating vocabulary learning has also been demonstrated empirically (see, for instance, Read).

Another cultural phenomenon cashing in on rhyme's narrowing of options is Cockney rhyming slang, common in the United Kingdom and Australia, in which a word is replaced by a word with which it rhymes. Antonio Lillo notes that rhyming slang often employs racial and ethnic slurs and explains that "this slang manages to hide the target word behind the false front of rhyme" ("From Alsatian Dog" 337–38). So, instead of saying *Jew,* the speaker is able to use such phrases as "tea for two," "ten to two" and "wooden shoe" (340–46). The difference between this rhyming slang and "Sweet Violets" or Barbara Bush's insult is in the condition of cuing: the hearer who is not in the immediate social circle will most likely not recognize that this is a rhyme-based code and will not be able to make sense of the phrase. As such, rhyming slang is often employed as a "secret language" within a well-defined group, such as American prison inmates (336), or in the British drug scene, where *Lou Reed* means "speed,"

Bob Hope means "dope," and *Uncle Mac* means "smack" (Lillo, "Rhyming Slang" 41–44). Poets who use systematic end rhyme have been quick to realize its inherent rigidity and have responded to it in a number of ways. Some have written explicitly about this rigidity, in poetry and prose. Alexander Pope, for example, in his "Essay on Criticism," warns against the "sure *Returns* of still *expected Rhymes,*" the kind of overexpectedness that in poetry can be a real concern:

> Where-e'er you find *the cooling Western Breeze,*
> In the next Line, it *whispers thro' the Trees;*
> If *Chrystal Streams with pleasing Murmurs creep,*
> The Reader's threaten'd (not in vain) with *Sleep.*
> (lines 349–53; emphasis in original)

The uninteresting poetry that Pope bemoans here is worse than the silly game of "Sweet Violets" because it supplies the all-too-obvious rhyming word that it leads the reader to expect.[4] In an earlier era, Ben Jonson's "A Fit of Rhyme Against Rhyme" (166–67) makes a number of arguments against rhyme, many underlining aspects of rhyme's rigidity:

> Rhyme, the rack of finest wits,
> That expresseth but by fits,
> True conceit,
> Spoiling senses of their treasure,
> Cozening judgment with a measure,
> But false weight.
> Wresting words from their true calling;
> Propping verse for fear of falling
> To the ground.
> Jointing syllables, drowning letters,
> Fastening vowels, as with fetters
> They were bound!
> . . . .
> Vulgar languages that want

Words, and sweetness, and be scant
Of true measure,
Tyrant rhyme hath so abused,
That they long since have refused
Other caesure.
He that first invented thee,
May his joints tormented be,
Cramp'd forever. . . .

Jonson is clearly alluding to the systematic, expected, and continuous end
rhyme, which he himself is employing, as is Pope. The terms and logic
echo the argument made by George Puttenham in the celebrated *Arte of
English Poesie* (published in 1589) to support rhyme. While for Puttenham
rhyme functions as a band that fastens the lines of the verse together as
in a building (89), for Jonson rhyme is "Propping verse for fear of falling /
To the ground," in a way that is reminiscent of T. S. Eliot's 1917 comment
that rhyme, when used poorly, has the "exacting task of supporting lame
verse" ("Reflections" 189). The difficulty of using rhyme, for the poet, expressed by Jonson in a tone that is at once humorous and complaining, is
a consequence of rhyme's rigidity. Some of the emotional import of that
difficulty is expressed in the humor of calling rhyme a tyrant and alluding
to binding and fetters.

The fetters of rhyme can offer poets gains as well. John Dryden, defending
his decision to employ rhyme in his play *The Rival Ladies,* homes in on the
same attribute of rhyme, but proposes a good use for writers:

But that benefit which I consider most in it [rhyme], because I have not sel-
dom found it, is, that it bounds and circumscribes the fancy. For imagination
in a poet is a faculty so wild and lawless, that, like an high-ranging spaniel it
must have clogs tied to it lest it outrun the judgment. The great easiness of
blank verse renders the poet too luxuriant. He is tempted to say many things,
which might be better omitted or at least shut up in fewer words. But when
the difficulty of artful rhyming is interposed—where the poet commonly
confines his sense to his couplet and must contrive that sense into such
words that the rhyme shall naturally follow them, not they the rhyme—the

fancy then gives leisure to the judgment to come in, which, seeing so heavy
a tax imposed, is ready to cut off all unnecessary expenses. (Dedication of
The Rival Ladies 3)

Some years later, in the prologue to another play, Dryden reversed his
position about the use of rhyme:

> Our author by experience finds it true
> 'Tis much more hard to please himself than you,
> And out of no feigned modesty this day
> Damns his laborious trifle of a play.
> Not that it's worse than what before he writ,
> But he has now another taste of wit,
> And . . . to confess a truth . . . though out of time,
> Grows weary of his long-loved mistress, rhyme.
> *Passion's too fierce to be in fetters bound,*
> And nature flies him like enchanted ground.
>   (Prologue to *Aureng-Zebe* 120, emphasis mine).[5]

In the earlier version of his sentiments on rhyme, the fetters are helpful
in binding the poet's words and fancy, which would go on and on if it
were not for rhyme's introduction of limitation and difficulty. In the later
version, precisely this curbing of passion is rejected. Passion should roam
free; it should not (or cannot) be limited by rhyme. Dryden's assessment
of the relative strength of the imagination versus that of rhyme has been
turned on its head, but the terms of the game, or the metaphor, have not
changed. In both his declarations, rhyme is perceived as binding fetters.

And John Milton perpetrates what is perhaps the most famous single
attack on rhyme in English, in a note attached to the second edition of
Paradise Lost (1674), explaining its lack of rhyme. The note employs the
same logic and the same metaphor: this "neglect" of rhyme, Milton writes,
is "an example set, the first in English, of ancient liberty recovered to heroic poem from the troublesome and modern bondage of rhyming" (457).[6]

Yet another major argument one finds against rhyme, which may seem
strange in our own time, is that it is vulgar or barbaric. This perspective

dates back to the (relative) lack of rhyme in classical Greek prosody. Rhyme becomes associated with a vulgarization of the Latin, compared to the purity of classical Greek, and is viewed as an inadequate late addition in the poetry of English and other languages. Milton expresses this idea in conjunction with the metaphor of rhyme as fetters. He wishes to recover "ancient liberty" and thus binds together the liberty from rhyme and the cultural prestige of the ancients.

In fact, the logic of liberty informs a much later poetic dispute. Peter McDonald's quote of Edward Thomas's grievance against Swinburne, that the latter "was too ready to let his words choose themselves" (McDonald, "Rhyme and Determination" 299), or of John Wilson Croker's unsigned attack on Keats, that Keats "seems . . . to write a line at random, and then . . . follows not the thought excited by this line, but that suggested by the rhyme" (McDonald, *Sound Intentions* 118), situates the discussion in the realm of mastery and control over rhyme, and by extension over language.

The lengths to which poets will go to find a rhyme and make it fit attest to rhyme's tyranny as well. Peter Dale (70–72) lists some of these "desperate measures," like Spenser's archaisms and Frenchifications and Keats's various syntactic inversions. It is hardly surprising that much later, in the American political-poetic arena that prototypically prizes liberty and freedom from tyrants, we have a carryover of this understanding of rhyme. An explicit bridge between ideology and aesthetics focused on rhyme is the accusation that rhyme, together with meter, is reflective of political neoconservatism, or is even un-American because it is unfree (though, incidentally, Walt Whitman's own views on rhyme are much more nuanced).[7]

SCHEMING RHYME

The rigidity of rhyme enables a text like "Sweet Violets" to hijack the hearer's associations and elicit a particular rhyming word. In subtler literary examples, it can be the rhyming sound that is evoked rather than the particular word, so that the reader knows a rhyme is coming and what its sound will be, but not the precise word that is coming. That is the tenor of Pope's warning to poets cited above, namely that they should avoid overused and obvious rhymes, not that they should avoid rhyme altogether.

But whether the expectation is for a specific rhyming word or just the rhyming sound, there can be no expectation developed without preliminary cuing to initiate it. In rhyming slang, for instance, the rhyming situation is cued by the social context and the otherwise nonsensical meaning of the words employed. But what about literary situations? What leads us to expect rhyme there?

In most traditional literary employments of rhyme, the rigidity inherent in rhyme is tightened because rhyme is put in a more or less rigid rhyme scheme, which creates expectations for more rhyme. More specifically, the expectation of a rhyme is generated in one of three ways. First, when the poem is written in a form that is easily recognizable because it has become institutionalized (for instance, in a sonnet, where the title, shape, paratextual, and contextual information can help identify the form or genre), the rhyme scheme is reasonably foreknown (such as the much-expected concluding couplet at the end of a Shakespearean sonnet). Second, sometimes the rhyme scheme is produced and then reproduced within the work itself, so that the second stanza will already entail an expectation for the return of the first. This is the case in nonce or rare rhyme schemes that are repeated in a long work, like Tennyson's "The Lady of Shalott," which rhymes /aaaabcccb/ in all nineteen stanzas. But a third and particularly interesting case has to do with how rhyme schemes, even when not foreknown and not repeated, rely on our cognitive tendency to create gestalts (shapes or forms) and are able to arouse expectations throughout our linear encounter with them.

Take the relatively simple rhyme scheme /aaba/ as an example. This is the rhyming of Edward Fitzgerald's translation of Omar Khayyam's *Rubaiyat*. Reuven Tsur makes the point that the gestalt law of good continuation leads us to expect that the couplet pattern established in the first two lines will repeat itself. In other words, after /aab/, our cognitive tendencies set up an expectation for another /b/. When we arrive at the fourth line and encounter the A-rhyme again, this surprise does not entirely disrupt our ability to form a gestalt, but it shifts the kind of gestalt we create. In fact, this rhyme scheme actualizes another gestalt law, the law of return. This "surprise," Tsur writes, "is perceptually justified only after the event" and has the effect of generating "a tightly closed and coherent unit" for the entire quatrain (*Toward a Theory* 124).

The same principles operate in other rhyme schemes. For example, the reader/hearer encountering /aba/ has a strong sense of necessity for a B-rhyme to come next, thus generating /abab/ and creating a strong gestalt for the quatrain as a whole (115). The rhyme scheme can generate cohesion, tying the four lines together, which is precisely one function of the use of end rhyme.

A reader's interaction with a rhyme scheme can be described as a continuous process of expectations and gestalt creation. In that sense, systematic rhyme is doubly rigid at the outset. It takes the rigidity in rhyme and further employs it in a structure that raises more specific expectations regarding the position of the rhyme to come. The creation of an expectation for a specific rhyme sound in a designated place is the basis for many of the closed verse forms, from the couplet to the ottava rima.[8] Rhyme's basic rigidity is at the heart of these forms.

Moreover, expectations are used and abused by poets in numerous ways, and often are harnessed for specific poetic means. Poets not only work creatively with given rhyme schemes; they also change them, subvert them, combine them, and invent new ones. Dryden will insert a triplet among couplets when he happens to be discussing triplicity (Ricks, "Dryden's Triplets" 94), Percy Bysshe Shelley will break an established rhyme scheme of the sonnet in order to convey the concept of fragmentation (Nänny 205–10), and William Butler Yeats will repeat the same word as the C-rhyme in the scheme /abc abc/ to demonstrate repetition with no change (Perloff, "Packed in Ice"). An insertion of a sporadic, unexpected element in a rhyme scheme, at times even threatening to undo the integrity of that rhyme scheme, relies on systematic rhyme's double rigidity.

Robert Creeley, a twentieth-century poet associated with Black Mountain College and projectivist verse—much indebted to William Carlos Williams but, unlike Williams, relying heavily on rhyme throughout his oeuvre—exploits rhyme's bondage in his poem "Oh No":

If you wander far enough	A
you will come to it	B
and when you get there	C
they will give you a place to sit	B

for yourself only, in a nice chair,	C
and all your friends will be there	C
with smiles on their faces	D
and they will likewise all have places.	D (158)

The rhyme in the first stanza is /abcb/, characteristic of common meter (4.3.4.3) used in ballads, hymns, and nursery rhymes, such as "Mary Had a Little Lamb." However, even though the second stanza shares the same number of lines with the first, the rhyme scheme changes and is made up of two couplets: /ccdd/. This rhyme scheme reaches sustained expression in works from the eighteenth century (Pope, Dryden, Jonathan Swift), and is also used in ballad stanzas of long meter (4.4.4.4), such as Marlowe's "The Passionate Shepherd to His Love." But the combination of the two different quatrain rhyme schemes in one poem is quite unique, and moreover, it is not repeated as a unit in a longer poem.[9] If the rhyme scheme were to recur, we would perhaps learn to expect it, but as it stands, the scheme is one of a kind.

A line-by-line stroll through the poem reveals the benefits of this particular rhyming, which exhibits a gradual tightening of pattern. To begin, the rhyme scheme of the first stanza is such that it delays the fact of rhyming to the last possible point. One reads the first, second, and third lines without encountering any rhyming. Only upon reaching the end of the fourth line do we realize, retrospectively, that we are dealing with a rhyme scheme at all. The word *sit* connects back to *it*, thus signifying it as its rhyming partner. The tightening of reins escalates quickly from that point on, as every one of the four next lines locks into a rhyme scheme, maximally tight. *Chair* and *there* not only form a couplet but also tie in more forcefully because one of its members has already appeared in the third line of the first stanza. The final two lines likewise rhyme prominently, due not only to proximity but also to the phonic addition of the plural suffix: *places* : *faces*. This final rhyme also ties back further, to the first appearance of the word *place,* in the first stanza. By the end, it becomes clear that the only line in the entire poem not to rhyme is the first.

As readers follow the constantly tightening rhyme scheme, the situation depicted in the poem may very well start to shift in their minds, from

inviting and heavenly to alarming and hellish. In that way, the poem uti-
lizes the predictability, or rigidity, inherent in rhyme, and it acts iconically
to manifest on the level of rhyme the increasing stifling uneasiness of the
situation presented. Through the enigmatic and insistent denial of exact
references (*you, it, there, they*), the poem's addressee and reader are led into
a designated place, assigned a seat, and forced into a position, not unlike
the way a rhyme scheme is an assignment of place for the rhyming word.

Creeley harnesses rhyme's rigidity toward creating the feeling of horrifying enclosure. If the poem's title ("Oh No") and choice of words signal
this uneasiness of enclosure on a semantic level, the rhyme employed
creates it on the sonic one. And the fact that Creeley's rhyme scheme is
not systematic at the outset but is constantly changing voids the poem
of a cushioning that perfectly systematic poems have. By taking more
liberties with the rhyme scheme, Creeley took liberties from the reader.

OPERATING UNDER THE SWAY OF RIGIDITY

Thomas Campion, fighting a losing battle for quantitative meter in English
in his *Observations in the Art of English Poesie* (1602), makes the following
intriguing argument against rhyme: "But there is yet another fault in rime
altogether intolerable, which is, that it enforceth a man oftentimes to
abjure his matter, and extend a short conceit beyond all bounds of art;
for in quatorzains, methinks, the poet handles his subject as tyrannically
as Procrustes the thief his prisoners, whom when he had taken, he used
to cast upon a bed, which if they were too short to fill, he would stretch
them longer, if too long, he would cut them shorter" (235).

Campion recruits the constraining power of rhyme and of poetic form
more generally (his example is quatorzains, fourteen-line poems) in his
effort to argue for a different, ideally less constraining, prosody, based not
on accent and rhyme but on syllabic length.[10] That rhyme "enforceth"—
holds sway over the poet—is a belief that Campion shares with others
who pronounce rhyme's tyranny, including Jonson, Milton, and Dryden.
Together with that, we can detect a new, less obvious aspect of rhyme's
tyranny, one that stands opposed to a claim made by Dryden. Whereas
Dryden suggested that rhyme will be helpful in delimiting the writing and
cutting off "expenses," Campion fears that rhyme, and by extension form

itself, will lead the writer to extend the writing beyond necessity. Rhyme can thus take over the writing and lead it to be more than it should. In a sense, this is not just the fear of rhyme taking over, but more precisely the fear of the temptation to succumb to rhyme's sway. The fear is, at root, the very same that Lord Byron acknowledges humorously when he, strangely and with no apparent reason, gives the Scottish pronunciation for the word *which* ("whilk") to form a rhyme with *milk,* and then uses the intimacy created by the parentheses to apologize for it[11]:

> Next with a virgin zone he was equipp'd,
> Which girt a slight chemise as white as milk;
> But tugging on his petticoat, he tripp'd,
> Which—as we say—or as the Scotch say, *whilk,*
> (The rhyme obliges me to this; sometimes
> Monarchs are less imperative than rhymes)—(*Don Juan* 5.77)

Milton combats rhyme's tyranny in *Paradise Lost* by avoiding the battle and opting for blank verse.[12] Others employ other poetic strategies in their combat. Working against the perils of rhyme's rigidity and sense of inevitability, poets may try to produce surprising rhymes that seem to escape the determinism and predictability inherent in the act of rhyming. Most famous, in the footsteps of Geoffrey Chaucer and Pope, are perhaps Byron's celebrated virtuoso rhymes, and later Ogden Nash's many humorous rhymes, sometimes too dismissively labeled doggerel. Byron's most celebrated rhyme comes at the end of the twenty-second stanza of *Don Juan*'s first canto:

'Tis pity learned virgins ever wed	A
With persons of no sort of education,	B
Or gentlemen, who, though well born and bred,	A
Grow tired of scientific conversation;	B
I don't choose to say much upon this head,	A
I'm a plain man, and in a single station,	B
But—Oh! ye lords of ladies intellectual,	C
Inform us truly, have they not hen-peck'd you all?	C (1.22)

The basic dynamic in these lines is that Byron's ottava rima manages "to stand for convention and to assault it at the same time, to signify rigidity and to couple it with flexibility" (Brownstein 181). Each ottava rima stanza has three rhyming sounds (see the markings for A, B, and C above). The first two rhyming sounds have three rhyming words each, the third only two. No easy task. But in this stanza, Byron is augmenting the difficulty of rhyming by making the B-rhyme a two-syllable rhyme (*education* : *conversation*) and the C-rhyme a virtually impossible three-syllable rhyme: *intellectual* : *hen-peck'd you all*. The result is a rhyme that is made to seem over the top and contrived, a demonstration of freedom against restriction. The effect is humorous because rhyme's rigidity is laid bare and the battle is laboriously won through considerable loosening of phonetic exactness.

The special challenge of rhyming place names offers ample opportunities to demonstrate the poet's combative efforts or liberty-loving inclinations. Byron is characteristically funny in "There's not a sea the passenger e'er pukes in, / Turns up more dangerous breakers than the Euxine" (*Don Juan* 5.5). Nash relished these maneuvers, as in the examples below from "The Dust Storm, or I've Got Texas in My Lungs":

Nobody minds
Dust storms in Lubbock;
They don't create havoc,
Just hubbubbock.
But I'm so full
Of Holy Texas
I'll be hallowed ground
When they annex us. (Nash 146)

It could be said that these kinds of examples by Nash and Byron exhibit not rhyme's rigidity but rhyme's creativeness or potential for flexibility. However, this demonstration of creativity and flexibility is only realizable against the background of rhyme's predictability and inflexibility. Flexibility is born out of tremendous effort—that is the point being played out—and the more contrived the rhyme seems, the more forcefully this point is made. In the case of Nash, the two names of places, Lubbock and Texas, are given first. Then there is an attempt to find a rhyme, an attempt that forces the poet to wrench words by adding a semantically vacuous syllable to an existing word to ridiculously create *hubbubbock* or to come up with a mosaic rhyme by rhyming *Texas* with the two words *annex us* (as Byron does with *pukes in* and *Euxine*). These rhyming instances are—and this is no small matter—two-syllable rhymes, just as Byron's celebrated example ("peck'd you all") is a three-syllable rhyme. Rhyming proper names, like producing two- and three-syllable mosaic rhymes, compound the difficulty and consequently the virtuosity, a sort of tongue-in-cheek skill under pressure.[13]

PLEASURABLE BUT/BECAUSE RIGID

As many poets have attested, rhyme is first among the linguistic enslavers. However, this tyrannical rigidity should not be taken to mean that rhyme is unpleasurable. In fact, there is much potential pleasure within and amid this rigidity. We have already seen how humor is generated by Byron and Nash exposing the rigidity in rhyme and demonstrating unruly flexibility in its face. This is the fun of waging war against rhyme's rigidity, with the absurdity of the rhyme employed ("hen-peck'd you all") a testimony to the hardships of the battle. There is a touch of sadomasochistic-like logic here, with the poet volunteering to put himself in shackles that are even tighter than necessary. If poetry is understood as a vocation one chooses, we can also take with a grain of salt the psychological merit of many of the antirhyme complaints by poets who, albeit begrudgingly, continue to rhyme.

Ultimately, though, such willing sadomasochism is not the end point and, at least for the poetic maneuvers represented here by Byron and Nash, the position is not one of passivity but rather one of gaining the upper hand over rhyme by producing those humorous and outrageous rhymes. We also can understand now why W. K. Wimsatt, in his celebrated essay on rhyme, attributes the pleasure in rhyme to an element of surprise—not the surprise of a fresh rhyme but the surprise that comes from "some incongruity or unlikelihood inherent in the coupling" (164). The more incongruous and outrageous the rhyme, the more pleasurable.

Related pleasure is also found in "Sweet Violets," where the incongruity between the two words of the rhyme is displaced onto that between the implied rhyme and the word actually supplied (for instance, *lecture* instead of *kiss*) and humor arises from the linguistic proximity to danger. Performer and hearer-victim share in setting into motion a mechanism of evoking, then suppressing, the expected; rushing into harm's way and then fleeing at the last minute. Rhyme's predictability is equated with taboo and danger because of the risqué nature of the words evoked, and the very mechanism of ducking taboo over and over again throughout the song-game produces victorious pleasure as one controls and plays with the rhyme as if with fire.

Contrarily, one can also think of the pleasure in rhyme as emanating not from difficulty but from ease. Nigel Fabb finds experimental evidence that suggests that because rhyme limits the number of words we must mentally search for in order to identify which word we heard ("selection space"), it adds to the fluency and ease of processing. This heightened fluency results in various psychological effects, including familiarity and pleasure (172, 189).[14] This is a kind of pleasure that results from lessening cognitive work, and it would probably not occur with the kinds of rhyme that Byron, Nash, and Pope (Wimsatt's chief example) employ. Here, instead of outsmarting rhyme's rigidity and tyranny, the goal would be to surrender to it.

We have seen how systematic rhyme creates expectations for rhyme (whether for a specific word or simply for the rhyming sound). The element of enjoyment can then emerge in the soothing, continuous meeting of expectations. There can be a sense of relief when the expected is reached, when one finally hears the other shoe drop, especially when a strong sense of requiredness has been created. This is evinced by Tsur's example: think of the effect on the reader when the rhyme scheme in a quatrain changes so that, after /aba/, one gets not the much-expected B-rhyme but a word that does not rhyme at all (*Toward a Theory* 115–16).

This would be a different economy of pleasure, the kind of pleasure that is epitomized in entirely regularized systematic rhyme. Systematic rhyme, deployed in a discernible rhyme scheme that frames the entire poem from beginning to end, produces a kind of pleasure in predictability,

pleasure in meeting expectations, and pleasure in form. William Wordsworth, defending his decision to write in verse rather than in prose, despite using "a selection of language really used by men," relies precisely on
this dimension of pleasure ("Preface" 446).[15] One section from the preface
to *Lyrical Ballads* is especially helpful in elucidating this point. Poetry's
end, Wordsworth writes, is to produce excitement "in co-existence with
an overbalance of pleasure," but excitement can be dangerous.

> If the words, however, by which this excitement is produced be in themselves
> powerful, or the images and feelings have an undue proportion of pain con
> nected with them, there is some danger that the excitement may be carried
> beyond its proper bounds. Now the co-presence of something regular, some
> thing to which the mind has been accustomed in various moods and in a less
> excited state, cannot but have great efficacy in tempering and restraining the
> passion by an intertexture of ordinary feeling, and of feeling not strictly and
> necessarily connected with the passion. . . . [T]here can be little doubt but
> that more pathetic situations and sentiments, that is, those which have a
> greater proportion of pain connected with them, may be endured in metrical
> composition, *especially in rhyme,* than in prose. (459, emphasis mine)

Like Dryden, Wordsworth understands rhyme (and verse in general)
as restraining, tempering, regulating, though the focus is on the reader's
side rather than the writer's; rhyme tempers the reader's pain rather than
the writer's fancy. This is the tempering effect of regularity in general,
of "metrical composition," in that, for example, the number of syllables
or feet or beats is roughly consistent per line, repeating throughout the
poem, with the end rhyme adding another regulating dimension at the
end of each line. That predictability has a soothing dimension is certainly
a commonplace, and poetical exploitations of this idea can be observed
in many types of discourse.

   Lullabies, in particular, fascinatingly show the sinister overtones of the
soothing aspect often associated with rhyme. The regularity of rhythm
and rhyme, as well as the accompanying physical gestures, characteristically act to put the baby to sleep. But, Nicholas Tucker writes, since "the
baby will not understand the actual words sung, and given that no other

audience is intended for these occasions, a mother on her own can be fairly uninhibited in what she croons to her infant" (18). Indeed, the often-times threatening, dark, or aggressive content of lullabies, Tucker claims, "stand[s] in such stark contrast to the way in which [the words] have to be delivered" (21).[16] Similarly, Edgar Allen Poe puts the reader to near sleep by lengthy repetition of elaborate metrical forms and regularized rhyming, which allows darker themes to slip in (as in, for example, "The Raven").

But there also is an additional source of rhyme's pleasure at work here, of which Wordsworth's qualification "especially in rhyme" is revealing. Like meter, rhyme can be a device for repetition or regularity. But what is that extra thing that rhyme has and that soothing metrical regularity does not? One place to home in on the answer is in discussions of blank verse, a form predicated precisely on the severing of ties between rhyme and meter, where, by definition, meter exists but (systematic) rhyme does not. Samuel Johnson, in his ambivalent assessment of Milton's versifica-tion in *Paradise Lost,* teases out the missing element: what rhyme is able to add to meter in English. Rhyme is unnecessary for languages "melo-diously constructed with a due proportion of long and short syllables," says Johnson. But English, with its "scanty and imperfect" meter, needs rhyme: "Poetry may subsist without rhyme, but English poetry will not often please" (112–13).

The connotations of rhyme as soothing, authoritative, and secure as-sign positive value terms to rhyme's stifling force. But there is more than just soothing regularity, more than just meeting expectations; rhyme also *delights.* Whether regularized throughout the poem (systematic) or even appearing once (sporadic), rhyme puts words in contact in a way that pro-duces harmonious fusion of sounds and can therefore be experienced as phonetically pleasurable. Early commentators on rhyme in English have justified this by positioning rhyme, together with accent, as equivalents to the Greek quantitative prosodic system. These defenders of rhyme want to show that rhyme and accent are able to perform the tasks that meter performs in Greek, and no less efficiently.

Harmony, and the comparison to music, become particularly salient features in these defenses. Samuel Daniel defends rhyme against Cam-pion's attacks by stating that it is "an excellencie added to this worke of measure, and a Harmonie, farre happier than any proportion Antiquitie could euer shew vs," and insists that it "dooth adde more grace, and hath more of delight than euer bare numbers" (7). Similarly, happy proportion and delight is crucial for Puttenham, who begins "The Second Booke" of the *Arte of English Poesie* by explaining "poeticall proportion": "a kind of Musicall vtterance, by reason of a certaine congruitie in sounds *pleasing the eare*" (64, emphasis mine). And in a transition from rhyme to metaphysics or theology, proportion takes on totalizing meaning: "All things stand by proportion, and . . . without it nothing could stand to be good or beautiful," Puttenham says, and he recruits a reference to the Judeo-Christian tradition (Wisdom of Solomon 11:20): "God made the world by number, measure, and weight" (64).

A modern scientific echo of the musical, though not the theological, analogy as the basis for the sonic pleasure in rhyme makes up Henry Lanz's *Physical Basis of Rime* (1931). Lanz uses early twentieth-century laboratory measurements of speech sounds in order to substantiate his claim that vowels are akin to tone clusters or musical chords and that rhyme exhibits in language the exact, literal pleasure of melody. Just as "a conventionally pleasing sensation" is created in music by melody's return to the same tone, so too does poetry return to the same vowel in rhyme, Lanz explains (36–37). Why rhyme? "Only in rime do we find the conditions of musical melody fulfilled: (1) the vowels are pronounced in exactly (or at least very nearly) the same way, because the consonants following them are identical; and (2) the musical phrase introduced by the vowels receives a definite melodic structure—it ends with the same tone with which it began" (Lanz 43).

I am less interested in the scientific correctness of Lanz's formulations than in the idea—coming from many different directions and eras—that rhyme pleases.[17] Just as it is the chief element in manifesting the rigidity that to some extent exists in all elements of a predetermined form, rhyme also has a prized status with regards to enjoyment. Even more than meter, rhyme foregrounds the signifier, its materiality, its musicality. The phonic dimension, rhyme's sonic rather than semantic value, is privileged by rhyme's very definition, since what constitutes rhyme is sound, not sense. Systematic rhyme, where the musicality inherent in every rhyming

instance is deployed systematically, endows the whole poem with an expected and regularly recurring sonic dimension, which can be perceived
either as mere annoying jingling or as harmonious pleasure.

RAP: PHONIC RIGIDITY AND LINGUISTIC DEXTERITY

Rhyme endows the text with a euphonious-harmonious dimension
through its phonetic features. It stands to reason, then, that when the exactness of the phonetic fit between the rhyming words is threatened, pleasure is threatened. It is here that rigidity reenters the scene. Rhyme, as we
already noted, is the head of a family of sound relationships among words,
consisting mostly of weaker connections like alliteration, consonance,
and assonance. Moreover, *full* or *perfect* rhyme is the head of the family
of rhyme, consisting of various degrees of imperfect or partial rhymes.
Far from a binary and discrete category, rhyme is rather a gradation of
phonic phenomena. This gradation creates the linguistic conditions for
rhyme's exactness to become a topic of debate and controversy focused on
rigidity and flexibility, tolerance to sameness and tolerance to difference.

Puttenham warns, "There can not be in a maker a fowler fault, then to
falsifie his accent to serve his cadence [the part of the line that includes the
rhyme], or by untrue orthographie to wrench his words to helpe his rime."
These two offenses are not equally bad, though. "It is somewhat more
tolerable to help rime by false orthographie, then to leaue an vnplesant
dissonance to the eare" (81). And it is particularly within the context of
regular, systematic end rhyme that phonetic inexactness, a "dissonance to
the eare," can be perceived as unpleasant, because the systematic element
gives a normative frame against which partial or wrenched rhyme can
seem a transgression, an emphatic refusal to fulfill expectations. Therefore, partial rhyme, that stubborn *almost* perfect rhyme, is prone to be perceived with hostility, as is evident, for example, by early reactions to Emily
Dickinson's slant rhymes. Though twentieth-century readers are more
accustomed to slant or partial rhyme, her first editors took the liberty to
"correct" some of her rhymes before publication.[18] And Margaret Morlier
highlights Victorian reviewers' reproving of Elizabeth Barrett Browning's
use of near rhyme, showing how this use served complex poetic goals for
the poet, as well as political goals pertaining to elitism and gender.

A prescriptive attitude easily enters the discourse around slant rhyme because of the fullness of enjoyment that is slighted when the rhyme is slant. These are the aesthetic and psychological dimensions underpinning the development of an anti–slant rhyme ideology, the responses to Dickinson's rhymes being but one example. Slant rhyme requires a normative, full and perfect rhyme as its other, and the practice of noted poets, together with rhyming dictionaries, supply that norm. The differences among rhyming dictionaries, or even among different editions of the same rhyming dictionary, with regard to permissible and nonpermissible rhymes, show that the whole topic is subject to historical change, due not just to changes in pronunciation but also to changes in taste (Morlier 101).

For instance, John Walker's eighteenth-century *Rhyming Dictionary* (first published in 1775) includes, immediately after the "perfect rhymes," two additional categories: rhymes that he calls "nearly perfect" and rhymes that are "allowable." Under the *oom* group, with words like *gloom* and *room,* we find *whom* and *womb* as nearly perfect rhymes and *come, drum,* and *home* as allowable rhymes, with an example from Pope to lend support (706). But a Victorian editor who published the book in a new edition was much less open and added in his editor's preface that "had we been producing a new work instead of a new edition of a work of the former century, all that refers to *allowable* rhymes would certainly have been cancelled, as no longer tolerable to a poetic ear" (vi). Rhyme is thus a benchmark for what the ear (of an individual or of an era) can and can no longer tolerate.

Even for the more tolerant Walker, the rhyming dictionary was less a handbook for poets than a thinly veiled (or not at all veiled) way to assist in promoting proper pronunciation.[19] The "Advertisement" preceding the index explains that "this collection of words is in some measure a dictionary of pronunciation, and may answer very useful purposes to foreigners and provincials, who, by understanding the sound of one word, may become acquainted with the pronunciation of a whole class" (672). Full, perfect rhyme in this way brings together language correctness and group (national) allegiance, with mispronunciations allocated to foreigners. If, for Puttenham, bad rhyme would be perceived almost as a transgression against God, correct rhyme is used here to ensure group affiliation. Both the embrace of, and the resistance to, slant rhyme thus can become a site to play out anxieties around authority, liberty, nationhood, and gender (perceptions associated with Dickinson and E. B. Browning's gender made them more subject to suspicion of poetic inadequacy).

In our own time, the issue of wrenching words to fit the rhyme, or loosening the very definition of rhyme, is played out in rap. Rap lyrics offer an interesting context, therefore, for an investigation of rhyme's rigidity, pleasure, and politics. Any cursory account of the basic tenets of hip-hop poetics cannot but mention rhyming, so central is it to this artistic endeavor. Adam Bradley is correct in writing that rap "celebrates rhyme like nothing else, hearkening back to a time when literary poetry still unabashedly embraced the simple pleasure and musicality of verse" (51).

Hip-hop artists have stretched the device well beyond what is found in (traditionally perceived) poetry. H. Samy Alim, examining the work of rapper Pharoahe Monch, shows that in order to begin to understand what is happening with rhyme in rap, one needs new terminology to account for the new usages, like multirhyming, sextuple rhymes, compound internal rhyme, back-to-back chain rhyme, and bridge rhyming (Alim, "On Some Serious"). At its best, this kind of inventiveness and complexity of rhyming, which Alim aptly calls "a multirhyme matrix," puts even Byron's rhyming to shame. But artistic ingenuity is not separate from larger concerns. As Richard Shusterman has written, many MCs "see their artistic expression of truth as part and parcel of a political struggle to achieve greater economic, social, political, and cultural power for the core hip-hop constituency of African American society" (55).[20] This struggle for power, which is rightly associated with African American society as the birthplace of hip-hop, even as hip-hop constituency now encompasses other societies and indeed other parts of the world, occurs on many levels, but rhyme has a crucial role to play within that struggle.

Why rhyme? In addition to echoing and continuing a long African American oral tradition,[21] rhyming, due to its inherent rigidity, requires skill, and so mastery of rhyme is a strong manifestation, in various cultures and languages, of mastery over language (Fabb 66). Rhyme is "one of the loudest announcements of authorial control" (McDonald, *Sound Intentions* 41). More specifically, rhyming well demonstrates mastery over a most material aspect of the language, and rhyming exceptionally well demonstrates an exceptionally high level of mastery.

The issue of mastery is particularly significant when an artistic endeavor tries to work against a dominant language/culture while employing the language of that culture—or a nonstandard form of it.[22] The tremendous lengths to which hip-hop artists have gone in rhyming attest to the importance of this mastery, to its success, even to the pleasure associated with it. And while the mastery is artistic, the significance and motivation go beyond it. Linguistic anthropologist Marcyliena Morgan has written the following on wordplay and word art, which, as I have been claiming about rhyme, are at once artistic and political: "The focus on words in hip hop is not only at the artistic level. It is an attempt to mark what is considered routine activity in African American communities. One aspect of these activities is the consumption of objects in public and popular culture and the reclaiming of the object once it is made 'black.' Word art then is the transforming of words to represent youth and artistic beliefs and practices by exploiting the referential and linguistic norms of the dominant society" (123).

Rhyming, like the creation of new words or the changing of old ones, represents action in speech, an active inter-action with language. As anyone who has listened to rap knows, a written version of the lyrics cannot always help in ascertaining which words will rhyme, especially if the spelling is standard. In performance, the MC will display the phonology and other aspects of what has been called Hip Hop Nation Language (Alim, "Bring It to the Cypher") and may also change, at times quite radically, the pronunciation of words in order to make them rhyme.[23]

Taking this liberty with pronunciation, teasing new rhymes from old words, constitutes a transformation of the words not on a lexical but on a phonetic level.[24] The MC proves linguistic dexterity by creating challenging combinations of rhyming words and at the same time employs pronunciations that change the very words used, with the consistency of the rhyming itself serving as a benchmark against which to derive pleasure and power from that linguistic audacity. Rather than being an error of falsifying accent in order to fit them into rhyme, as Puttenham decries, what is happening both showcases nonstandard English and treats standard

words not as givens but as material for play. The fact that hip-hop comes
from, and is still often enjoyed as, a live performance, adds much to this
display of dexterity, since it hints at the possibility that all this linguistic
maneuvering is done live, on the spot.

The skill involved in performing the lyrics (for instance, at a rapid pace)
is yet another aspect of the tremendous importance that the concept of
skill plays in hip-hop. David Caplan, in a book devoted to hip-hop and
rhyme, shows how the skill in rhyme is itself a theme in hip-hop. We can
see this nicely in hip-hop seduction songs, a genre that highlights the tradition of seduction in and by poetry. In one example, Caplan underlines
the argument made by Eminem to a rival that Eminem is the superior
lover because he is the superior rhymer. The ability to rhyme better, to
get into the woman's ear, is equated with lovemaking itself. Eminem's
forcing of words into rhyme exhibits, Caplan writes, not an inability to
find "correct" rhymes but rather power and domination over the language
(*Rhyme's Challenge* 96–100).

What kind of rhyme does one find in rap? Rather than answer the
question in its entirety (because rhyme in the rap tradition is tremendously varied), I wish to focus on a particular type of rhyming that represents an extreme demonstration of the rigid and pleasurable sides of
rhyme, as well as the dexterity involved. Situated between systematic-
regular rhyming and sporadic rhyming, in this type, the contemporary
rapper Jay-Z uses a recurrence of rhymes on the same sound. A short
excerpt from his "99 Problems" will demonstrate:

> The year is ninety-<u>four</u> and my trunk is <u>raw</u>,
> In my rearview mirror is the motherfuckin' <u>law</u>,
> Got two choices <u>y'all</u>, pull over the car <u>or</u>
> Bounce on the double put the pedal to the <u>floor</u>.[25]

In this excerpt and throughout, rhyme dominates the soundscape,
though the orthography does not tell the whole story. In these four lines,
while it is evident from the outset that *raw* and *law* rhyme, and that *four,
or,* and *floor* do as well, only the performance of the words shows how,
with Jay-Z, all five words come very close to rhyming with one another.

To these five he also adds the word *y'all.* There is thus a succession of six rhyming words (in addition to *double : pedal*), and for clarity's sake I have underlined these rhymes as performed in the excerpts.

Not just at the beginning but also throughout Jay-Z's verse there is an impressive succession of the same rhyming sound. He will rhyme and rhyme again on a certain sound—for various spans within the verse—and then move to another rhyming sound and do the same. The lyrics are therefore quite naturally divisible into what we might call "rhyme stretches," a stretch of language that is dominated by the recurrence of a specific rhyme sound and is fairly devoid of others. Here are the first three (out of six) lines of another such rhyme stretch, from a little later in the song:

> So I pull over to the side of the <u>road</u>.
> I heard "Son do you know why I'm stoppin' you <u>for</u>?"
> 'Cause I'm young and I'm black and my hat's real <u>low</u>?

While we are never far from a rhyme here, and never far from expecting one, other variables concerning the rhyme are less regular and more sporadic. For example, the exact number of rhymes and their position is not always predictable from one instance to the next. It would be difficult to assign an overall and specific rhyme scheme to the lines, because the listener does not know when the rhyme will occur or when the rhyme stretch will end; some rhyme stretches are only two lines long and some may be as long as six lines or more. In addition, the number of rhymes and their proximity are not entirely dependent upon the total length of the rhyming stretch. In the first stretch, four lines contain six tightly squeezed rhyming words (I count only the rhymes of the sound that defines the stretch), namely *ninety-four : raw : law : y'all : or : floor,* whereas in the second stretch six rhyming words are spread out across six lines. The rhyme that is external to the sound of the stretch, *double : pedal* (in the first stretch), also contributes and varies, as do some of the more subtle sonic elements, such as the echoing of *year : rearview,* and sporadic alliterations.

Of particular interest is that the rhyme stretches do not always coincide with other divisions within the text. The second stretch, we notice, folds within its rhyming lines the speaker's narration of the events (line 1), the police officer's address to him (line 2), and his reply to the officer (lines 3). The rhyming in this case overrides diegetic and presumably racial divides.

Overall, rhyming here serves as the principal means of controlling the song, the words, and the situation, and provides the disparate events and speakers with a frame. The final rhyme stretch of this part of the song makes this clear, when Jay-Z seals off the officer's warning by rhyming it with the line that is the song's refrain ("I've got ninety-nine problems, but a bitch ain't one"). Rhyme itself has the last, resounding word.

Finding and fitting many rhyming words in a short span of text takes not only linguistic dexterity but also a capacity for innovation and linguistic maneuvering. One rhyme stretch in "Run This Town," also by Jay-Z and performed by Kanye West, includes the following rhymes: *G-string* : *bee stings* : *beasting* : *Riesling* : *precinct*.

In this rhyming group, Jay-Z ties together by rhyme a verb (*beasting*), a proper noun (*Riesling*), a two-word noun phrase (*bee stings*), and a compound word (*G-string*)—an implausible assortment that is as far as imaginable from Wimsatt's "tame" rhymes (which he associates with Chaucer) or Hugh Kenner's "normal" or "reasonable" rhymes (which he associates with some of Pope). To add to the abundance, the two rhyme stretches on each side of this stretch use sounds not entirely dissimilar to these. If we concede some inaccuracies of rhyme within and across the three stretches, we get a chain of thirteen (!) two-syllable rhymes: *stunting* : *one thing* : *hunting* : *cumming* : *G-string* : *bee stings* : *beasting* : *Riesling* : *precinct* : *do bring* : *mood ring* : *new things* : *shoe string*.

The departures from standard English on the level of prosody (for instance, West stresses the *one* in "one thing" so as to fit with the other trochaic rhymes) and phonology (such as when *precinct* is truncated into *precin*) are important, not accidental; taking liberties with pronunciation simultaneously attests to the difficulty of so much rhyming and celebrates the control over the language that is the overcoming of this difficulty. This chain represents a predominance of rhyme and control over rhyme, and by extension a form of mastery over language, with the profound political significance this carries in the case of hip-hop culture. Rhyme in the poetry that is rap shows that poetry can bespeak freedom not by foregoing artistic constraints (as a naive view of "free" verse would have it) but by taking on very elaborate constraints while taking liberties with and within them.

THE RISKS OF MONORHYME

With so many words rhyming on the same sound, there is also a risk of saturation, an emotional or cognitive fatigue. Barbara Herrnstein Smith identifies this risk as present in a long series of couplets. A series of closed couplets, she states, like any other systematic repetition, entails a force for continuation. But "when a stimulus continues to be repeated exactly over a considerable period of time, our expectation of further repetition ultimately must contend with our desire for closure or at least for change. Up to a certain point, this produces a heightening of tension; but after that, it is as if the nerves 'give up' and simply fail to respond altogether" (75). Smith offers variation within the form as a safeguard against saturation.

In the rap examples given here, even though the danger of saturation is even more plausible than in the couplet form, saturation or boredom are kept at bay. If "Run This Town," with so many instances of the same or similar rhyming sound, does not fall into monotony, it is thanks to the degrees of variation that the lyrics employ, which effectively counter this danger. The rhyming stretches are of varying lengths and unexpected durations, and they even sometimes include other rhymes within them (such as in the first stretch of "99 Problems").

Of the utmost significance in the dynamic of this type of rhyming is its sporadicity, which means that one does not know how long a rhyme stretch is going to last or how many rhyming words it will include. With each new word added to the growing list of rhyming words, the ante is upped: How long can this go on? Not unlike freestyle, in which the mastery of rhyme is tested in a live and improvised competition of linguistic capability, it is verbal skill that is foregrounded, judged, and responsible for keeping rhyme—and the audience's interest—going.

The appreciation of the verbal dexterity involved in producing these rhyme stretches is augmented when we consider the relative difficulty of forming many rhymes of the same sound in English, in contradistinction to languages such as Hebrew, Arabic, or Slavic languages, in which

features of the language facilitate the creation of such rhymes. One pa-
rameter is the degree to which the language is flectional, though this linguistic feature is mediated by the degree to which poetry in that language
admits as legitimate rhymes based on these suffixal endings ("grammatical
rhymes"). In classical Arabic poetry, for instance, there are poems that
rhyme on the same sound ("monorhyme") for dozens if not hundreds of
lines. Sustaining the same rhyme sound throughout the poem is in fact
the norm, but morphological suffixes alone are not usually taken as suf-
ficient, and they need to be added to the root consonant (Drory 66–67).

   Several other variables affect the relative difficulty of the creation
of rhymes in a language. For example, it has been noted that "riming
chances will increase as the number of phonemes available for rime becomes smaller" (Eekman 61). It is therefore more difficult to find rhymes
for a given rhyming sound in English than in Hebrew, because English has
more end sounds; modern Hebrew has only five vowel sounds, as opposed
to thirteen in English (Hrushovski 729). And it has been suggested that
English fares worse than Romance languages because English words end
in more ways than words in those languages (Steele 196–97).[26]

   Unlike Arabic, no consistent monorhyming form developed in English,
whose institutional forms of poetry, save for some curious exceptions,[27]
require relatively few repetitions of the same rhyming sounds. While
employing the Italian sonnet form in English demands four A-rhymes
and four B-rhymes for the octave (abbaabba), and the Spenserian sonnet
likewise needs four B- and C-rhyming words, most popular verse forms
used in English demand less. The Shakespearean sonnet and all popular
quatrain forms need only two, and ottava rima, rhyme royal, terza rima,
and the limerick up to three.

   Successive use of the same rhyming sound, brought to a peak with rap
lyrics, represents an extreme form of rigidity in rhyme, though the performance strives, paradoxically, to appear as effortless as possible. There are
precedents in English poetry, though the risk there is doggerel, excessive
rhyming that seems hard to take seriously. An early example is John Skelton's "skeltonics," relatively irregularly metered and irregularly rhyming
poems that sometimes rhyme on the same sound for five, six, or even

twelve lines. Here is an example of Skelton's satirical "Why Come Ye Nat to Courte?" from 1552:

> Than have good daye. Adewe!
> For defaute of rescew,
> Some men may happely rew,
> And some theyr hedes mew.
> The tyme dothe fast ensew
> That bales begynne to brew.
> I drede, by swete Jesu,
> This tale will be to trew:
> "In faythe, Dycken, thou krew,
> In faith, Dicken, thou krew, etc." (280)

The Victorian prosodist George Saintsbury explains, assuming a critical tone, "He [Skelton] wants to run up and down all the gamut from aureate to familiar diction," and for the sake of the exorbitant, over-the-top rhyming, he "falls in the habit either of positively inventing words, or of selecting and heaping together the most out-of-the-way and burlesque examples that he can find" (1:242–44).

While poets often use rhyming dictionaries when searching for a specific rhyme (Fig. 1), Skelton, a forerunner of twentieth-century procedural or rule-based poetry, seems almost to challenge himself to exhaust an entire entry in a rhyming dictionary. What becomes evident while looking through the words lumped together because of their rhyming is precisely how semantically distant they are; after all, a rhyming dictionary's very structure privileges the sonic over the semantic.

It is interesting that, in his attempt to escape the constraint of more regular rhyming schemes, Skelton used a procedure that is more demanding in that it requires more rhyming words, more innovation. This is the same dynamic of rigidity and pleasure, upping the ante, that is operative in rap. If we understand the arduous task of producing more and more words that rhyme on the same sound as a play with and against the rigidity of rhyme, it is not surprising that this play has the effect of humor.

A
DICTIONARY
OF
RHYMES.

AB.

B{Lab, Crab}
Stab
Scab

ACE.

Brace
Chace
Face
Grace
Lace
Mace
Pace
Place
Race
Trace
Apace
Deface
Efface
Disgrace
Displace
Misplace
Embrace
Grimmace
Interlace
Retrace

Base
Case
Abase
Debase
Enchase

AGH.

Ach
Attach
Detach

ACK.

Back
Black
Crack
Hack
Knack
Lack
Pack
Quack
Rack
Sack
Slack
Smack
Snack
Stack
Tack
Track
Wrack
Attack

ACT.

Act
Tract
Attract
Abstract
Compact
Contract
Detract
Distract
Enact

Extract
Exact
Protract
Substract
Transact
Cataract
And the Participles of the Verbs in ACK.

AD.

Add
Bad
Clad
Gad
Glad
Had
Lad
Mad
Sad
Pad

ADE.

Blade
Fade
Glade
Jade
Lade
Made
Shade
Spade
Trade
Wade
Degrade
Diſwade

Evade
Invade
Perswade
Blocade
Brigade
Cavalcade
Masquerade
Renegade
Retrograde
Serenade
Ambuscade
Cannonade
Palisade

Aid
Braid
Maid
Afraid
Upbraid
And the Participles of the Verbs in AY, EY, and EIGH.

AFE.

Chafe
Safe
Vouchsafe

AFF.

Chaff
Draff
Graff
Quaff
Staff
Engraff
Epitaph

(2)

Fig. 1. First page of Edward Bysshe's *Dictionary of Rhymes*, which is part of his *Art of English Poetry*, 4th ed. (London 1710). Columbia University Libraries, Eighteenth Century Collections Online.

But monorhyme, due to its markedness, can be used to signal more than humor. Even the shortest instance of monorhyme, repeating the rhyme sound three times, is conspicuous. If a couplet is two lines held together by rhyme, a triplet already entails excess, since it goes beyond the minimal number of two that rhyme needs by definition. Monorhyme thus signals more insistence or deliberateness, and this extra bit of deliberateness lends the triplet emphatic "formness." It foregrounds form and can potentially be converted into a statement *about* form itself, as in Robert Frost's enigmatic poem "Pertinax," which takes form as its subject matter:

> Let chaos storm!
> Let cloud shapes swarm!
> I wait for form. (308)

Monorhyme as a form raises fundamental questions about rhyme, about its very definition. Rhyme relies upon the perception of similitude in dissimilitude or dissimilitude in similitude.[28] In English, at least most of the time, both similitude and dissimilitude manifest on the phonemic level: rhyming words share an ending but must differ in their beginning. If the rhyming syllable at the end of the two words shared a beginning *and* an ending (*light* : *delight, vice* : *advice*), the danger is, as Edward Bysshe warns in his influential eighteenth-century handbook *The Art of English Poetry,* that rhymes will be "too perfect" and there cannot be "Musick in one single Note" (21). Some languages, like French, readily accept homonym rhymes, but even those have the element of dissimilitude, now on the level of the disparate meaning of the two phonetically identical words.

"Tautological" rhymes, featuring exact identity of sound *and* meaning, are the very last frontier and are recognized as rhyme "only with difficulty" (Lotman 58). In that sense, then, rhyme is different from mere repetition. It is also different from a pun. "Rhyme and pun are twins," writes Debra Fried (83), but they are different in terms of their temporality: pun is simultaneous while rhyme is sequential (96). For there to be rhyme, there needs to be separation and difference, both between the two rhyming words and across time.

A long succession of the same rhyming sound comes dangerously close

to stepping outside this definition. Though it fulfills the requirement of
sequentiality, it threatens the expectation for difference or change across
time, especially when the rhyming words themselves are close or even
identical in meaning as well as sound. Again Frost exploits this risk mar-
velously in "The Rose Family," an interesting and rare example of an entirely monorhymed poem:

> The rose is a rose,
> And was always a rose.
> But the theory now goes
> That the apple's a rose,
> And the pear is, and so's
> The plum, I suppose.
> The dear only knows
> What will next prove a rose.
> You, of course, are a rose—
> But were always a rose. (246)

In its ten lines, the poem pushes its language in the direction of pure
rhyme or pure identity. Thus, six of the ten lines end with the same word
(or tautological rhyme), *rose*, a word present also in the title and first line.
The remaining four lines offer four different rhymes for the word: *goes* :
so's : *suppose* : *knows*, the middle two contributing to the poem's tone of
understatement, humor, and casualness. The rhyming is highly repetitive
and circular, as the poem commences with two lines ending on *rose*, and
ends with three.

While a word chimes with itself too perfectly or purely to be considered
a rhyme, such repetition evokes the rhetorical figure of tautology that
Frost's allusion to Gertrude Stein's "Rose is a rose is a rose is a rose" immediately brings to mind. With the rhyming engulfing the poem around a
single word and rhyming sound, issues of identity and connectedness are
brought to the fore. It is no surprise, if we stay on theme but move from
rhyme to figuration, that Judith Oster uses the poem in her discussion
of Frost's metaphors and reads the poem as dealing with metaphor itself,
a figure so central to Frost's conceptualization of poetry. Oster asks, in

part for Frost and in part for herself as a reader of the poem: "What constitutes legitimate metaphor? Why is it that a woman can be a rose but an apple cannot be?" And also "How close can metaphor come to being identity?" (168).

Though these questions do not explicitly involve rhyme, a significant way the poem evokes them is through its deft handling of rhyming, and more precisely, through its choice of monorhyme. If rhyme is a metaphor on the level of sound, then by using the same rhyming sound over and over again, Frost is performing the very act that he is describing in the poem: a deliberation about the possible inclusion of new concepts (apple, pear, plum) under the heading of "rose," or under a rhyme with the word *rose*. In the poem, these new inclusions are contrasted with two things that have "always been" a rose: a rose, and *you*. The temporality of "always been" wins out over the new "theory," and it is this never-changing temporality that we find cyclically at the poem's beginning and end: the tautological "rose is a rose," and the ultimate realization that "you . . . are a rose." This is a timeless, continuous present, pure identity of sound and concept that is never untrue, enacted by the repetitive monorhyme approximating identical, intransitive, solipsistic solorhyme.[29]

3

Organizing and Disrupting

Rhyme's Schematic Duplicity

RHYME AS THE AGENT AND OBJECT OF ORGANIZATION
Rhyme's rigidity, or even tyranny, has to do with a narrowing of options: once the first of the two rhyming words is selected (from the poet's side) or given (from the reader's side), there are severe limitations for its partner. And that very narrowing is further traditionally organized in poems via rhyme schemes. Rhyme schemes are the prototypical instance of what I am calling systematic rhyme. In schemes, expectations for the rhyme to come are generated, a fact that poets use creatively.

The rhyme scheme serves the poem by organizing the poetic material. Instead of a series of lines grouped by grammar or theme, as a paragraph is said to be in expository prose, rhyme groups lines into stanzas, and the rhyme schemes organize the stanzas internally. This organizing is perhaps the most recognized function of rhyme, dubbed the "organizational" or the "schematic" (Hollander, *Vision and Resonance* 121) or even the "metrical" function (Wellek and Warren 160). The term *metrical* speaks to the affinity between rhyme and meter; by default, metrical poetry in English is rhymed (blank verse stands as the prototypical alternative).

In rhyme schemes, rhyming has a structural, prosodic function; it is part of the poem's makeup. Rhyme schemes often scheme or plot the poem. Think of the Shakespearean sonnet, with its characteristic /abab cdcd efef gg/ end rhyming. This rhyme scheme materially, sonically, and cognitively turns a fourteen-line poem into a sonnet, made up of three quatrains and a concluding couplet, an internal division that individual sonnets work with and against. Or think of the rhyme scheme of a Petrarchan sonnet (for instance, abba abba cde cde), which, alternatively, organizes the same fourteen lines into an octave and a sestet.

So prevalent is this organizational function of rhyme that, for Viktor Zhirmunsky, it makes up rhyme's very definition; for him, rhyme is "every phonetic repetition . . . that claims a functional (in other words, structural) meaning in the metrical composition of a poem" (121). Sporadic rhyme, one might quickly add, calls this definition into question: it is phonetic repetition that does *not* claim a structural role in the composition of the poem. And although rhyme seems a natural device with which to organize the poem, one should not be too quick to accept this naturalness. Rhyme was not always part of the organization of the poem and does not have to be.

Before rhyme became integral to English versification, it was on the sidelines, appearing sporadically, and on occasion accidentally, in poems whose prosody was based on alliteration and a fixed number of stresses. Likewise, in classical, highly inflected Greek and Latin, rhyming was external to the poem's structural features, which were based on quantity. Instead of rhyme, in those cases, it is more accurate to speak of two close designations: homoeoteleuton (similar word endings when the words are indeclinable) and homoeoptoton (words in the same case and with like case inflections). These like endings were not simply outside of the prosodic system (and sometimes outside of verse altogether and used in prose as an embellishment); they also could be distracting. The author of *Rhetorica ad Herennium,* the classical Latin book on rhetoric, warns that both homoeoteleuton and homoeoptoton "are to be used very sparingly when we speak in an actual cause, because their invention seems impossible without labour and pains" (4.20.28, 4.20.32).[1]

This is an early instance of an old and persistent fear: the idea that rhyme, as the place where sound is brought to the fore *as sound,* is potentially so distracting that it threatens the functioning of language. The fear is close to the pleasurable dimension of rhyme; as a locus of harmony and pulsation of sound, rhyme punctures "normal" language, threatening to take over sense.[2] If we take this fear seriously, it's possible to come to see the organizational function of rhyme as essentially an act of curbing (that is, organizing and scheming) this distracting element. Rather than rhyme organizing the poem, which is the common account, an alternative view is that the poet is attempting to organize rhyme. Thus, the very element that potentially distracts us is brought into the poem in an organized way (via rhyme schemes), and then, by extension, helps to organize the poetic material as a whole.

Rhyme always straddles the line between harmonizing, settling, and organizing and distracting, confusing, and disorganizing. The paradoxical nature of the (dis)organizational function of rhyme is latent in each rhyme instance, but it surfaces especially clearly in sporadic rhyme situations, as much of the rhyme in twentieth-century poems makes abundantly clear. How is this duplicity played out?

To anticipate what we will see, the duplicity at the heart of sporadic rhyme means that it can be put to contradictory uses. Sporadic rhyme can be used to secure the integrity of a single line as well as contrarily, to puncture a text by counterpointing its lineation. And when a poem has both a rhyme scheme and sporadic rhyme, that sporadic internal rhyme, perceived as a subversive element vis-à-vis that rhyme scheme, can interact with the scheme in order to augment or deflate it. The location of the rhyme within the poem is just as crucial: a single rhyme at the end of the poem can be tremendously potent in signaling closure, but sporadic rhyme manages, in the same poem and in the same instance, to mark the end of the poem and to leave it void of excessive conclusiveness. Similarly, sporadic rhyme connects two stanzas or units of the poem while keeping them separate, offering a subtle sonic bridge without converting the two into one.

The tension between organizing and disrupting, then, gives rise to some of the most compelling work with rhyme, from rigid rhyme schemes to complete irregularity of rhyme. The range from systematic to sporadic is wide, and I start with one rhyming strategy that is situated smack in the middle.

IRREGULAR END RHYMING

Even more than meter, rhyme schemes reflect both rhyme's rigidity and the freeing, creative, pleasurable responses to that rigidity. While many poets write within an existing rhyme scheme or vary the scheme to a certain extent, thus introducing a sporadic and unexpected element, others will invent a new scheme altogether, or adopt one from poetry of a different language. John Donne and George Herbert were particularly creative in inventing rhyme schemes, often coupled with heterometrical lines, as were such later poets as Algernon Swinburne, Gerard Manley Hopkins, William Butler Yeats, and W. H. Auden.[3] Inventiveness may come in the rhyme scheme of a single-stanza poem, or the scheme may be repeated throughout many stanzas in a single poem (as in Alfred, Lord Tennyson's /abba/ in "In Memoriam" or Matthew Arnold's slightly extended version, /abbba/, in "On the Rhine") or across poems (such as John Keats's stanza /abab cdecde/, which he employed in several of his odes). Keats's scheme is a combination of a quatrain with the sestet of a Petrarchan sonnet, a novel combination of old forms (Robert Creeley's "Oh No," discussed in chapter 2, would be another example). Poets can also create distinctions or divisions within a poem via the changing of the rhyme scheme. For instance, John Milton's "L'Allegro" and "Il Penseroso" start with a ten-line rhyme scheme of /abba cddeec/, in which he addresses and dispenses with Melancholy and Joys, respectively, before turning to dozens of couplet lines that host the main focus of each poem.

Whether it is foreknown or realized only in retrospect, whether it takes a simple form or a more convoluted one, all of these rhyme schemes, by definition, include some gestalt created by the rhyming, some measure of regularity in the rhyming. At the other end of the spectrum are poems either entirely devoid of rhyme or in which the little bit of rhyming is so scantily distributed that it is unable to form a rhyme scheme. I call the kind of rhyming at the former end of the spectrum systematic and the kind at the latter end, sporadic. But there is another possibility that stands between the two. This is irregular end rhyming, by which I mean poems in which rhyming is consistent but so intricate or irregular that no clear gestalt can be created in the reader's mind.[4] In different ways, this rhyming is both systematic and sporadic. It is systematic in that nearly every single line rhymes with some other. Yet there is no regularity other than this fact of rhyming, so the rhyming pattern is unpredictable and unreplicable. While the dividing line between regular and irregular is ultimately a question of the reader's perception, the poems considered here are cases in which the sheer length of the stanzas prohibits an easy gestalt from emerging.

There are many examples of this kind of irregular end rhyming. In English, they include some of the most celebrated poems, like Edmund Spenser's "Epithalamion," Donne's "The Dissolution," Milton's "Lycidas," John Dryden's "A Song for St. Cecilia's Day," William Wordsworth's "Intimations of Immortality," and Percy Bysshe Shelley's "Mont Blanc." But taking liberties with rhyming, rhyming elaborately and irregularly, is not an English invention. The troubadours' examples of ingenuity in inventing ever-increasing permutations of rhyming is well documented,[5] and freedom with rhyming is explicitly endorsed by Dante, too. When discussing rhyme and stanza organization in the second book of *De vulgari eloquentia,* Dante states, "First of all you must know that almost all poets grant themselves a considerable degree of license in this matter," though he does go on to detail certain "rules of organization [that] are to be observed" (85).

English poets employing this kind of irregular rhyming could thus comfortably rely on Italian irregular forms as precedent. In fact, many of the exemplary uses in English, like those by Spenser, Milton, and Richard Crashaw, are versions and adaptations of influential Italian models, especially the canzone.[6] Another, no less salient context for a poet wanting to use irregular and idiosyncratic rhyme is the tradition of the ode, both Horatian and, even more so, Pindaric, associated in particular with Abraham Cowley's celebration of irregularity in his *Pindarick Odes* of 1656.[7] Pindar's precedent combines with "a certain growing weariness of the stanza," which George Saintsbury traces throughout the seventeenth century. The irregular stanzas were attractive, Saintsbury explains, because they offered "the variety and sweetness of rhyme without tying the poet down to the necessity of giving it at absolutely regular intervals" (2:339).

These longer irregularly rhyming poems have a unique set of variables with which to work. For one, what is the distance between two rhyming sounds? Are there lines, or whole sections, that do not rhyme? And, more generally, what is the relationship between the rhyming and the verse paragraph, a unit that some of these poems use? Moreover, since the poems are defined by an irregularity of their end rhyming, are there still local gestalts or patterns for the reader to seize upon? Is the whole more regular than it may appear? These last two questions are pertinent because a persistent feature of this kind of intriguing rhyming technique is that it resists regularity while at the same time evoking in readers a strong desire to seek one out, to explain or explain away the irregularity.[8]

PROXIMITY

T. S. Eliot employs various rhyming techniques, and he provides a strong modern example of regularity of rhyme with irregularity of rhyme scheme in such early poems as "The Love Song of J. Alfred Prufrock," "Portrait of a Lady," and "Preludes." Here, more than anywhere else, Eliot is heavily influenced by Jules Laforgue's brand of French vers libre, not just in a tone that combines self-pity and irony (Soldo 140) but also in this precise technique of rhyming, which Eliot describes, when acknowledging his debt to Laforgue, as "rhyming lines of irregular length, with the rhyme coming in irregular places" (quoted in Soldo 146). A great many of the potential exploitations of this irregular rhyming can be seen in the following lines spoken by the nervous and obsessive Prufrock:

For I have known them all already, known them all—	A
Have known the evenings, mornings, afternoons,	B
I have measured out my life with coffee spoons;	B
I know the voices dying with a dying fall	A
Beneath the music from a farther room.	C
So how should I presume?	C
And I have known the eyes already, known them all—	A
The eyes that fix you in a formulated phrase,	D
And when I am formulated, sprawling on a pin,	E
When I am pinned and wriggling on the wall,	A
Then how should I begin	E

To spit out all the butt-ends of my days and ways?	D
And how should I presume?	C
And I have known the arms already, known them all—	A
Arms that are braceleted and white and bare	F
(But in the lamplight, downed with light brown hair!)	F
Is it perfume from a dress	G
That makes me so digress?	G
Arms that lie along a table, or wrap about a shawl.	A
And should I then presume?	C
And how should I begin?	E

(Eliot, *Collected Poems* 4–5)

These three "I have known" stanzas, following two "And indeed there will be time" stanzas, form a cohesive rhythmic group both internally and in relation to one another. Each starts similarly, with a declaration of experience and knowledge, and ends similarly, with an anxious question that seems to derive from that declaration. Among the three stanzas there is basic parallelism, as well as progression: between the first ("For I have known") and the last ("And I have known"), the number of lines increases from six to seven to eight, and the number of questions increases from one to two to three.

Affixing our attention now on end rhymes, we see that no line remains unrhymed. In total, there are seven terminal rhyme sounds (A–G) in twenty-one lines, and though loose patterns can be detected, there is no rhyme scheme as such:

1. ABBACC
2. ADEAEDC
3. AFFGGACE

The first stanza has the A-, B-, and C-rhymes in an envelope rhyme followed by a couplet, while the other two stanzas keep the A-rhyme and add two new rhyming sounds: D and E in the second stanza, F and G in the third. The fact that for every terminal word there is a rhyming partner can be exploited through shifting the variable of proximity, and indeed some rhyming pairs follow each other in maximal proximity (BB and CC in the first stanza, FF and GG in the third), while others are separated by quite a few lines.

Interesting effects of this irregularity of recurrence are seen when tracing the recurring crucial word *presume* in relation to the stanza and the rhyming in which it is embedded. In the first stanza, the word is fastened by its close proximity to its rhyming partner *room* (CC) and further secured by the B-rhyme (*afternoons* and *spoons*) with which it shares a vowel and a close consonant. But in the second stanza, *presume* has no rhyming partner within the stanza, and so for it to be integrated into the web of rhyme, one needs to shift backwards seven lines, all the way to the last line of the first stanza. The word has drifted far from its rhyming partner. The same thing happens upon encountering *presume* in the penultimate line of the third stanza, with the small difference of having an internal sporadic rhyming partner three lines up, *perfume*. In short, the word starts as part of a closely knit rhyme and becomes more distant and detached. The effect is a progressive loosening or weakening of the question itself, which undergoes a slight but significant change from "So how should I presume?" to the less confident "And should I then presume?"

The key word of the other recurring question, "How should I *begin*?," undergoes similar treatment. In the second stanza, *begin* is only one line apart from its rhyming partner *pin* (the E-rhyme), but it reappears without a rhyming partner in the last line of the third stanza, requiring the reader to look back ten lines and cross a stanzaic boundary in order to reach the same sound. *Begin* in the third stanza becomes an echo or faint memory of a rhyme from an earlier stanza. The perceived effect is an increase in hesitancy, a drifting away from pattern and security in rhyme and emotional tone. Rhyme in "Prufrock" is perfectly suited to represent the duality of the neurotic speaker: rhyme's recurrence underscores the obsessive, repetitive nature of the questioning, while its uncertain and loosening scheme underscores a sense of hesitant insecurity.[9]

Above all else, the variable of proximity, how close a word is to its rhyming partner, is at play in the dynamic afforded by consistently using rhyme in inconsistent order. The reader learns that every line rhymes, or, in other words, that this is a rhyming poem. This contractual realization is synonymous with the expectation that every new rhyming sound introduced will find its rhyming partner, somewhere, sometime, hopefully before a sound has disappeared from active memory.[10] The question of how long the first rhyming word will linger before the reader encounters its partner is at the very heart of the sporadic game.

Since in this kind of rhyming almost every line rhymes with some other, each line will either close a rhyme that is already in motion or open a new one. These are essentially two kinds of lines: lines that do not—at the point of encounter—rhyme with any line, and lines that do. Therefore, a question related to that of proximity is a question about the distribution of these two kinds of lines.

In the example here, the fifth stanza of Wordsworth's "Ode: Intimations of Immortality from Recollections of Early Childhood," I have marked the lines to represent this dynamic, so that the number at the end of each line tallies the number of lines so far endured in anticipation of a closing rhyme. The first line, since it does not rhyme with any previous line, starts the count at 1. The next line does not rhyme with the first, and so the number is now 2, representing two successive lines without a rhyme. When a line is reached that rhymes back, with whichever previous line, the number goes back to zero, the clock starting over, as in line 3.

Our birth is but a sleep and a forgetting:	1
The Soul that rises with us, our life's Star,	2
Hath had elsewhere its setting,	0
And cometh from afar:	0
Not in entire forgetfulness,	1
And not in utter nakedness,	0
But trailing clouds of glory do we come	1
From God, who is our home:	0
Heaven lies about us in our infancy!	1
Shades of the prison-house begin to close	2
Upon the growing Boy,	3
But he beholds the light, and whence it flows,	0
He sees it in his joy;	0

The Youth, who daily farther from the east	1
Must travel, still is Nature's Priest,	0
And by the vision splendid	1
Is on his way attended;	0
At length the Man perceives it die away,	1
And fade into the light of common day.	0
(Wordsworth, *Poems* 525–26)	

The stanza moves chronologically from birth to manhood, with stops at infancy, boyhood, and youth. Wordsworth uses vision and light as a guiding benchmark to trace this process of maturing, displaying, as Lionel Trilling has written, "the reminiscence of the light of heaven and its gradual evanescence through the maturing years" (149).

In terms of rhyming, sixteen out of nineteen lines are marked by either a zero or a one. In fact, most of the stanza consists of alternating zeros and ones. This means that the baseline is no more than a single-line wait for a rhyme, a temporal structure characteristic of the couplet. But there are two places in the stanza (indicated by bold type) where the reader must endure more lines before a rhyme. First, at the very beginning of the stanza, where the second line joins the first in not rhyming. The second and more intriguing place is in the middle, where there are three consecutive nonrhyming lines. In both cases, this nonrhyming stretch is immediately compensated for with two zero-marked lines.

These are moments of potential threat to the rhyming, and represent opportunities for places of tense or convoluted material. The temporal dynamic is one of mounting tension: the longer the deferral of the rhyme, the higher tensions rise, until they are resolved with the arrival of rhyme. This tension-resolution is particularly exploited in the second highlighted case:

Heaven lies about us in our infancy!	1
Shades of the prison-house begin to close	2
Upon the growing Boy,	3
But he beholds the light, and whence it flows,	0
He sees it in his joy;	0

The first line presents the imagined beginning, the heavenly state of infancy, while the two following lines depict a battle between the boy and the prison-house, the boy's growth curbed by the prison closing in. All of this is rendered in three successive nonrhyming lines in a poem that has already established itself as consistently rhyming. The rhyme then returns, after the temporary three-line nonrhyming wasteland, in what turns out to be a pivotal moment. It starts with the boy's defiant rebuttal ("But he"), initiating two insistently rhyming lines to compensate for the three nonrhyming ones, the last occurrence of such a rhyming succession in the stanza. These two lines continue with "beholds," which echoes "But he" (*But he : Be holds*), and end with the rhyme that realizes the boy's *joy*. The "shades of the prison-house" are answered by the light the boy still beholds; the prison's attempt to *close* is answered by the rhyming partner, *flows,* realizing the conflict between closing in and growing.

If rhyme is understood as rigid, there is an ironic discrepancy between the rhyming and the proposition: the lines depicting the prison-house closing in on the boy are the ones temporarily free of rhyme. It could be that the sense of tension and mounting expectation for a return to rhyme is lurking just below consciousness and *via negativa* confirms the prison-house. Perhaps the frustration of not having the rhyme come back mirrors the disorienting feeling of loss of harmony with the world that comes with imprisonment. At any rate, the linguistic joy in rhyme, maximized at the point of return to rhyme after a long wait, coincides with the boy's own joy and temporary triumph over the prison-house. In these six lines, the rhyming works to differentiate the two warring elements on both sides of the discourse marker *but.* Temporarily switching the rhyme off and then switching it back on adds a dramatic countermovement to the linear progression of ever-fading light of which the entire stanza speaks.[11]

THORN LINES: SPORADIC NONRHYMING

In theory, there are two extreme possibilities of proximity in irregular end rhyming: *maximal proximity,* when the rhyming partner arrives as fast as possible, that is, in the very next line,[12] and *zero proximity,* when the rhyming partner never arrives. The second kind is sometimes called a "thorn line," and it could be described as sporadic nonrhyming. Thorn lines are not limited to situations of long irregular rhyming, and they also exist as a breach of systematic rhyme, a deviation from or variation on a set rhyme scheme—imagine a series of couplets and then, suddenly, a line *not* followed by its rhyming partner.[13]

However, when the reader does not anticipate a specific rhyme in a specific position, only that it will come *somewhere,* the thorn line works differently. The strong expectation of a rhyme is not conspicuously disappointed; rather, an expectation lingers and becomes diffused. The letdown is not localized so much as it is gradual. Or there may not be letdown at all. In fact, Thomas Shaw shows that there are two contradictory pragmatic effects of unexpected nonrhyming within a larger rhyming work (his corpus is Alexander Pushkin's rhyming works): it can invite the reader to supply the missing word or it can signal a continuation, a lack of closure, as when Pushkin ends a catalog or list with a nonrhyming word, implying that the list has not ended and could be extended (*Pushkin's Poetics* 68).

In Matthew Arnold's irregularly rhyming "Dover Beach," the ninth line in the first, fourteen-line sonnet-like section is the only one not to find a rhyming partner anywhere in that section. Curiously, this is the very line in which the speaker calls on his addressee to "Listen!":

The sea is calm to-night.	A
The tide is full, the moon lies fair	B
Upon the straits;—on the French coast the light	A
Gleams and is gone; the cliffs of England stand,	C
Glimmering and vast, out in the tranquil bay.	D
Come to the window, sweet is the night-air!	B
Only, from the long line of spray	D
Where the sea meets the moon-blanch'd land,	C
Listen! you hear the grating roar	E
Of pebbles which the waves draw back, and fling,	F
At their return, up the high strand,	C
Begin, and cease, and then again begin,	G
With tremulous cadence slow, and bring	F
The eternal note of sadness in.	G (Arnold 211–12)

Since there is no clear rhyme scheme in the poem, the prick of the thorn, the denial of rhyme, is rather gentle. By the ninth line, the reader has twice had to wait four whole lines for a rhyming partner (for the B- and C-rhymes), and so the lack of an immediate rhyming partner for *roar* is not necessarily remarkable, the sonic distinction of the word among other rhyming words in the section notwithstanding. When, in the following lines, all rhyming sounds receive partners, as happens in the next, six-line section of the poem, we may feel a lack of resolution for the *roar* line. Or this line, which "was once," may be awakened in the reader only in retrospect, upon reaching the second line of the third section, the one to rhyme twelve lines back. If this retroactive rhyming was missed, the word *roar* itself is re-evoked two lines down, again in sonic remembrance of things past ("Its melancholy, long, withdrawing roar"):

> The Sea of Faith
> **Was once, too, at the full, and round earth's shore**   E
> Lay like the folds of a bright girdle furl'd
> But now I only hear
> **Its melancholy, long, withdrawing roar,**   E
> Retreating, to the breath
> Of the night-wind, down the vast edges drear
> And naked shingles of the world. (211)

The rhyme of words is also a rhyme of events and locales: the sea that the speaker can see out the window rhymes with the "Sea of Faith." Sound is always literal (the word *roar* is literally literalized sound because of onomatopoeia), but here sound connects the literal roar of the sea to the metaphorical, imagined roar of the metaphorical, imagined "Sea of Faith." It connects but also separates, since in the time span between the first roar and the second, *roar* itself turns from grating ("you hear the grating roar" in the first section) to retreating ("Its melancholy, long, withdrawing roar" in the third section).

"Dover Beach" thus makes good use of the much-deferred rhyme on *roar*, first to lend it markedness, due to its missing rhyming partner,[14] and then, with the eventual arrival of rhyme, to convey a sense of looking back, or listening back. Both the organizing and the disrupting aspects of this kind of rhyming are essential. If rhyme is supposed to mark the end of each line, it is somewhat disorienting to have a line that does not rhyme. The expectation for rhyme makes the lack of it stand out in the first section. And the unexpected stretching of the variable of proximity, not knowing when the rhyme will come, facilitates the long wait, or retrospective surprise, in the third section.

INTERNAL RHYME AND SPORADIC RHYME

It is customary to think of end rhyme as regularized, systematic rhyme and of internal rhyme as more sporadic. This certainly makes sense, if we rely on empirical evidence, since so much of what has counted as poetry employs end rhyme systematically; all institutionalized rhyme scheme forms and genres, like ottava rima, belong to this category. But the dimension of end/internal and the dimension of systematic/sporadic, at least in theory, are entirely independent.

	Systematic Rhyme	Sporadic Rhyme
End rhyme	Poetic genres and forms that have specific rhyme schemes as part of their generic repertoire (for example, couplets, terza rima, sonnet, or ottava rima)	Poems in which nearly every line rhymes with some other line but no rhyme scheme emerges because rhyming patterns are irregular and unpredictable (for example, Milton's "Lycidas," Wordsworth's "Intimations," Eliot's "Prufrock")
Internal rhyme	Poetic genres and forms that regularize rhymes in places other than (just) the end of the line (for example, Leonine verse and the Czech Gothic epic)	Poems in which rhyme appears, irregularly and unpredictably, anywhere in (some of) the lines

At the beginning of this chapter, we analyzed Eliot's "Prufrock" and Wordsworth's "Intimations" as instances of sporadic end rhyme, and Leonine verse, in which a word at line end regularly rhymes with the word preceding the caesura of the same line in a hexameter, is an example of systematic internal rhyme. Another example is Czech Gothic epic, made up of rhymed quatrains in which there is a regularly recurring internal rhyme in the third line (Worth, "Roman Jakobson" 521). Still, the most common instances of sporadic rhyme are internal rhymes, and vice versa. Sporadic internal rhyme is, in a sense, a double affront, carrying the risks both of internal rhyme and of sporadic rhyme.

One of the biggest challenges that rhyme can pose to the poem's organization is to appear in the middle of a line and thus refuse to quietly overlap with the line unit. Still, not all internal rhymes are born equal. B. J. Pendlebury, in an insightful chapter on rhyme in modern poetry, makes an important distinction between two kinds of internal rhymes. The first is the kind found often in ballads, where the rhymes, though internal, come at points in the line where there is a natural pause; the second is internal rhymes that "cannot be thought of as breaking the line in half" (89–90). The renowned prosodist George Saintsbury, early in the twentieth century, made the same distinction, with an added judgment on the desirability of internal rhyme "at other than these natural pauses." He ends his account of rhyme by saying conclusively, "On the whole, rhyme should come at the end of something" (3:539).

The source of this aesthetic preference for internal rhyme that marks an "end of something" is not difficult to gauge. Rhyme traditionally comes at the end of metrical lines; indeed, marking the end is a major function of rhyme. Thus, if rhyme comes not at the end of the typographical/metrical unit that is the line, one still wants it to preserve part of its original function by at least coming at the end of a syntactic unit or of a lesser metrical unit, like the half-line. The more rhyme departs from this expectation, the more it seems autonomous, unwarranted, or sporadic, and the resistance to it increases accordingly. Generally, it is better to talk of different degrees of sporadicity when considering various options for internal rhyming.

Oscar Wilde's "Ballad of Reading Gaol" can help demonstrate the function of internal rhymes. Here is the second stanza:

He walked amongst the Trial Men
  In a suit of shabby grey;
A cricket cap was on his head,
  And his step seemed light and gay;
But I never saw a man who looked
  So wistfully at the day. (Wilde, *Complete Poetry* 152)

Wilde expands the common-meter four-line ballad stanza to six lines; the
odd lines rhyme with one another and the even lines do not, producing
the rhyming /xaxaxa/. Though the number of syllables varies somewhat
in each of the two line types, the odd lines consistently contain four beats,
and the even, rhyming lines, only three. In the above stanza, no other
rhyme exists, but quite often one finds in the poem stanzas such as the
following two, in which I have highlighted only the internal rhymes and
not the systematic end rhyming:

He does not rise in piteous haste
  To put on convict-clothes,
While some coarse-mouthed Doctor gloats, and notes
  Each new and nerve-twitched pose,
Fingering a watch whose little ticks
  Are like horrible hammer-blows. (154)

. . . .

With slouch and swing around the ring
  We trod the Fool's Parade!
We did not care: we knew we were
  The Devil's Own Brigade:
And shaven head and feet of lead
  Make a merry masquerade. (158)

Stanzas like these exhibit internal sporadic rhyming, rhyme that is not part of the rhyme scheme. These internal rhymes constitute a surprise or surplus compared to the rhyming of the more moderate end rhyme–only stanzas.[15] The internal rhyme is far less systematized than the regular end rhyme, and to add to the irregularity, these kinds of stanzas are unsystematically dispersed amid the stanzas that have no such internal rhyming.

But are these internal rhymes truly so irregular? In the quoted stanzas, internal rhymes, when they appear, are not arbitrarily placed. They are restricted to the odd, four-beat lines that do not rhyme as part of the rhyme scheme; they are never in the even, three-beat A-lines. Moreover, the place within the line where rhyme appears is not arbitrary, either. In the second of the two stanzas, which represents the majority of cases with internal rhyming, the first rhyming word comes exactly at the middle of the line, on the second beat, and its partner appears at the end of the line, on the fourth beat:

With **slouch** and **<u>swing</u>** around the **<u>ring</u>**[16]

This internal rhyming also comes at the strongest syntactic break in the line ("With slouch and swing // around the ring"), thus fulfilling Saintsbury's requirement that it come "at the end of something." In the "He does not rise" stanza quoted, it seems that the internal rhyme is more disruptive because it does not halve the line so symmetrically. Yet the rhyme still coincides with a major syntactic break within the line and falls only on the beats—in this case, the third and fourth rather than the second and fourth:

While some **coarse**-mouthed Doctor **<u>gloats</u>**, and **<u>notes</u>**

These internal rhymes are sporadic in that they do not occur in all stanzas and are not part of the scheme per se, yet they are highly constrained. When they occur, it is always in these potential places: on odd lines, on the beat, and at the ends of syntactic or phrasal units within the line. As the long poem continues and stanzas with such rhyming accumulate, the level of sporadicity diminishes somewhat. In fact, we can speak of a rhyme scheme with two levels: obligatory end rhyming on three of the stanza's

lines, and optional internal rhyming in the other three lines. Using Robert
Abernathy's helpful distinction, the optional internal rhyming lines can
be said to be normally "rhymeless" but not "antirhyme" with respect to
the places of prominence within them (3). Such optional rhymes lend
local emphasis and embellishment, a variation highly needed in a poem
consisting of so many recurring stanzas.

INTERACTING WITH THE RHYME SCHEME
Wilde's internal rhymes fall in foreknown and designated places within
the line and coexist in harmony with the rhyme scheme. But this relatively
restrained nature is not true for many internal rhymes. An example of less
harmoniously integrated rhymes can be found in the opening stanza of
William Blake's "The Chimney Sweeper," from *Songs of Innocence:*

When my mother died I was very <u>young</u>,	A
And my father sold me while yet my <u>tongue</u>	A
Could scarcely cry <u>weep weep weep weep</u>.	B
So your chimneys I <u>sweep</u> & in soot I <u>sleep</u>.[17]	B (Blake 10)

Blake uses the four-by-four and /aabb/ form of the ballad meter ("long meter").[18] This form continues throughout the poem's next five stanzas and
determines its systematic end rhyming, but in the last line of this stanza
there an internal rhyme: *sweep : sleep.* Similar to the examples from Wilde,
here the rhyming falls at the end of a metrical and syntactic break, dividing the last line into two symmetrical hemistiches. Unlike Wilde's rhymes,
however, this internal rhyming is implicated in the rhyme scheme itself:
the word *sweep* intervenes as an extra rhyming partner between two B-
rhymes, *weep* and *sleep.* The interaction between *sweep* and the third line
is further accentuated because of the repetition of the rhyming word
weep, so that the end and internal rhyming join forces to create a lengthy
and highly marked rhyming group: *weep : weep : weep : weep : sweep : sleep,*
ironically and bitterly accentuating the very cry that the speaker's tongue
could "scarcely cry."

Blake has the speaker's tongue work hard on rhythmic grounds, too.
While other lines easily fall into the four-beat scheme, exhibiting a mix

of iambs and anapests (for instance, "When my **mo**ther **died** I was **very young**"), it is very difficult to envision a vocalization (or subvocalization) of the third line ("Could scarcely cry weep weep weep weep") without exceeding the expected four beats. The place of extreme repetition, which retroactively, upon reaching the fourth line ("So your chimneys I *sweep* & in soot I *sleep*"), also turns out to be a place of extreme rhyming, is also the very place where rhythmic regularity ceases. The eruption of the speaker's cry exceeds the regularizing effect of rhythm and carries further, outside of regular bounds, the poem's systematic rhyme.[19]

Using internal rhyme that rhymes with the systematic end rhyming of the stanza has double-edged potentiality. In Blake's case, it worked to cumulate and augment the existing rhyming. In his poem "Death," Yeats uses it to the opposite effect, namely robbing the end rhyming of its force.

Nor dread nor hope attend	A
A dying animal;	B
A man awaits his end	A
Dreading and hoping all;	B
Many times he died,	C
Many times rose again.	D
A great man in his pride	C
Confronting murderous men	D
Casts derision upon	E
Supersession of <u>breath</u>;	F
He knows <u>death</u> to the bone—	E
Man has created <u>death</u>.	F (Yeats 234)

Listening to the rhyming, even before attending to what the poem "means," we see that the end rhyming divides the poem's twelve lines into three parts, each a quatrain with an alternating rhyme scheme, such as /abab/. Allowing for Yeats's partial rhymes, the final four lines realize the rhyme scheme with the words *upon : breath : bone : death.* And yet the word *death* appears first internally, in the penultimate line, before its appearance as part of the rhyme scheme, and much closer to its rhyming partner, *breath.* This sporadic internal rhyming of *breath : death* competes with the end rhyming *breath : death,* first because it comes first, and second because it is made up of the same words. Death's first appearance thus steals the second's thunder and greatly deemphasizes the rhyme scheme, as if the rhyme escaped, or rather preceded, its bounds.

By the time *death* recurs at the end of the poem, in accordance with the rhyme scheme, we may be less impressed, having already encountered the word. And the way in which the second half of the poem characterizes a "great man in his pride" is entirely fitting to this rhyming strategy. Unlike the dying animal or the man in the first half of the poem, the "great man" has no fear of death; he has control over it, and knows it, Yeats writes, "to the bone." The early rhyme on the word *death* manifests the foreknowledge of death or the control over it by which the "great man" is characterized, as if the lines themselves take control of death by placing it earlier than anticipated.

In a poem laden with other rhymes, the sporadic internal rhyme will always stand out when proximity and other variables work in its favor. And one can also make use of the rhyme scheme in order to further prop up the internal rhyme, including when the two do not share a sound. An example in miniature is Howard Nemerov's poem "The Common Wisdom," an ironic and bitter piece of proverbial wisdom on marriage, culminating in a final line that teases the potential atrocity out of the "common wisdom":

Their marriage is a good one. In our eyes	A
What makes a marriage *good?* Well, that the tether	B
<u>Fray</u> but not break, and that they <u>stay</u> together.	B
One should be watching while the other dies.	A (Nemerov 67)

The rhyme scheme, /abba/, represents two proximities for the end rhyme, either at a distance of two lines (the A-rhyme) or immediately at the next line (the B-rhyme). The internal sporadic rhyme, *fray : stay,* supported somewhat by the unstressed *they* that precedes the word *stay,* stands out because of its positioning within the same line, with the proximity much greater than for the other two systematic rhymes (and for the other sporadic rhyme, *good : should*). The sporadic rhyme is situated between the two B-rhymes, which are themselves situated between the two A-rhymes:

eyes   dies
    tether   together
        fray   stay

This positioning puts much emphasis on the doubly nested and semantically incongruent rhyme *fray* : *stay,* the last rhyme of the three to be
introduced, and the first to find its ending.

INTERNAL RHYME DOMINATING THE LINE

If rhyme schemes are taken as attempts to organize the poem and to curb
the unruly rhyme, or sound stratum, by way of organizing it, it becomes
clear that a poem will be sensitive to additional rhyming that escapes the
scheme. In the earlier examples, therefore, where a rhyme scheme exists,
the internal rhyme is perceived as external to it, a transgression of the rules.
And while internal rhyme can interact with the scheme and accentuate it
(as in Blake) or be accentuated by it (as in Nemerov), in the sprung rhythm
of Hopkins—perhaps the master of such internal rhyming—internal
rhyming is so pronounced that it dominates the line; thus, transgression
almost becomes the rule.[20]

W. H. Gardner takes great pains to elucidate the influence of early
Welsh poetry on Hopkins, in addition to the other important sources
of rhythmic influence, which include classical Greek poetry, Old English, nursery rhymes, and earlier English poets (143–54). Though Hopkins did not follow the system to the letter, the centrality of *cynghanedd*
("harmony"), the systematization of internal rhymes and other sounds
in Welsh poetry, undoubtedly impacted his use of those sound devices.
While these were systematic in the Welsh, however, Hopkins's use, transported to English poetry, is sporadic. The octave of the sonnet "God's
Grandeur" exhibits much of his technique:

The world is charged with the grandeur of <u>God</u>.	A
It will flame out, like shining from shook <u>foil</u>;	B
It gathers to a greatness, like the ooze of <u>oil</u>	B
Crushed. Why do <u>men then</u> now not reck his <u>rod</u>?	A
Generations have <u>trod</u>, have <u>trod</u>, have <u>trod</u>;	A

And all is <u>seared</u> with trade; <u>bleared</u>, <u>smeared</u> with <u>toil</u>;   B
And <u>wears</u> man's smudge and <u>shares</u> man's smell: the <u>soil</u>   B
Is bare now, nor can foot feel, being <u>shod</u>.   A (Hopkins 70)

First, the sheer abundance of rhyming in the lines has a global effect: the internal sporadic rhyming is a participant in the tight repetition of sound and phrase that starts with the systematic rhyme scheme of the Petrarchan sonnet, itself more tightly rhymed than its Shakespearean counterpart because it contains more rhyming words on fewer sounds. When we add the other sound devices, functioning in nearly every line (for instance, the multiple consonances in *grandeur* : *God, shining from* : *shook foil, gathers* : *greatness,* to take the first three lines), we come to perceive the lines as a web of sound repetitions of which rhyme is the most obtrusive.

How do the internal rhymes operate? In part, they interact with the end rhyming in ways discussed earlier. The word *trod* in line 5 is part of the A-rhyme, but it is reached much before its expected time to chime with *rod*:

Crushed. Why do men then now not reck his <u>rod</u>?   A
Generations have <u>trod</u>, have <u>trod</u>, have <u>trod</u>;   A

It is not just that *trod* repeats three times. By the time we arrive at *trod* we already have its rhyming partner *rod* in mind, so every time *trod* repeats, the rhyme recurs, resulting in three identical and successive rhymes (*rod* : *trod, rod* : *trod, rod* : *trod*), an emphatic icon for the repetitious treading (and trading) itself.

But, to my ear, the most salient and curious rhyming is found in the antepenultimate and penultimate lines:

And all is <u>seared</u> with trade; <u>bleared</u>, <u>smeared</u> with <u>toil</u>;
And <u>wears</u> man's smudge and <u>shares</u> man's smell: the <u>soil</u>

In these lines the sporadic rhymes are fully internal: the words *seared* : *bleared* : *smeared* and *wears* : *shares* are all inside the line, not reaching the line's end. Unlike the Yeats example from earlier, or the rhyming of *rod* : *trod* : *trod* in this stanza, this rhyming does not ricochet off the end rhyming. The rhyming is independent and, in its sheer quantity, dominates the lines. In the first line the internal rhyming overtakes the line both sonically (three of the ten words rhyme internally) and rhythmically, particularly in the anti-iambic stress clash of the pair *bleared* : *smeared*, only partly reduced by the comma intervening between them.

Proximate and parallel content words that rhyme cannot but be stressed, as they reinforce each other in an emphatic stressing above and beyond the constraints of their metrical environment, which explains Hopkins's abundant use of internal rhymes in such highly sprung poems as the celebrated "The Wreck of the Deutschland." To this I add that "with toil" picks up "with trade," resulting in an almost entirely repetitious line. The command of the line by the rhyme is aided further by the semantic congruency of the rhymes themselves. Since the triple rhyme *seared* : *bleared* : *smeared* binds together three verbs that agree in sense as well as in sound, the sporadic rhyme is used to augment, reinforce, and emphasize this sense. This semantic layer and the mass of rhyming glue together the material in the line, making the line a cohesive mass.

In the second line, *wears* and *shares* are likewise connected semantically, and the phrasal and sonic repetition epitomized in the rhyming is again enriched by surrounding sounds, namely the "and" before the verbs and the /m-s-m/ sequence after them: "wears man's smudge" and "shares man's smell." This line's cohesion is slightly weaker, though, than the previous line's, for several reasons. First, only two words participate in the rhyming, as opposed to three in the previous line. Second, the variable of proximity is lessened, as the distance between *wears* and *shares* is greater than the maximal proximity of *bleared* : *smeared*. Finally, *wears* and *shares* occur in rhythmically prominent positions, requiring less of a strain than the stress clash in the previous line.

What is the effect of this conspicuous internal rhyming? The organizational function of rhyme is transferred from fastening together different lines into stanzas to underscoring the line unit itself, strengthening its autonomy against other lines (and, in the process, competing with the organization the rhyme scheme achieves throughout the poem). With so much of the rhyming focused inside a line, the sheer sonic noise of the line "springs" it up, pulls it out from the poem, affording it extra weight and definition. As should be clear by now, the attribute *extra*, by definition, requires that the rhyme be sporadic, since if it were systematic and expected it would remain the default. Because rhyme schemes sanction rhyme in certain places and forbid it in others, an overabundance of internal, sporadic, transgressive rhyming is perceived as an irruption, a "flaming out," perhaps out of control.

RHYME ACROSS LINES OR STANZAS

When a line is host to so much rhyming, as in Hopkins, the effect is to make the line stand out, underlining its integrity by gluing its words together. When the internal sporadic rhymes are positioned across different lines or even stanzas, with reasonable distance, the rhyme strives to do the same. In these cases, rhyme fastens together not the words of one line but certain stanzas or lines, bridging the lineal or stanzaic divide. This organizational function is different from that of systematic end rhyme, where rhyme is a strong participant in the very creation of stanzas. Rather than create or define the stanzaic form of the poem, sporadic rhyme has the potential to undermine the integrity of the stanza.

May Swenson, a poet whose work exhibits extensive sporadic rhyming, uses this (dis)organizational function of sporadic rhyming across the first two stanzas of the poem "Close-Up of a Couple on a Couch":

> Creases in his clothes
> creases in his flesh
> creases in his arteries
> The inner walls shrinking
> while the outer walls slip and shift flabbily
> Pepper grains in the chin-furrows
> in the pale ear-basins
> the inelastic lobes sagging <u>tits</u>
>
> She <u>sits</u> still
> until it is over
> holding her breath her tongue curled back
> like a fastidious animal

aloof before an old cur
circling and sniffing her (Swenson 112)[21]

This too-close-for-comfort close-up of the couple starts with the man,
the focal point of the poem, penetrating progressively inward, from his
clothes to his flesh to his arteries. Much of the characterization, in this
stanza and in later ones, is centered around the man's weight, the stanza
ending with his "sagging tits." By the second stanza, focalization has
shifted to the woman, still and fastidious, waiting out the sexual interaction with obvious displeasure. The cross-stanzaic rhyme, *tits : sits,* is
reached quickly within the new stanza.

On a semantic level, the rhyme connects the couple—the *tits* his, the
sits hers—and participates in the blurring that results from the very use
of *tits* to characterize the man rather than the woman. On an organizational level, the rhyme, with one leg in the first stanza and the other in
the second, formally connects the two (stanzas and people), sonically lit-
eralizing a bridge. Sporadic rhyming dispersed this way allows for the two
protagonists to sit separately in two separate stanzas but to be connected
in a fairly marked manner. The rhyme schemes of some poetic forms, like
the terza rima (/aba/, /bcb/, and so forth), have a more consistent and
therefore blatant interlocking function, which can be put to good use,[22]
but Swenson manages to achieve a suggestion of interlocking by using
sporadic internal rhyme in a free verse poem.

Lyn Hejinian also uses sporadic rhyme across different lines, images, or
sections to create transitions. Her 1992 book *The Cell* comprises a series
of highly associative and challenging pieces, each given a date between
October 6, 1986, and January 21, 1989. In these enigmatic works, which
operate on the verge of incomprehensibility, transitions carry much
weight. Here is one example:

> I meet myself rarely to
>   experience the coincidence of my
>   objectivity with my subjectivity
> This incongruence is independent of
>   the possibility that a person

had an articulate organ which
    he called a <u>lung</u>
The blunt November summer—I
    could have only <u>said</u> <u>so</u>
<u>Red</u> and <u>yellow</u> language coming
    with the <u>tongue</u>
A big one
The year is <u>thick</u> and
    long and thrust
The label <u>sticks</u> up from
    the collar but the hair
    hides it
The <u>place</u> <u>warm</u>
The <u>space</u> bar <u>worn</u>
There's no such thing as
    yesterday which rolls under and
    holds its information up and
    forward for long
The <u>information</u> is like a
    balmy <u>palpitation</u>
I like everything at a
    level below its name
            November 13, 1986 (Hejinian, *The Cell* 31)

On one level, this is a succession of non sequitur units, each one assuming a relative autonomy, at least visually, by its left alignment. Such a succession evokes a hermeneutic desire to make the whole cohere, which means finding a common thread or threads running through the units. Though the desire is only partly fulfilled (bringing to mind Wallace Stevens's notion that the poem should resist the intelligence "almost successfully"), nearly every unit in this sequence is somehow connected to its neighbor in some semilogical way. More often than not, sound accompanies or actualizes the poem's loose connections. This can be seen, for example, in the move from the first unit ("I meet myself rarely to experience the coincidence of my objectivity with my subjectivity") to the second unit ("This incongruence is independent of the possibility that a person had an articulate organ which he called a lung"). "This incongruence" may or may not refer to "the coincidence of my objectivity with my subjectivity," but the strong homoeoteleuton of *experience* : *coincidence* : *incongruence* and of *objectivity* : *subjectivity* : *possibility* secures the connectedness between the two units.

A similar thing occurs between the third and fourth units:

> The blunt November summer—I
>   could have only <u>said</u> <u>so</u>
> <u>Red</u> and <u>yellow</u> language coming
>   with the tongue

The two units seem to share the general theme of speech, but again, any semantic connection between them is reinforced by, if not born out of, the rhyming of *said* : *red* and *so* : *yellow*. Moreover, the word *tongue* connects back to the end of the second unit to create the rhyme *lung* : *tongue,* a late explication of the "articulate organ," since speech requires both tongue and air from the lung (*lung* : *tongue* in this context may also pun on *langue*).

Though not all units connect in this way, most do, and when rhyme accompanies the connection, it eases it. The poem therefore makes use of sonic *and* conceptual associations, sometimes simultaneously, as in *worn,* which refers to wearing out the space bar ("The space bar worn") as well as to wearing clothes, like the shirt alluded to two units earlier ("The label sticks up from the collar but the hair hides it").

Ultimately, the poem shows that all such associations or connections, whether conceptual or sonic, are at root *language-based,* and the nature of linguistic connections (or the nature of connections as linguistic) becomes a focal point for Hejinian in many of the pieces in the book. Sporadic rhyme aids in joining the units while leaving the connections loose, organizing while marking that organization as tentative, a poetic task that could not be achieved with a more intrusive means such as systematic rhyming. Imposing its own soft logic, the rhyming reaches from one unit to an adjacent one, assuring their distinction and their conjoining.

Sporadic rhyme, peppered throughout a poem unsystematically, displays looseness. This could be considered its iconic dimension, to represent looseness itself. Yet a distinction must be made between two levels of the iconic potential of sporadic rhyming. Judy Jo Small, in a tremendously insightful book devoted to Emily Dickinson's rhyming, analyzes the internal (and sporadic) rhyming with a focus on "particular expressive effects," often ad hoc and iconic (112). Small claims that, in a poem by Dickinson about the wind, "the capriciousness of the wind is nicely correlated with the apparent randomness of the rhymes that recur insistently but unpredictably" (122). This is iconic in a fairly direct and narrow sense and is different from Hejinian's use. Accepting Simon Jarvis's assertion that "poetics need not subserve hermeneutics" opens the door to understanding poetical elements in ways that go beyond the obvious result of reading hermeneutically, the directly iconic ("For a Poetics of Verse" 932). In Hejinian's less straightforward iconicity, sporadic rhyme does not come to strictly represent a loose symbol or theme (like the wind) but to perform looseness vis-à-vis language. This looser iconicity has far greater potential, inasmuch as it seizes upon rhyme's dual, even duplicitous, nature: to impose order upon the language of the poem and to mark that order as fundamentally precarious.

COUNTERPOINTING LINEATION

When rhyme extends from one stanza to the next, or when it abounds in a certain line, it strives to create cohesion, to unify, to lend to the stanzas or lines its inherent rigidity by solidifying them. But much of the time sporadic rhyme, with an emphasis more on *sporadic* than on *rhyme,* fulfills the opposite goal: to cut, puncture, and divide. When this is the main (dis)organizational functioning of sporadic rhyme, it competes with other means of parsing the language of the poem, like the line, meter, and phrasing. As we have seen in Blake and Yeats, sporadic rhyme also can compete or interact with another means of parsing the material of verse, systematic end rhyme.

In the unremarkable case that rhyme comes at the end of an end-stopped line in a metrical poem, it reinforces the breaks that all these other means created: the end of the line is the end of the rhyme *and* the end of the metrical unit *and* the end of the grammatical phrase. But in the most radical forms of sporadic rhyme, instead of further enforcing a preexisting break, rhyme *creates* a break in an otherwise unmarked point in the linguistic fabric of the poem. Therefore—to paraphrase and negate Saintsbury—rhyme comes not at the end of something but marks something as an end. While systematic end rhyming can counterpoint phrasing (the ur-example is enjambment in a rhymed poem, where end rhymes join the line in counterpointing grammatical units),[23] internal rhyme can further counterpoint the line unit itself.

Why is rhyme in the middle of the line so "dangerous"? Russian poet Vasilij Trediakovskij, in his 1735 treatise on versification, answers this question clearly: "The rhyming of the caesura syllable with the end syllable of a heroic verse line is clumsy and uncalled for, because this produces not one but two lines of verse" (45). Rhyme in the middle of the line threatens the integrity of the line, so much so that it may give the impression of making one line into two. And this would be the case not only when the rhyme is between the caesura and the end of the line but also in many other sporadic cases. Counterpointing the line unit becomes especially significant if we accept prosodists' centralization of lineation in the prosody of much of free verse, a form whose rhythm may rely almost entirely on lineation.[24]

Emily Dickinson uses rhyme's disruptive potential in the interaction with lineation in the final, fourth stanza of the poem "'Twas the old—road—through pain":

> Another bed - a short one -
> Women make - <u>tonight</u> -
> In Chambers <u>bright</u> -
> Too out of <u>sight</u> - though -
> For our hoarse Good <u>Night</u> -
> To touch her Head! (Dickinson 401)[25]

In the four internal lines of this six-line stanza, Dickinson uses four rhyming words, *tonight : bright : sight : night,* three at line ends and one internally. The internal rhyming word, coming third in the series of four, finds an unexpected place in the line; rather than ending the line, like its two predecessors, *tonight* and *bright,* the line continues with another word (*though*) after the rhyming one. The internal rhyme is thus a subversive agent in the prosody of the line, marking an end that turns out *not* to coincide with the typographical lineal end, which results in an accentuation of the surprising non-ending. The word *though,* the rhetorical pivot of the stanza, is lent special emphasis. If it were repositioned and placed at the beginning of the next line, everything would be resolved, but as it is, it lingers (a reverberation via rhyme of a nonrhyming word).[26]

We can observe a similar maneuver if we add the last line of the previous stanza:

Herself - though - <u>fled</u>!

Another <u>bed</u> - a short one -

Due to the rhyme, there is a likely pause after *bed*; the word is perceived as a sonic end, a closing of rhyme that started with *fled.* This sense of an ending is aided by the phrasal and rhetorical break that is represented by the subsequent dash, a hallmark of Dickinson's poetics. And yet there is an alternative end close at hand, that of the line unit, with which this end does *not* coincide. The ending of rhyme is counterbalanced by the continuation of the line.

In this way, rhyme is akin to punctuation, sonically punctuating the line. Internal rhyme has a rhythmic effect on the pacing of the line: rhyme is a cue for accenting and pausing. If the second of the two rhyming partners cues for pause, it does so in this poem by joining the numerous dashes, line ends, and phrasal ends. The entire stanza becomes acutely disjointed at each step, and the poem rarely lets us go more than two or three words before forcing some kind of halt. The overall effect, quite typical of Dickinson, is that fraught admixture of high bursts of energy amid much hesitation.

SPORADIC RHYME, ENDINGS, AND CLOSURES

Finally, I would like to turn to the employment of sporadic rhyme in the most strategic of places in a poem: its ending. When rhyme comes at the

poem's end, at least two endings overlap: the end of the rhyme—reached
with the second of the two rhyming words—and the end of the poem.
Barbara Herrnstein Smith has shown that poems tend toward "terminal
modification," a change that comes at the end of the poem to strengthen
closure and break the expectation for the continuation of the same. In a
consistently rhyming poem, terminal modification can be achieved with
a change in the rhyme scheme. A prime example is the Shakespearean
sonnet: after three quatrains in a row, one is set up to expect more quatrains, but then the poem signals its ending by switching to a couplet. The
concluding couplet, Smith writes, is a terminal modification that has become "incorporated into the convention of the sonnet" (53). And the same
concluding couplet can just as easily signal an ending in other contexts. A
nonrhyming speech in a play, for instance, could end ceremoniously with
a rhyme that would reinforce the fact that it is an ending.[27]

Free verse poets writing poems that do not regularly rhyme have not
forsaken rhyme's potential to conclude, or even the concluding couplet,
although using sporadic rhyme frees up more possibilities, including a
more inclusive definition of what constitutes a couplet. This is evident in
Sylvia Plath's poem "A Birthday Present," written in thirty-one two-line
stanzas, with almost no internal rhyming and not a single end rhyme
throughout. The poem's speaker makes several attempts to guess what is
behind a veiled birthday present, to contemplate it, and even to talk to
it. The speaker then ends the poem with a final expression of what she
wants the birthday present (referred to here as "it") to be:[28]

> If it were death
>
> I would admire the deep gravity of it, its timeless eyes.
> I would know you were serious.
>
> There would be a nobility then, there would be a birthday.
> And the knife not carve, but enter
>
> Pure and clean as the cry of a baby,
> And the universe slide from my side. (Plath 67)

There is an undeniable concentration of novel rhyming at the very end of the poem, a shocking and elegant accompaniment to the disturbing "pure and clean" cut of the knife and the suicidal desire. Interestingly, rhyme counterpoints the two-line stanza, with *cry* : *my* being purely internal and *slide* : *side* contained within the second of the two lines (the two rhymes are strongly related, too, as they share the diphthong [aɪ]).

What we have, then, is a rhyming two-line stanza that is *not* a couplet in the regular sense; it is a visual couplet in which the rhyming *slide* : *side* is more proximate than in a regular couplet. The misalignment between rhyme and line, and rhyme and stanza, does not diminish the rhyme, but it changes its effect. Irrespective of and unsupported by the (visual) couplet—a form so associated with systematic end rhyming—rhyme packs a stronger punch, particularly because it appears in an otherwise rhyme-free poem.

A different take on the concluding couplet in a free verse poem is seen in Louise Glück's "Firstborn":

> The weeks go by. I shelve them,
> They are all the same, like peeled soup cans . . .
> Beans sour in their pot. I watch the lone onion
> Floating like Ophelia, caked with grease:
> You listless, fidget with the spoon.
> What now? You miss my care? Your yard ripens
> To a ward of roses, like a year ago when staff nuns
> Wheeled me down the aisle . . .
> You couldn't look. I saw
> Converted love, your son,
> Drooling under glass, starving . . .
>
> We are eating well.
> Today my meatman turns his trained <u>knife</u>
> On veal, your favorite. I pay with my <u>life</u>. (Glück 38)

Formally, the rhyming at the end of "Firstborn" resembles the concluding couplet of a sonnet. As almost the only rhyme in the poem, it is even more marked than the couplet at the end of a Shakespearean sonnet, since it introduces rhyming itself rather than introducing a mere change *in* the rhyming. The poem's fourteen lines further hint at the traditional sonnet as a formal intertext to this piece, and a fainter echo is found in Shakespeare's use of these same rhyming words in the concluding couplet of Sonnet 100, addressed to the Muse:

> Give my love fame faster than Time wastes <u>life</u>;
> So thou prevent'st his scythe and crooked <u>knife</u>. (Shakespeare 52)

Shakespeare and Glück exploit the strong semantic incongruity between *knife* and *life*.[29] For Shakespeare, the heart of the couplet is the contrast between Time's knife (death) and the eternal life (fame) that the muse can grant. For Glück, the couplet becomes a comment on the bleak nature of the relationship between the meatman and the speaker. The shocking, incongruous rhyme is used to suggest the horrifying situation the speaker is in, forced to pay with her life, perhaps with her body. By the end, "Firstborn" pushes the reader to a grimmer understanding of the action of the meatman. We may come to see his turning of the knife on veal not as trimming meat for a customer but as metaphorically describing a sexual and emotional action performed on the speaker herself.

On a formal level, though, the concluding couplet is handled differently in the two poems. In Shakespeare, the rhyming couplet is relatively autonomous within the sonnet, resembling an aphorism or epigram, a detachable conclusion of the sonnet, whose immediate context it transcends. There is a full stop before it, and the couplet could be read in isolation. The two lines are also logically balanced, with the line break coming at a natural point of pause in the sentence:

> Give my love fame faster than Time wastes <u>life</u>;
> So thou prevent'st his scythe and crooked <u>knife</u>.

In "Firstborn," too, there is something of that detachability at play, though the couplet is less detachable than in the typical sonnet. Typographically, the two rhyming lines stand out because they are longer than the lines immediately above them. Yet these two lines are part of a three-line stanza, a fact that somewhat curbs the aphoristic feel while retaining the chilling reality that rhyme signals:

> We are eating well.
> Today my meatman turns his trained <u>knife</u>
> On veal, your favorite. I pay with my <u>life</u>.

The distinction of the couplet as an autonomous unit is further curbed because there is nothing of the phrasal and rhythmic balance one finds in Shakespeare. The first line of the couplet is heavily enjambed and the second line is punctured by the period in its middle.

Ending a poem on a rhyme can make for a very strong concluding note, and it is hard for rhyme, even sporadic, not to import something of the "ring of authority and conclusiveness" (Wesling, *Chances of Rhyme* 129) that is associated with systematic rhyme. But authoritative conclusiveness is not desirable for some poets. In her formative essay "The Rejection of Closure," Hejinian, a contemporary of Glück who, though associated with very different poetic orientations, shares with her a reliance on rhyme in nonmetrical poetry, advocates for an open rather than a closed text. "Open," Hejinian clarifies, does not at all mean "without form." In fact, she seeks out "a conjunction of form with radical openness" (42), writing whose formal features are foregrounded without being closed or static— two adjectives that are often, and wrongly, associated with form. Rhyme would seem to be the worst possible candidate for exhibiting radical openness, though we have already seen how poets, Hejinian included, employ *sporadic* rhyme precisely for this potential.

What if a poet wishes to use rhyme at the end of the poem but at the same time to lessen its epigrammatic effect, preventing it from ringing too conclusively? Deemphasizing the couplet unit is one technique to achieve this, which we saw with Glück. Another is to add something *after* the rhyme, so that rhyme comes *almost* at the end of the poem but does not coincide with its exact ending. Eliot's "Morning at the Window" is an example:

> They are rattling breakfast <u>plates</u> in basement kitchens,
> And along the trampled edges of the street
> I am aware of the damp souls of housemaids
> Sprouting despondently at area <u>gates</u>
>
> The brown waves of fog toss up to me
> Twisted faces from the bottom of the street,
> And <u>tear</u> from a passer-by with muddy skirts
> An aimless smile that hovers in the <u>air</u>
> And vanishes along the level of the roofs. (Eliot, *Collected Poems* 19)

Eliot makes sporadic rhyme work in a comparative manner. *Gates* at the end of the first stanza closes the line, stanza, and sentence, and reaches back to close the rhyme begun by *plates*. In the second stanza, *air* does the same: it appears at the end of four lines and could easily have been the ending of the sentence. However, this time rhyme fails to coincide with the end of stanza, sentence, or poem. Under such differential circumstances, the final, fifth line—the extra mile after the close of rhyme—becomes highly marked, as if the poem needs another line for the final vanishing of the "aimless smile."

These differential circumstances are a background against which the basic similarity of movement in both stanzas is highlighted. In both, something emerges from below: the "souls of housemaids" sprouting from basement kitchens (first stanza) and the smile that hovers in the air up to the "level of the roofs" (second stanza). When the poem completes its journey from basement kitchens (first line) to roofs (last line), we may very well understand the stanzas as comprising one continuous movement upward. The places of rhyme puncture the continuity of movement, offering temporary moments of pause, but the continuation after the second rhyme ultimately shows the flow to be stronger than the puncturing halts. The poem ends by returning to the nonrhyming norm.[30] Like the "aimless smile," rhyme, too, vanishes in the last line, since a world that, to quote Eliot in "The Hollow Men," ends "not with a bang but a whimper" cannot give to rhyme the last word.

Finally, a poet *can* give rhyme the last word but strategically position the first of the rhyming partners much earlier in the poem, where it is barely reached by short-term memory. This is another way to have one's cake and eat it, too, to take advantage of rhyme's sense of an ending while restricting its teleological and authoritative force and leaving things open.

This is the technique of choice in Jordan Rice's poem "My Life." The speaker is involved in the process of gender transition; the poem starts with the physician, who gives scientific validation to what the speaker already knows, and continues, in the second and third stanzas, with voices of anonymous people who offer advice:

> The physician tells me much I know already:
> These structures of your mind correspond
> with women's, his illustrations clearly lined
> in color quadrants, lobes lit up, explain.
>
> Life won't be simple either way and, it's an
> impossible choice. I take a year. Then advice.
> Lose weight now. Grow out your hair. Unlearn
> hiding. Mostly fear will pass. Passing's always
> a state of mind, though you may require surgery.
> The list of surgeons lengthens without end.
>
> Choose. This one Boston. This one
> Wisconsin. Save your money. How's your wife? (Rice 19).

The poem is emotionally compelling due to the asymmetry between the barrage of well-meaning advice and the speaker's own silence. What is the speaker's reaction, one wonders, to all these pieces of advice bordering on commands? "Lose weight now. Grow out your hair. Unlearn / hiding. . . . Save your money." The speaker never responds directly, but something of the immensity of the task awaiting her is revealed through the discrepancy between the urgency that the imperative voice suggests and the speaker's own need to slow down and deliberate ("I take a year").

The most arresting element of all seems to be not any of the advice imperatives but the seemingly innocent question that ends the poem:

"How's your wife?" This is an arresting question, we could say, because the poem rests (ends) with it. It is also arresting in its implications, suggesting that the transition from biological male involves not just the speaker but also someone very close to her and, by extension, an entire familial and social life. Finally, it is arresting because it is the point of ending for the rhyme that we now retrospectively know started with the word *life*, eight whole lines earlier (or even earlier than that, with the poem's title). Quite crucially, the distance between the rhyming partners is such that rhyme will barely be registered, and thus much of the closure-inducing snap is kept at bay, while a more diffuse, open, lingering echo remains. Openness is further guaranteed by the choice to end the poem on a question, a rhetorical form that leaves readers waiting for an impossible-to-provide, never-to-arrive answer. What rhyme, to a certain degree, closes, the question leaves open.

4

Accidental and Motivated

Rhyme's Semantic Trap

THE LANGUAGE OF GOD

Most of the words one uses and encounters in most discursive situations do not rhyme. Relative to the nonrhyming norm, rhyme is qualitatively different: it is *marked* and can catch one's attention and ear.[1] As an important part of their phonological development, children typically develop awareness of rhyme very early. One empirical study showed that infants from English-speaking households could be taught to identify rhyme when they were as young as seven and a half months old. The infants were able to indicate, by turning their heads, when a change was made from one group of rhyming words to another (Hayes, Slater, and Brown). Rhyme awareness in children has also been linked to their reading skills, and rhyme awareness tasks are regularly used in schools and in diagnostic settings (Wagensveld et al., "Nature of Rhyme Processing").

The way in which rhyme stands out has also been given neurological confirmation. In 1984, researcher Michael Rugg had subjects look at pairs of words, some rhyming and some nonrhyming, and measured their brains' response to both types of pairs, using electrodes placed on the subjects' scalps. He found that the brain's response differed measurably between the rhymed and nonrhymed conditions. In other words, the recognition of rhyme empirically and measurably jolts the brain. Interest-

ingly, Rugg found the same effect on waveform even when the rhyming
pair consisted of a real word and a made-up nonword, in a pair like *sighs* :
mize. The brain's response to semantic incongruity (such as a sentence
that ends on an unexpected and illogical word, like "He spread the warm
bread with *socks*") is also measurable.

Rugg found that the exact time in which the brain's response to a rhyme
occurs, peaking at 450 milliseconds after the stimulus, differs from the
time in which the brain responds to semantic incongruity. He concluded
not only that the brain's response to rhyme can be recorded but also that
the response relies not on semantic or orthographic processing but on a
phonological one. Since then, many other studies have been carried out
to confirm and further investigate the so-called rhyming effect.[2]

Neurology can tell us that rhyme stands out, but it cannot speak to
how it does this, in the way that practitioners of rhyme can, always with
an eye to changing historical and cultural attitudes. Attuning to these
practitioners, better known simply as poets, we can say that rhyme not
only stands out but that it stands out as signaling a different kind of
language. Some, like John Milton, resisted rhyme, in part because it was
perceived as an "invention of a barbarous age" and contrasted with the
much-admired nonrhyming classic Greek and Latin poetic forms. But
for others, and quite persistently, rhyme signals a perfect, harmonious,
magical, even fully motivated (nonarbitrary) language. This view of rhyme
is entirely linked to the mix of rigidity with pleasure and musicality that
was discussed in the chapter 2. In this vein, rhyme, like poetic language
more broadly, operates in the vicinity of old myths and fantasies about
language.

Gerald Bruns opines that it is "perhaps impossible to speak of language
without at some point invoking the myth of a primordial sign, which is to
say the myth of an ideal unity of word and being" (190). The accumulating
work that keeps countering Ferdinand de Saussure's famous claim that
the linguistic sign is arbitrary, by amassing evidence for the pervasiveness
of iconicity and systematicity, much beyond just strict onomatopoeia,
speaks to the pervasiveness of this myth.[3]

The myth of a "unity of word and being" or of a perfect language finds
a special home in poetics, never more clearly than in Dante's *De vulgari*

eloquentia. Dante sought to recover the *forma locutionis* of Eden, a meta-language lost after Babel, "whose principles permitted the creation of language capable of reflecting the true essence of things" (Eco, *Perfect Language* 45). Rather than resort, as some did, to Hebrew as that originary language, Dante strove for a modern invention, an "illustrious vernacular," which he saw as potentially existing in poetry: "The illustrious vernacular would take from the perfect language its necessity (as opposed to conventionality) because, just as the perfect *forma locutionis* permitted Adam to speak with God, so the illustrious vernacular would permit the poet to make his words adequate to express what he wished, and what could not be expressed otherwise" (46). In Dante's thinking, poetry comes to be seen as a place where language is not arbitrary but motivated, where words mean and do what they say.

The heightened iconicity that literary criticism is so keen to find in poetic language on all its levels, from onomatopoeia all the way to the entire form of the poem, underscores Dante's idea.[4] But what about rhyme specifically? How does rhyme represent well notions of the nonarbitrary, motivated, perfect language? Lawrence McCauley suggests one answer, which goes back to Eden's prelapsarian language and world, a world "of fully motivated signs," where Adam was able to name the animals simply because he knew their nature (256). Rhyme, McCauley explains, also invites a view of language as motivated, in that the fortuitous phonological relationship between two rhyming words is so striking that it triggers a consideration of their semantic relationship. Rhyme makes us think, beyond our control, that there is some inherent reason, some logical or semantic or metaphysical grounds, for it.

Hugh Kenner draws a similar connection between rhyme and other "fantasies of linguistic order," such as John Wilkins's suggested universal nonarbitrary language,[5] though he limits this connection to what he calls "normal" or "congruous" rhymes. These are rhymes like *high : sky* and *spring : sing,* rhymes "that for some reason or another persuade us that they inhere in the workings of the normal mind." Kenner writes, "In the light of such fantasies of linguistic order as Wilkins's project illustrates, every real language, every language accessible to poets, affirms hints of a shattered perfection. Order, congruence, universal truth, these a poet might hint at by careful exploitation of such few congruous rhymes as his tongue placed at his disposal. They are what we have been calling the normal rhymes, and the sense of propriety they denote can seem to come from beyond the world" (87).[6]

There is something magical and fantastic in the sense of propriety that rhyme connotes. Rhyme does this by virtue of its sonic congruity, regardless of its semantics. (Infants are fascinated by rhyme without understanding the words' meaning or even knowing that words *have* meaning.) And so, while in a given culture and period certain rhyme clusters can recur and seem particularly salient and congruent,[7] I would add to Kenner that the fantastic applies on a deeper level to *all* rhymes, to rhyme itself, not just to the semantically congruent rhymes. Oscar Wilde, in writing that rhyme "can turn man's utterance to the speech of gods," echoes the same notion, that rhyme is "beyond the world," that rhyme belongs to a qualitatively different linguistic order ("Critic as Artist" 244). The various chants, spells, and incantations that employ the magic of rhyme and that form one of the early roots of lyric poetry are an explicit manifestation of this, as is the overabundance of sound repetition and patterning in forms of glossolalia, that language touched by divine spirit (see Jakobson and Waugh 211–15). Rhyme is "the language of God" because in it the sense of propriety, of harmony on the level of sound and (by extension, suggestively) on the level of meaning, combine to evoke a notion of a perfectly eerie language, rigidly and mystically fitting everything together.[8]

MOTIVATED AND ACCIDENTAL

The magical harmony in rhyme is carried over from the perceptual level to the conceptual, against our better judgment. A good place to observe the effect of rhyme is in people's assessment of rhyming aphorisms' truth value. In fascinating research designed to check this, Matthew McGlone and Jessica Tofighbakhsh asked participants to assess the accuracy of unfamiliar aphorisms, both rhyming and nonrhyming, and found that they deemed rhyming aphorisms to be more accurate descriptors of human behavior than a nonrhyming aphorism of the exact same propositional content.

Why would "Woes unite foes" be perceived as any truer than "Woes unite enemies"? In the discussion of their results, McGlone and Tofighbakhsh surmised that the aesthetic quality of the message is used as a heuristic for the assessment of its truth value ("Keats Heuristic" 240), or that rhyme affords the aphorism an enhanced processing fluency, which then translates to an enhanced assessment of its accuracy ("Birds of a Feather" 426–27). Either way, the fact is that rhyme's sonic features are carried over into a semantic level. While the implications far exceed rhyme and have to do with questions of aesthetics and ethics, these findings surely attest to rhyme's strong, indiscriminate conscious and unconscious hold.[9] Rhyme can still "ring true," even in an era that by and large is hostile to systematic rhyme.

That rhyme's hold is partly unconscious became evident when participants were asked whether they believed that rhyming aphorisms were more accurate than nonrhyming ones. They unanimously answered in the negative, though their own choices proved otherwise (McGlone and Tofighbakhsh, "Keats Heuristic" 239). An interesting duplicity is revealed: the conscious, rational mind knows that rhyme is pure happenstance and does not prove anything, but rhyme speaks to us subliminally. Within the finite number of sounds that combine to form words, rhyme will, if the language allows, make an appearance sooner or later. This chance aspect of rhyme should weaken the hold that rhyme may have on us, because it augments rhyme's nonsensical sense, but paradoxically it strengthens that hold. The duplicity of sense and nonsense, of motivated and arbitrary, raises the stakes of what is involved in any rhyming pair.

The stakes become manifest in culture and politics. On September 10, 2007, the advocacy group MoveOn.org placed an ad in the *New York Times* with the all-caps title "GENERAL PETRAEUS OR GENERAL BETRAY US?" (Fig. 2). Their stated argument was that the general was being disingenuous in his testimony before Congress about the real situation in Iraq, but the rhyme *Petraeus : betray us* carries that argument beyond the stated. The resistance that the ad raised across partisan lines attests to the uneasiness with this "juvenile name-calling" and to the sense that the ad went too far.[10] But too far in what way? Its overreach was not, I would argue, in what the ad said but in what it implied: that the general's very name rhymes with *betray us* proffers a signal of some hidden truth about the man himself, almost as if we are hearing God speaking through the name.

GENERAL PETRAEUS OR GENERAL BETRAY US?

Cooking the Books for the White House

General Petraeus is a military man constantly at war with the facts. In 2004, just before the election, he said there was "tangible progress" in Iraq and that "Iraqi leaders are stepping forward." And last week Petraeus, the architect of the escalation of troops in Iraq, said, "We say we have achieved progress, and we are obviously going to do everything we can to build on that progress."

Every independent report on the ground situation in Iraq shows that the surge strategy has failed. Yet the General claims a reduction in violence. That's because, according to the *New York Times*, the Pentagon has adopted a bizarre formula for keeping tabs on violence. For example, deaths by car bombs don't count. The *Washington Post* reported that assassinations only count if you're shot in the back of the head — not the front. According to the Associated Press, there have been more civilian deaths and more American soldier deaths in the past three months than in any other summer we've been there. We'll hear of neighborhoods where violence has decreased. But we won't hear that those neighborhoods have been ethnically cleansed.

Most importantly, General Petraeus will not admit what everyone knows: Iraq is mired in an unwinnable religious civil war. We may hear of a plan to withdraw a few thousand American troops. But we won't hear what Americans are desperate to hear: a timetable for withdrawing all our troops. General Petraeus has actually said American troops will need to stay in Iraq for as long as ten years.

Today, before Congress and before the American people, General Petraeus is likely to become General Betray Us.

MoveOn.ORG
POLITICAL ACTION

Paid for by Moveon.org Political Action, political.moveon.org, not authorized by any candidate or candidate's committee.

Fig. 2. MoveOn.org ad, *New York Times*, September 10, 2007.

Like advertisers and sloganeers, poets can make use of the randomness of language, rhyme included, and bring it into their poetic conception. In Thomas Hardy's "The Man He Killed," the speaker is a soldier contemplating having shot and killed his enemy at war. Here is the third stanza:

"I shot him dead because—
Because he was my foe,
Just so: my foe of course he was;
That's clear enough; although   (Hardy 287)

On one level, the senseless arbitrariness of killing in war is subliminally echoed in the rhyme itself, since all rhyme is an arbitrary connection between words. Furthermore, the randomness is augmented by the fact that the rhyme appears in a seemingly random place within the line, sporadically: "just so." And yet rhyme has such force that it can dubiously lure us to see the arbitrary as purposeful, so that the randomness of it is thought meaningful and the rhyme itself is perceived as rigid after the fact, an unforeseen inevitability. Thus, the rhyme "Just so: my foe" creates a sense of a proverb, epigram, or aphorism that locks together elegantly and inevitably, like the aphorisms that researchers invented to entice people to believe in their truth value. Hardy is using the epigrammatism to invent a new, nonce epigram, which is used ironically and tautologically to convey the senselessness of the situation of death that the poem is describing, namely shooting a man in combat for no reason but the situation of combat. Randomness and meaningfulness, the accidental and the motivated, mix in a disturbing way, and the fact of rhyme serves to make the tone duplicitous, to justify the killing while pointing to its absurdity.

Giving place to the contingencies of language, making the contingent meaningful, is nothing new. Think of Shakespeare's puns, for example; every pun is a harnessing of an accidental sound relation between words toward making some point. But in the twentieth century, it was promoted in some regions of the poetry sphere to a central principle, even to a hallmark of what literature is and where it should go. In "procedural" forms of writing, a more or less arbitrary rule is imposed at the outset and writing takes place within this rule, letting the poem go where it will. (One thinks of the Oulipo group in France, from the 1960s, but also of some of the practitioners of L=A=N=G=U=A=G=E poetry, in the American context, from the mid-1970s.) What happens is that language is torqued out of its normal operation in ways that facilitate exposing those very operations. "Averting apparently 'natural' writing styles" and moving "toward opacity and away from transparency," Language writing is less interested in creating specific meanings, and more in underscoring the way language makes meanings (Bernstein, "Expanded Field" 70, 68).

Gertrude Stein was an early practitioner of this radical modern poetics, targeting language itself in its thickness and outwardly relishing in its twists and random turns. When a poem records thought contours and associative leaps or operates according to a contrived procedure or constraint that lessens authorial control, rhyme—as a quirk of language—is fairly likely to enter the scene, though the way in which rhyme appears in such texts is very different from its traditional manifestations. Here is an excerpt from the piece "Sacred Emily," immediately after the famous "Rose is a rose is a rose is a rose" line:

> Loveliness extreme.
> Extra gaiters.
> Loveliness extreme.
> Sweetest ice-cream.
> Page ages page ages page ages.
> Wiped Wiped wire wire.
> Sweeter than peaches and pears and cream.
> Wiped wire wiped wire.
> Extra extreme.
> Put measure treasure.
> Measure treasure. (Stein 187)

It may be possible, though somewhat beside the point, to offer an entirely logical paraphrase of these lines, but in fact the poem is, to borrow the title of a study about Language poet Susan Howe, "led by language." Reading the lines, it becomes evident that many of Stein's attempts at this kind of Wittgensteinian "game of testing the limits of language," to borrow a theorization by Perloff (*Wittgenstein's Ladder* 85), focus on sonic features. In this lineated excerpt, a word is never more than two or three words away from another that echoes it, by either exact repetition, rhyme, alliteration, or assonance. In fact, the entire piece is a web of tightly knit sonic units. For example, the word *extreme* is picked up by its variant *extra* as well as by its rhyming partner *cream,* which in turn receives further echoing by the vowel sound it shares with *sweeter, sweetest,* and *peaches.*

From the reader's or hearer's side, being presented with words that entail phonemic overlap has an effect that cognitive psychologists have dubbed "acoustic confusion," a kind of mixing of the words in short-term memory. Studies have consistently found that presenting subjects with series of words that share sounds erodes the words' distinctive qualities and makes the lists difficult to reproduce (see Baddeley, and Lange and Oberauer; for application to poetry, see Tartakovsky). In serial recall tests, when participants are asked to repeat such sequences, they are less likely to reproduce them in full and in the correct order than they are words that sound nothing alike. The confusion, or fusion, of the distinct words may threaten the sense level of the words, a sign of sound taking center stage and pushing comprehension to the back. Essentially, the very autonomy of the individual word is threatened (*Petraeus* and *betray us* edge to become one in our echoic memory), and the sequence as a whole becomes a confusing or fused mass of sound.

Harryette Mullen, a contemporary poet who, like Stein, is deeply invested in the notion of poetic language as productive linguistic play, lets rhyming and other sonic devices overtake her poem "Jinglejangle." In her case, the poem contains a long list of rhymes that infiltrate the current American soundscape. The extreme succession of rhymes, with almost nothing intervening between them, is joined by another element of rigidity, the alphabetization running from A to Z, thus signaling an affinity with rule-based procedural poetic forms. Take, for example, the Ds:

> date rape deadhead deep sleep dikes on bikes dilly-dally
> ding-a-ling ding-dang dingle-dangle
> ding-dong dirty birdy Dizzy Lizzy dog log Don Juan
> Donut Hut double trouble downtown dramarama

drape shape dream team Dress for Success drill & kill
drip-drop drunk skunk dry eye (Mullen, *Sleeping with the Dictionary* 35)

As would be expected, much of the rhyming included in the lines is drawn from the public sphere and is recognizable from commercial contexts, such as the names of brands or bands (*Donut Hut, Dizzy Lizzy*). Even the story of the pharmaceutical industry's hijacking of language for gain by creating, or naming, catchy-sounding symptoms (*dry eye*) is represented. Many of the rhymes are catch phrases, which were probably given an evolutionary advantage by the fortuitousness of their like-sounding elements (*Dress for Success, double trouble, dream team*). Others, such as *downtown* or *deep sleep,* are in such common use that their rhyming might go unnoticed were it not for their inclusion in this list, in this poem, which brings out the rhyme in them and causes us to suspect that they have enjoyed popularity because of the rhyming.

The constraints of the self-imposed form, a list of found rhymes, and the cognitive phenomenon of acoustic confusion, would seem to sanction an obliviousness to the meaning of the rhymes, as if rhyme itself is the point, a kind of equalizer of the items included. But a careful listen to the items offers moments of surprise and shock, especially when the less innocuous terms, like *date rape,* with which the list opens, resound. Consequently, even the seemingly innocuous terms, like *deadhead* and *drill & kill* (an educational term for repetitive drilling before mastering a skill), come to be questioned, their rhyming causing us to hear them anew, to hear the *dead* in *deadhead* and the *kill* in *drill & kill.* Taken as a whole, the list elicits a realization not just of the sheer amount of rhyming but also of the fact that all rhymes are situated on an imagined spectrum from contingent to purposeful, none entirely innocuous.

Stein and Mullen, like Lyn Hejinian in the poem from chapter 3, are not at all invested in an authorial lyrical "I" as a coherent center around which the poem is organized. In its stead, they place accidentals and quirks of language, making the random purposeful or understanding the purposeful as ultimately random. It is somewhat paradoxical, and not at all accidental, that these avant-garde practitioners are open to rhyme, a metonym for traditional poetry, which is precisely what the avant-garde sees itself as turning its back on. The reason for rhyme's ability to cross over from traditional to the most avant-garde, to be at once the most avant-garde and the most conventional, may hinge on the understanding of "literariness," that dividing line, if there is one, between the literary and the nonliterary.[11]

A topic of acute interest to Russian formalists, the question of literariness received one of the most succinct answers from Viktor Shklovsky, not in the justly celebrated "Art as Device" and the notion of estrangement but in the earlier "Resurrecting the Word." In that essay, Shklovsky makes the point that poetic or artistic perception "is such perception in which form is experienced" (64). Rhyme, one hastens to add, can readily epitomize this foregrounding of form; it is heard form, or form temporalized and concretized when the poem is read or heard. Shklovsky's emphasis here, as Todorov (137) remarks when glossing this very sentence, is on the poetic as conditioned by the process of perception.

Rhyme, if it is perceived as form, would thus be the epitome of the poetic or literary. In most metrical verse, systematic rhyme and meter frame the text as prose's other and confer form upon it. In those cases, literariness as perceived form is actualized and the poem is seen as a highly designed object (or a well-wrought urn, to borrow a phrase from a neighboring theoretical tradition). But later, when tides change and randomness and the accidental become poetic desiderata, rhyme—now of the sporadic version—can fit the bill just as precisely because of its accidental nature. By moving from rhyme as authority to rhyme as coincidental, avant-gardists are able to keep the notion that rhyme is a foregrounding of form and that a foregrounding of form epitomizes the literary, while offering a very different praxis of the literary.

THE SEMANTIC DYSFUNCTION OF RHYME

Like Shklovsky, Roman Jakobson theorizes the line between poetic and nonpoetic, in his case by positing a poetic function that "projects the principle of equivalence from the axis of selection into the axis of combination" ("Linguistics and Poetics" 71). This formulation offers us yet another path by which to situate rhyme, as a palpable form of equivalence between words, at the very heart of the poetic function, and to explain its centrality to poetry.

But rhyme is not just any textual equivalence or parallelism; it is equivalence or parallelism on the level of sound, and as a sound device, there is a danger that rhyme might be relegated to the realm of sound alone. Indeed, in some regions of formalism, inspired by the Russian Futurists' notion of *zaum* or transrational (illogical) language, poetry was defined precisely by its being a form of discourse that disregards sense altogether and succumbs to the contingencies of sound (Steiner 167). Jakobson is adamant about rejecting such notions: "It would be an unsound over-simplification to treat rhyme merely from the standpoint of sound" is Jakobson's clever articulation of his position in a pun, a device that is itself based on the very relation between sound and sense that Jakobson is advocating ("Linguistics and Poetics" 81). For him, sound must be tied to sense: "In poetry, any conspicuous similarity in sound is evaluated in respect to similarity and/or dissimilarity in meaning" (87). Parallelism operates between, as well as within, each level. Not only are two rhyming words parallel because of their sounds, but also there is parallelism between the sonic and the semantic levels; rhyme brings up an equivalence between the two words' meanings just as it does between their sounds.

Although there are rhymes that seem semantically logical (*high : sky*), there are many more that do not, such as semantic opposites (*glad : sad*). Some, perhaps most, rhymes offer no ready-made or obvious semantic connection (*clip : trip, computer : looter, ring : wing*). This critical avenue, the investigation of the semantic relationship between rhyming words, is most widely recognized as originating with W. K. Wimsatt's now classic essay "One Relation of Rhyme to Reason," which Jakobson mentions favorably in his own piece. In it, Wimsatt wishes to lead away from the view of rhyme as merely "a form of phonetic harmony" and to advance rhyme studies through the attempt to "connect rhyme with reason" (163). By comparing Pope and Chaucer, Wimsatt shows that rhyme essentially "impose[s] upon the logical pattern of expressed argument a kind of fixative counterpattern of alogical implication" (153).

Marjorie Perloff takes this basic orientation as a point of departure in a detailed analysis of the semantic function of rhyme in Yeats. She divides "semantically functional" rhymes into "semantic congruity," when the rhyming words agree semantically, and "semantic disparity," when they do not, and then enumerates different relationships under each category (Perloff, *Rhyme and Meaning*). In practice, much of the work involves plucking the rhyming words out of the poem and analyzing the specific semantic relationships among them, then applying the insights gained by this effort to the entire poem. Therefore, a premise is created that the rhyming words are more central, and potentially more illuminating to the poem as a whole, than other words. A similar study has been conducted for the rhyming of the twelfth-century trouvère poet Gace Brulé, from a very different poetic tradition. Here, rather than defining precise relations, Susan Bécam groups together rhyming words throughout the poet's corpus by semantic association, according to prevalent motifs and themes like loyalty/disloyalty and joy/grief.

Interestingly, though, the kinds of rhymes that Wimsatt (and to a certain extent Jakobson, too) had in mind, and that Perloff and Bécam analyze, are almost always systematic rhymes. The prevalence of systematic rhyme for the poets they research certainly warrants that decision, as does the attention that poets surely allot the rhyming words. But what happens to the semantic function when it is not restricted to systematic rhyme but rather is exhibited in sporadic rhyme? One such sporadic rhyme is found in the penultimate line of Donald Justice's short, sad poem "On the Death of Friends in Childhood":

> We shall not ever meet them bearded in heaven,
> Nor sunning themselves among the bald of hell;
> If anywhere, in the deserted schoolyard at twilight,
> Forming a ring, perhaps, or joining hands
> In <u>games</u> whose very <u>names</u> we have forgotten.
> Come, memory, let us seek them there in the shadows.
>   (Justice, *Collected Poems* 12)

Though instances of lesser sonic relations, like assonance, exist in the poem (*death* : *friends, meet* : *bearded, perhaps* : *hands*), the only full rhyme is *games* : *names*. Rhyme is the most marked of these sound devices, and the sporadicity and singularity seem to maximize its markedness. With no competition, this single rhyme reverberates longer, and its poetic potential is thus drastically increased. As the pairing reverberates—not unlike memory itself, which is the poem's theme—the rhyme, intralineal and separated by only two words and three syllables, lends extra markedness to the two words and creates semantic excess around them. Since rhyme sonically blurs the boundaries between the two rhyming words and fuses them, it invites the stretching of semantic possibilities: Is it the games that are forgotten? The names of the games? The friends' names? Perhaps the friends themselves? In a poem preoccupied with childhood and memory, this last question becomes pertinent. Like an aural shadow, rhyme spreads and echoes semantic possibilities, evoking childhood memories while speaking of forgetting.

Moreover, the poem capitalizes on the association between rhyme and childhood, a metonymy born out of rhyme's salience in children's games, in jump-rope rhymes, in counting rhymes, and in nursery rhymes. Rhyming is often itself a children's linguistic game, and this, more than any other attribute, is evoked by the sporadic rhyme in this poem; it is a harnessing of the pleasure found in rhyme. The introduction of this single sporadic and highly marked rhyme in the poem offers the reader a glimpse into the forgotten world of childhood, into something of the reality of childhood. Rhyme is the inclusion of childhood within the words of the adult speaker, a world within the words.

And so, in addition to the two solitary words *names* : *games,* it becomes possible to talk of a separate world, dimension, or layer that the rhyming creates, a layer that systematic rhyme would find it harder to engender because of its prevalence in the poem. This layer is a development of the semantic function of rhyme, beyond the relationship between the two rhyming words and toward a relationship between the rhyme itself and the unmarked, the nonrhyming. Sporadic rhyme highlights the semantics of the words against the background of their sonic similarity (as in the traditional semantic function), as well as the very rhyming against nonrhyming. With this operation, rhyme makes some comment, implicit as it may be, about the possibility of rhyming itself. This comment is worth making and is worth listening to, especially when a poem is written, or read, at a time when rhyming is no longer the norm in poetry.

Sporadic rhyme enhances the semantic function of (any) rhyme, then proceeds to extend the poetic markedness and harness it for the purpose of creating a distinct conceptual layer within the poem. Another example of this operation in contemporary verse appears in Ruth Stone's "In the Next Galaxy":

Things will be different.
No one will lose their sight,
their hearing, their gallbladder.
It will be all Catskills with brand-
new wraparound verandas.
The idea of Hitler will not
have vibrated yet.
While back here,
they are still cleaning out
pockets of wrinkled
Nazis hiding in Argentina.
But in the next galaxy,
certain planets will have <u>true</u>
<u>blue</u> skies and drinking water. (Stone 8)

In a poem dealing with the distinction between this galaxy and an imagined "next galaxy," rhyme serves to subtly entrench and polarize the two opposing galaxies by attaching itself to one but not the other. The "next galaxy," the host of rhyme (*true : blue,* faintly echoed also by the earlier *new*), is described as a utopia, devoid of personal, historical, and environmental disasters. And so, within the various differentiations drawn out throughout the poem, rhyme comes at the end as a linguistic stamp to mark the items and characteristics of the next galaxy: the physical health and agelessness, the verandas, the skies, the water. In this case, the rhyme is maximally proximate, in that the two words follow each other yet are separated by a line break. The enjambment has the advantage of forcing a slight pause between *true* and *blue,* thus defamiliarizing the otherwise common expression and underscoring its rhyming. Placing *blue* at the beginning of the line also has a rhythmic effect, making it harder to avoid stressing the word, presenting us with a conspicuous succession of three stresses: "true blue skies."

That the skies in the next galaxy are the color of "true / blue" contributes to the vividness of its utopia. But it is the rhyming of the two words that *makes* this utopia a linguistic reality, and not just because of the emphasis lent to the words by their rhyme. There is a strong though latent fit between utopia and rhyme, as if rhyme is a phonic equivalent of a naive utopian world of things falling into place, fitting together. With its euphonious function, rhyme affords a glimpse into a distinct phonological reality, harmonious and fantastic, the very basis for its association with the prelapsarian or Edenic language. The congruence between a sonic harmony that rhyme manifests and a semantic harmony is the basis for rhyme's employment in this instance, and the creation of a separate layer is taken in the direction not of childhood but of a related semantic field of perfection or fantasy.

Similarly, Wallace Stevens, dubbed by Hollander the "modern master of occasional rhyme" (*Vision and Resonance* 132), has sporadic rhyme fulfill its potential to create a distinct layer that engulf different parts of his poem "Anecdote of the Jar" (Stevens 76). The poem's first eight lines include not a single pair but a sporadic cluster of five like-sounding words: *round, surround, around, round* (again), and *ground.* First and foremost, the jar itself, the focal point, is said to be round. The jar then causes the wilderness to surround the hill, which is to say, to be around the hill, or to round it. The hill, we can surmise by following the rhyming beyond what is explicitly stated in the poem, is also round, due to its ground, not only because *ground* rhymes with the very word *round* but also because of the geographic features of all hills. Together, the words fulfill this expanded semantic function, which Benjamin Harshav calls "focusing sound patterns," linking clusters of sounds across several words to draw attention to potential thematic links ("Meaning of Sound Patterns" 154–56).

Noticeable, too, is how all of these rhymes include the prevocalic /r/, so that they exceed the minimal requirement for rhyme in English (an identity of the vowel of the last stressed syllable and everything following it), which in the context of Russian verse is called "enrichment" or "instrumentation."[12] In fact, this rhyme cluster is particularly rich, since the entire word *round* is contained in *surround, around,* and *ground* (echo rhyme). Together, via this accumulation of rhyming words, roundness itself achieves a distinction and sounding out, much as the jar's roundness achieves a standing out that organizes everything around it.

Later in the poem, though in a less pronounced manner, another rich rhyming group, consisting of *air* : *everywhere* : *bare,* gathers together another key feature of the jar, its emptiness and dominion (the jar is bare, has nothing much but air, and therefore is everywhere). The poem confirms the augmented functioning that Michael McKie ascribes to some semantic rhymes: rhyme "may assist in relating one circle of ideas to another, not merely single words" ("Semantic Rhyme" 351).

Helen Vendler reads Stevens's jar vis-à-vis Keats's Grecian urn, and the poem's language as a kind of battleground that reflects "the absurdity of the American artist's attempt to write a lyric," an American artist who, unlike Keats, "cannot feel confidently the possessor . . . of the Western cultural tradition" (*Wallace Stevens* 45–46). Vendler cites the line "The jar was round upon the ground" as an example of "plain American," as opposed to the language imported from Europe, such as the expression "to give of." Interestingly, Vendler does not reference the rhyme in that very line, which in a convoluted way is relevant to her reading. Rhyme itself, as metonym for older poetry, is inherited from Europe, so "round upon the ground" is not simply American language. But rhyme's employment in the line and in the poem—namely, as sporadic—bespeaks the Americanization of rhyme and therefore manifests poetically the tension she is describing between inherited form and American language.[13]

The inclusion of rhyme in a poem by poets writing in a poetic culture that does not take rhyme as a given is never merely the inclusion of those specific rhyming words. It is an invitation, it seems, to read rhyme itself, to read what rhyme brings with it into the poem. Sometimes, rhyme can allude to poetic genres associated with it, such as nursery rhymes.[14]

Lorine Niedecker makes use of this possibility in her series of short and usually untitled poems, like the poems grouped together under the heading "For Paul." In this series of forty-three poems, some are devoid of rhyme, some abound in it (at times completely systematically), and some exhibit sporadic rhyming. The poems contain a great deal of slant rhyming, which adds a phonemic dimension of sporadicity, and are varied rhythmically. And so, even though a number of the poems have systematic rhyme, the principle of rhyming that dominates the series as a whole is sporadic, and in addition, quite a few poems are also individually sporadically rhymed.

The "For Paul" poems exemplify Niedecker's ongoing interest in the brevity of haiku-like poetics, in folk poetry, and in nursery rhymes. As poems in which a woman addresses a young boy (Louis Zukofsky's son, Paul), there is potential, at least, for a maternal tone, perhaps a maternal longing, which could find a comfortable materialization in the form of nursery rhymes. And yet these poems are never fully or simply nursery rhymes, and so it is crucial that the rhymes across the series be sporadic, that they include enough rhyme to allude to nursery rhymes but not so much as to make the poems nursery rhymes themselves.

>   Ten o'clock
>   and Paul's not in <u>bed</u>!
>   He's reading Twelfth Night
>   all Viola <u>said</u>.
>
>   Drink to <u>three</u>, the <u>family</u>
>   around the bathroom tap.
>   Little Paul—<u>Corelli</u>,
>   what's that?—<u>belly</u>!
>
>   Wash and say good night
>   to variants and quarto texts,
>   <u>emendations</u>, close <u>relations</u>.
>   Let me hear good night. (Niedecker 151)

Typographically, this poem shares with the nursery rhyme ballad the four-lines-per-stanza structure. And although the rhyming of the first stanza is consistent with the ballad and the rhythm of each of the lines can reasonably be performed with two beats, the rhyme and rhythm of the rest of the poem reveal a departure from this familiar form. For example, in the second stanza, the expected rhyme scheme /abcb/ has been replaced by a surprising /abaa/ scheme, and the third stanza has even less traditional rhyme. The rhyme in the second stanza also may be forced, especially when the stanza is read in the over-the-top, affected way one typically reads nursery rhymes to small children. In order to preserve a rhythmic parallel between the two parts of the first line, and in order to rhyme *three* with *family,* the latter needs to be pronounced with an unusual and emphatic stress on its last syllable: "Drink to **three**, the fa-mi-**ly**." If we then want the other two rhyming words, violinist *Corelli* and *belly,* to follow suit, they too need to be pronounced with a stress on their normally unstressed final syllables: Co-rel-**li**, bel-**ly**.

Rhyme in the poem is thus used to signal the poem's affinity with the nursery rhyme, to call upon that rhyming layer, *and* to demonstrate a departure from it. This kind of queer nursery rhyme that sporadic rhyme facilitates can have a comic effect, a consequence of the forced and self-consciously failed rhyming. But while rhyme easily lends itself to humor, one is constantly aware that in many Niedecker poems, we are hearing "bitterly comic undertones" (Figlerowicz 68). In fact, sporadic rhyme can sound a melancholic note, as in the following, more enigmatic poem, which is phrased as a direct address to Paul:

<u>Paul</u>
      when the leaves
         <u>fall</u>

from their stems
      that lie thick
         on the walk

in the light
      of the full note
         the moon

playing
>   to leaves
>   >   when they leave

the little
>   thin things
>   >   Paul (Niedecker 156)

The poem starts with the semantically troubling single rhyme *Paul* : *fall*
and ends with *Paul,* though syntactic ambiguity denies the poem stable
closure. The rhyme on a name adds a faint allusion to nursery rhymes,
and the short, often anapestic lines organized in stanzas of three, with
the triple indentation, carry all the way to the end the brisk and choppy
rhythm that is often associated with the genre. Though other sound devices appear, like the pun on *leaves* and the sonically striking "thin things,"
Paul : *fall* stands out not just because of its singularity and strategic location at the start of the poem but also because of its absence at the poem's
end. *Paul* recurs, but this time without a rhyming partner, underlining the
fact that the constant appeal to Paul remains unreciprocated.

OVER-READING RHYME

Rhymes are sonically strong; they stand out by bringing together two
words and showing them to fit, to melt into each other, to reverberate
together in short-term memory. The harmony and echo, turning the two
into one, is part of the reason some commentators on rhyme refer to it
as magical or otherworldly. Rather than an arbitrary system that merely
represents or describes, the surprising sonic harmony that rhyme seeks
to impose on the words' meanings links it to fantasies of a language that
can *do* things in the world, such as cast a spell.

And yet we know that the relationship between rhyming words is arbitrary. Most rhymes, after all, are not a result of some logical relationship,
nor do they show a clear semantic agreement (*bright, sight, light*) or dis-
agreement (*light, night*). As sense-pursuing beings, many readers strive to
find meanings in rhymes that, more often than not, exhibit a relationship
that is cryptic and enigmatic. And so the excess around rhyme, both sonic

and semantic, lends it tremendous interest, which translates to poetic potential. This poetic potential is what sustains rhyme and pushes us, if we are so inclined, to hear it and then read it, to find its reason or impose one on it, rather than ignore it.

Peter McDonald precisely articulates the war between chance and choice involved in the employment of rhyme, and how rhyme and repetition, as "points of intersection between the composing will and its linguistic medium," assume particular resonance for a number of nineteenth-century poets (*Sound Intentions* 58). The following, centering on determination, is taken from his discussion of the significance of rhyme in William Wordsworth's "Intimations of Immortality" ode, though the general point is much larger in its applicability: "Rhyme is determined, in so far as a rhyming relation used by the poetic voice is something which *pre*-exists in the available language; at the same time, the exercise of choice in a poet's use of rhyme, and pursuit of the semantic courses which rhyme might offer, is proof of the self's determination, of its exercise of the will in language" (McDonald, *Sound Intentions* 112).

Rhyme is a quirk of language turned poetic device. It can signal language's randomness or the determination of its user to employ that randomness; it can be planned and harnessed for poetic means or it may occur accidentally ("a hymen between rule and chance" is Jacques Derrida's formulation).[15] While the question of control and determination, chance or choice, can always be raised, when rhyme recurs systematically, there is a stronger pull in the direction of choice.

Indeed, demonstrating control, however tenuous, over the language of the poem is one of the functions that rhyming fulfills; an authorial hand or ear seems to be lurking behind, when rhyme is conspicuous and recurring, flaunting its organization. However, when we approach the more sporadic of rhyme's manifestations, we find ourselves more and more distant from a conspicuous sense of controlling the rhyme. The random element is brought to the fore when we encounter situations of, for instance, a single rhyme in a poem, as with "On the Death of Friends in Childhood" or "In the Next Galaxy."

The issue is not just that the rhyming or nonrhyming of any two given words is accidental. In the case of nonsystematic rhyme, one may wonder

whether the very appearance of rhyme in the poem is not simply accidental too. And if it is accidental, the argument might go, is it not also insig-
nificant? After all, even a poem that includes the two common words *he*
and *be* has some rhyming in it. Are we not, by reading rhyme, falling into
what Umberto Eco has called "hermetic semiosis" or "paranoiac interpretation," obsessively finding loose connections and exercising the "uncon-
trollable drives of the reader" (*Interpretation and Overinterpretation* 48, 65)?

It is important to remember that, within poetry, with its tradition of
attention to form and sound, one would be hard-pressed to imagine a
poet allowing rhyme to occur in a poem without at least a high level of
awareness. The relative difficulty of rhyming in English is another argument for affording sporadic rhyme due critical attention, especially
when focusing on exact rhyme and not simply any form of loose or partial
alliteration or assonance. Ultimately, though, my reasoning for treating
even a single rhyme in a poem as potentially significant lies not in authorial intention but in the result that such attention can produce. On this
issue, I side with Jonathan Culler, who, in a rebuttal of Eco and a defense
of "overinterpretation," says that this interpretative excess is potentially
"the best source of the insights into language and literature that we seek"
("In Defence" 123).

Culler shifts the emphasis from interpretations of a single work to se-
miotics: "to identify the codes and mechanisms through which meaning is
produced" (115–16). On this level, I consider every single rhyme significant
(even *he* and *be*), as it concretizes in incubated form the dynamic play of
accidental/motivated as well as the earlier pairings discussed, organizing/
disrupting and rigid/pleasurable. But while any poem that has the two
words *he* and *be* will have rhyming, the rhyming is more easily overlooked
in some texts than in others. Some poems will harness the sporadic rhyme
toward hermeneutic goals—or, to state it differently, some poems will
show rhyme as highly active. Those poems take advantage of the linguistic markedness of rhyme itself to underscore, for example, a conceptual
markedness or to exploit some characteristic inherent in the structure of
rhyme, in terms of its intertextual or connotational import.

The markedness of sporadic rhyming, the way it sticks out of the
sound strata of the poem, is aided by doubts concerning its intentionality.

The admixture of accident and markedness always involved in sporadic rhyme thus lures our interpretive strategies and affords rhyme tremendous potential, including potential to strongly affect our understanding of what the poem suggests. In the following, final stanza of Theodore Roethke's mainly nonrhyming poem "Elegy for Jane," the fact of rhyming competes with the manifest content of the stanza:

> If only I could nudge you from this sleep,
> My maimed darling, my skittery pigeon.
> Over this damp grave I speak the words of my love:
> I, with no rights in this <u>matter</u>,
> <u>Neither</u> <u>father</u> nor <u>lover</u>. (Roethke 102)

After an entire poem addressing Jane, his student thrown by a horse, replete with intimate observations and reminiscences of her smiles and sadness, Roethke's speaker turns in the last two lines to himself, to question his own position or right to elegize. The cluster of words, homoeoteleuton elevated to the level of rhyme by bulk, consists of all the principal words of the last line, together with the last word of the penultimate line: *matter* : *neither* : *father* : *lover*. The overwhelming concentration of sound at the close of the poem suggests that there is something more to listen to, that the speaker's words cannot be taken completely at face value (when can they ever?). Indeed, while the speaker *negates* ("I am neither your father nor your lover"), something in the very presence of rhyming holds these words together and *affirms*. In a way, perhaps in keeping with the common stereotype of the attitude of an older male teacher to a younger female student, the speaker imagines himself to be precisely both father and lover. Acoustic confusion mixes *father* and *lover*, blending with and negating the word *neither* that tries to negate them. The poem thus offers a contrast between the fact of rhyme, or something inherent in the rhyme, and what is stated.

And the rhyming affirms more. The speaker's self-deprecation at the end of the poem—who am I, "neither father nor lover," to "speak the words of my love" over the grave—stands opposed to the very speech act of saying these words of love. Indeed, these words are given to us in

a poem rather than spoken over the open grave. The sonic markedness
at the end of these words in this poem, at the exact place of supposed
doubt over the expression of words, is a marker of the poetic. So an answer suggests itself: the speaker, neither father nor lover, is a poet, and
as such has rights in this matter, if we understand the "matter" to be that
of producing the elegy as poetic text.[16]

Russian formalist Yuri Tynianov has claimed that semantics are "deformed" in verse, such as in the way the meaning of a word is "lexically
colored," or changed, by its appearance in an intimate relationship with
contiguous words in the same verse line (70–84). Rhyming, too, exhibits this deformation of the semantic. By putting the two rhyming words
together, the result is semantic blurriness and indeterminacy. And with
sporadic rhyme, not only does the sense of a word change but also other
parts of the poem change as well, due to the rhyming words or the rhyming itself. Such is the case in David Ignatow's poem "Peace for Awhile:"

> Peace for awhile,
> but there is no such thing as peace forever.
> The calm suburbs you see
> while passing by on a train,
> the children riding their bikes under trees,
> are only interludes between the strain
> of coming to grips with what we wish to do
> and the failure to do it. (Ignatow 38)

The poem itself, in logical form, sets out to substantiate its own thesis
given at the outset: "there is no such thing as peace forever." The proof
consists of saying that "the calm suburbs," which we might mistakenly
think of as calm or peaceful forever, are in fact "only interludes" between
two things that are not calm at all, namely (a) "coming to grips with what
we wish to do" and (b) "the failure to do it." The main part of the poem
can thus be represented in skeletal form as saying, "The calm suburbs are
only interludes between (a) and (b)."

The rhyming words, *train* and *strain,* though prominent in their position at the end of two lines, are fairly tangential with respect to the

semantic skeleton of the poem. The *train* is but the instrument we use to see the suburbs, and the *strain* belongs very limitedly to the (a) part of the extract. Yet the emphatic rhyme, if we attune to it, picks *strain* out of its literal context and expands its relevance. The markedness and excess of the rhyme helps to push *strain* beyond the strain "of coming to grips with what we wish to do" and associates this phrase with everything that lies outside the temporary peace. Since *strain* receives such sonic attention, by the close of the poem it stands opposed to *peace,* and by sonic metonymy colors the idea of the supposedly calm suburbs themselves; it is all a strain.

Like a drop of red dye placed into a container of clear water, sporadic rhyme has an "ecological" effect on the poem it inhabits.[17] As a linguistic site that is both materially and historically rich, as an enactment of the alluring mix of the magical and accidental, sporadic rhyme can grab the reader's attention and reach beyond itself to transform much of one's understanding of the poem; it becomes a focal point that affects the whole poem, often backwards in correlation with rhyme's own backwards-looking temporality (the topic of the next chapter).

Kay Ryan, another twentieth-century free verse poet for whom rhyme is important, has talked about a related effect. She is comfortably far from any injunction to rhyme ("When I started writing nobody rhymed—it was in utter disrepute," she says), so her rhyming is heavy but nonsystematic. In a *Paris Review* interview from 2008, she discussed her use of "recombinant rhyme": "What's recombinant rhyme? It's like how they add a snip of the jellyfish's glow-in-the-dark gene to bunnies and make them glow green; by snipping up pieces of sound and redistributing them throughout a poem I found I could get the poem to go a little bit luminescent" (Fay, "Kay Ryan").

Ryan's poem "Spring" is characteristic of her work in both its brevity and its great reliance on rhyme:

> Winter, like a set opinion,
> is routed. What gets it <u>out</u>?
> The imposition of some external season
> or some internal <u>doubt</u>?

I see the yellow maculations <u>spread</u>
across bleak hills of what I <u>said</u>
I'd always <u>think</u>; a stippling of white
upon the <u>grey</u>; a <u>pink</u> the shade
of what I said I'd never <u>say</u>. (Ryan 60)

In addition to rhyming, the poem is full of weaker partial or approximate rhymes and other sound devices (including *set* : *gets, routed* : *What* : *out, imposition* : *opinion* : *season, what* : *white, said* : *shade*). Among the rhymes underlined here are four pairs of full rhymes that, while phonetically perfect, are varied in other ways. Of the four, two pairs are end rhymes, with the first pair (*out* : *doubt*) separated by a line while the second pair (*spread* : *said*) is not, and two pairs are internal rhymes, one (*think* : *pink*) purely internal and the other (*grey* : *say*) ending with the poem. The sheer abundance of rhyming and other sound devices in such short a poem runs the risk of turning it from luminescent to overlit, perhaps too close to light verse. If this challenge is met, it is in large part thanks to the sporadicity of the rhyming. When we do not know if or when a rhyme will come, there is a dynamic that resists easy organization and works counter to stifling systematic rigidity, which is manifest in light, singsong verse.

While the poem is not at all light or overlit verse, a comic tone is nonetheless apparent, most clearly in the gentle self-deprecation, as the speaker comes to think and say new things, things she said she would "never say." In the poem's first sentence, this process of relinquishing or routing one's "set opinion" is likened to the change of seasons. While the opening simile keeps its two parts separate, however, the rest of the poem elaborates upon and unites the two.

Take, for instance, the image of "yellow maculations" that "spread / across bleak hills of what I said / I'd always think." The first part of the image belongs to the realm of seasonal change, with the yellow spots of new spring flowers slowly overtaking the bleak hills of winter. But in the second part of the sentence, the reader understands that the bleak hills are "hills of what I said." Simile seamlessly turns to metaphor, the more radical of the two figures of speech. And as the color imagery continues, so does the metaphor, as in the ending phrase: "a pink the shade / of what

I said I'd never say." The pink is at once the literal result of the "white / upon the grey" in the hills of winter changing with the arrival of spring, and the figurative shade of newness in the realm of opinions and sayings.

The rhyming strategy used in this poem deftly contributes to this mixing of semantic spheres on at least two levels. First, the fact that these rhymes are "spread," dispersed sporadically throughout the poem, creates a sonic correlate not just to the spreading of the yellow maculations but also to the confusion of tenor and vehicle, the human and the natural spheres. Second, in terms of the semantic functioning, we note that in the rhyming pairs, one of the words belongs to the tenor and pertains to the human agent (*doubt, say, think*) while the other belongs to the vehicle pertaining to the field and flowers (*spread, grey, pink*). Each rhyme therefore belongs at once to tenor and to vehicle, becoming a sonic bridge between them, or a literal manifestation of their conceptual blending.

When the last word of the poem rhymes, this rhyme is particularly resounding and adds semantic richness to sonic markedness. John Logan, another poet to use much sporadic rhyme, ends his pentametric poem "Two Brothers: Two Saltimbanques" with the rhyming pair *red* : *bed*. The poem is a lengthy account of the speaker's observations of two teenage brothers, first on the train on their way back from the ballpark and then, at the end, as they get off the train and "start home together for supper and bed."

Two boys stand at the end of the full train
Looking out the back, out the sides, turning
Toward each other. Their arms and shoulders brush
As the train shakes. They've been to the ballpark
Together, and can prove it with the huge
Red and blue scorecards in their hands. A sense
Of repeating in the shapes of the ears,
In the bearing of the clefted, young chins.
The older brother is perhaps fifteen,
The other, twelve? A gold of Indians
In summer faces, the color of <u>their</u>
Like <u>hair</u>, which is cut short, though with more bronze

In the younger. The brows of the older
Are surprisingly rich. And this young man
Is ripe with strength, his long face keen shaped,
Arrogant, rather sad about the eyes,
The face not yet tight. They wear green T-shirts
(Perhaps for some school sports?), their khaki pants
Sagging from the day in the sun. The two
Brothers slowly sway together with the
Motion of the train. The younger works <u>hard</u>
At his great <u>scorecard</u>. Now the older <u>son</u>
Bends to whisper: mixed, uncontrolled higher
And lower laughter runs over the train's
Screams, and raises heads out of newspapers.
Suddenly we strike a curve. The small <u>one</u>
Loses balance, and the other moves to
Steady him, leg and thigh muscles tight a-
gainst the steel weight of cars. They straighten. They
Smile, and the older boy's hand rests awhile
At his brother's side. Now as the train slows
A school of jets wings at the left windows
Tracking flame from the late sun. The boys lean
To the glass and the small one grins, gestur-
ing toward the planes, his long young arm poised,
Giving the lie to awkwardness at twelve
Catching for a passing moment the grace
Of what he felt. Now they move to the front
And get off. I watch them walk the platform
At the <u>station</u>. On the <u>invitation</u>
Of a vendor they buy Coke. They won't look
At the penciled dirty word, with its figure,
On the margin of a sign scorecard <u>red</u>.
They start home together for supper and <u>bed</u>. (Logan 86–87)

"Supper and bed," the poem's ending, is the typical schedule for American children come evening, though these are not small children but teenagers, who are, by definition, positioned between childhood and adulthood. Indeed, much of the speaker's interest in these two brothers hinges upon this positioning, as when he estimates their ages at fifteen and twelve. From the first line the brothers are referred to as boys, but at one point the older of the two is referred to as a "young man," and the issue of age and maturing is ever present, as in the "awkwardness" of gesture, so characteristic of teenagers, which the speaker picks up on toward the end.

The poem ends with a highly emphatic and almost exclusive rhyme: *red* : *bed*. The rhyme initiates a backwards movement from the word *bed*. This is the inevitable phenomenology of rhyme. But the backwards movement does not stop with *red*; it continues past it, launching a reading of the poem in reverse, from end to beginning. Inclusion in a rhyme puts much pressure on the word *bed,* and given its already weighty status as the poem's final word, we are invited to read more into it.

With this in mind, this sporadic rhyme unleashes homoerotic connotations that were more or less latent throughout the poem. We may now notice the careful attention earlier given to the brothers' physicality (the references to their arms, shoulders, hands, ears, chins, hair, brows, face, eyes, and muscles quickly accumulate). We likewise take heed of certain words, phrases, and images which, though innocent enough in isolation, nonetheless lend themselves to an erotic reading, such as the two brothers' "slowly sway[ing] together with the / Motion of the train," or the older brother being "ripe with strength," or the young brother's "long young arm poised." In this reading, propelled and retroactively justified by the accidental/motivated rhyming at the end, even potentially innocent phrases like "get off" (as when the brothers get off the train) become "dirty words" like the "penciled dirty word" on the margin of the scorecard that the brothers will not look at—the very "scorecard red" that rhymes with *bed.*

Logan's rhyme *red* : *bed* is resounding. It is an end rhyme, but not a systematic one, because the poem as a whole is only peppered with a few rhymes here and there. Like Logan, all the poets investigated in this chapter (except Hardy) are twentieth- or twenty-first-century poets who do not at all, or do not exclusively, use systematic rhyme. In their sporadically rhymed poems, the appearance of rhyme can be taken as an invitation to read not only the semantic relationship between the rhyming words but also the appearance of rhyme itself. In the more interesting cases, the rhyme becomes a comment on itself or on specific features of itself, such as an allusion to rhymed poetry (Niedecker), childhood (Justice), utopia (Stone), its own markedness (Stevens), its own randomness (Hardy, Stein), or its own pervasiveness (Mullen). In other cases, the sporadic rhyme has a ripple effect that "awakens" or overwhelms the words and opens up possibilities of expanding their meanings (Ignatow, Ryan), realizing latent semantic potentialities in the poem as a whole (Logan), or casting doubt on what is explicitly said (Roethke). In the twentieth century, a surprising number of poets choose to allow rhyme to enter the poem, therefore allowing us to read that allowance.

5

Progressive and Regressive

Rhyme's Traumatic Kernel

BACK AND FORTH, FORTH AND BACK

Previous chapters have demonstrated how rhyme entails a mixing of rigidity and pleasure, how it is at once an agent of organization and disruption, and how it teases the reader with a sense of the accidental and the motivated. Any instance of rhyme has been taken to be not a static given but the result of a dynamic of opposing forces. Rhyme is a privileged poetic device because underlying it are these pairings of seeming contradictions, and each rhyme, to varying degrees, harbors all of them.

In this chapter, I wish to uncover one additional pair, which underlies these other pairs. I am less concerned here with unpacking poetic examples; my goal is to offer a new, admittedly speculative understanding of what rhyme *is,* in both its systematic and sporadic varieties. This will entail foregrounding what has so far, for the most part, been left in the background: rhyme's temporal dimension. And while there are different directions from which to theorize rhyme's temporality, I rely heavily on Sigmund Freud's notion of the temporality of the unconscious because I have found that—when considered in conjunction with a host of other discourses—it offers the richest rewards in its application to rhyme.

Here, I suggest that rhyme can be understood as a material-linguistic manifestation of a specific temporal logic that operates in the unconscious. And while it is evident that this temporal logic resonates in many other arenas besides poetry and rhyme, the latter, for reasons that will become clear, is an exceptional exemplar of it. In addition, the fact that Freud founded the grain of the psychoanalytic theory of temporality on a case of trauma opens the door to uncovering, as I do toward the end of the chapter, the theoretical gains of the problematic coupling of rhyme and trauma.

To start at the beginning, rhyme, whether sporadic or systematic, is a relation or structure realized *in time.* Many of the accounts of rhyme are oblivious to this dimension. But an appreciation of rhyme's rigidity brings it to the fore, because this rigidity depends on linearly unfolding language: the reader can become aware of the rigidity after the first rhyming word is evoked, and in the anticipation of the second. From the perceiver's point of view, we can speak more generally, with Yuri Tynianov, of two complementary features: "a progressive feature (the first rhymed member) and a regressive feature (the second rhymed member)." For Tynianov, more than for many of his contemporaries, verse is anything but static. Like meter, rhyme is "a result of dynamic, progressive preparation and dynamic, regressive license" (53). In numerous poetic forms, rhyme plays this progressive and regressive, back and forth (or rather forth and back) movement. The first rhyming word of the pair initiates the forward orientation or anticipation, and the second word, when reached, connects back to its earlier partner.

Entangled with reader's expectations, this double movement, a form of Edmund Husserl's protention and retention, reaches its peak in poetic forms that are relatively simple and systematic, such as the couplet. These, for example, are the first lines from Christopher Marlowe's translation of one of Ovid's elegies (Elegia 4), where the speaker is about to attend a banquet with the lover's husband:

> Thy husband to a banquet goes with me,
> Pray God it may his latest supper be,
> Shall I sit gazing as a bashfull guest,
> While others touch the damsell I love best?
> Wilt lying under him his bosome clippe?
> About thy neck shall he at pleasure skippe?

Marveile not though the faire Bride did incite
The drunken *Centaures* to a sodaine fight.
I am not halfe horse, nor in woods I dwell,
Yet scarse my hands from thee containe I well. (Marlowe 1.4.1–10)

Ovid wrote these poems in elegiacs, nonrhyming couplets made up of an hexameter followed by a pentameter. In Marlowe's translation, all the lines are pentameters, and it is the rhyming that serves the function of creating couplets. A reader who is attentive to sound and rhythm, whether reading aloud or silently, will very likely come to grasp and anticipate the recurrence of rhyme at the end of each line, with the first rhyming word an opening up and the second a closing, a dropping of the second shoe. Thus *me* waits for its partner *be, guest* is an opening of expectation that is made good with *best, clippe* sets us on an anticipation that ends with *skippe,* and so on. We can understand here Donald Wesling's use of the term "teleological effects" with regard to rhyme (*Chances of Rhyme* 129); we are in a world of anticipation and fulfillment, stifling rigidity or, to put the same dynamic in positive terms, comforting regularity.

Yet this opening-then-closing thrust of rhyme deserves a closer look. Let us focus, with Barbara Herrnstein Smith, on the first of the couplets above. In her classic study *Poetic Closure,* Smith examines an isolated couplet and dispels the popular misconception that rhyme is the sine qua non of closure. She writes, "One cannot say that the second rhyme-word . . . has fulfilled an expectation set up by the first because there is nothing in the lines to create such an expectation (always excepting the effect of the reader's previous experience with English distichs)" (48). Smith forks two aspects of systematic rhyme that usually come together: first, systematic rhyme is rhyme occurring in a rhyme scheme (in this case couplets); and second, there is an expectation for rhyme in situations of systematic rhyme. In the case of the first encounter with the first couplet, or in the case of an epigram (an isolated couplet), just the first of these two aspects of systematic rhyme applies. We can speak of a rhyme scheme, but only one that we are made aware of in hindsight, a posteriori.

Of course, this theoretical innocent encounter with rhyme is an empirical rarity, for exactly the reason Smith herself acknowledges parenthetically: many readers are aware, however subliminally, of the conventions of English distichs, and for such readers there are elements in the lines that cue one to the fact that this is a rhyming situation. The awareness of rhymes to come is certainly stronger when we encounter many rhyming lines in a row. In the Marlowe example, for instance, even if it takes one or two couplets to create the expectation, soon enough rhymes will come to be anticipated with growing certainty, and both aspects of systematic rhyme will thus be fulfilled. Once we know we are in a rhyming form, and that the form recurs, the forward-and-backwards dynamic kicks in. But Smith nevertheless points to a basic characteristic of rhyme that is always true: one never knows for sure that a rhyme is coming. In other words, there is an asymmetry at the heart of rhyme. The "forward" part of the forward and backwards is always provisional, while the "backwards" part is the only certainty.

This crucial attribute relies on foregrounding the diachronic or temporal dimension of rhyme. Simply stated, a key tenet of rhyme manifested in the phenomenology of reading or listening is that a rhyme is realized *in retrospect*. The unfolding rhyme exhibits the fascinating, though not often mentioned attribute of being split across time, with the attainment of the very status of rhyme deferred until the second word of the rhyming pair is reached. When this happens, the status of the first word is changed and the two words (one at present, one reverberating in our active memory) join to form a rhyme.[1]

Though rhyme that is incorporated into a foreknown and easily discernible rhyme scheme conceals this fact and misleads us into a kind of bi-directionality of forth and back, even the purest systematic rhyme cannot do away with it completely. There are never hard and fast guarantees about the future, and so this belated realization is true for any rhyme. In fact, sometimes the rhyme to come does not come, as when a rhyme scheme is "broken" for various specific reasons. Imagine the effect if Marlowe had left a line without a rhyming partner, or had introduced a triplet amid the many couplets. Whether this happens or does not is something the reader will only ever know after one's encounter with it, never in advance.

Theoretically, then, each and every rhyme is a retrospective construction. But there is still a difference between systematic and sporadic rhyme.

While in systematic rhyme this fact is overtly exposed only when an un-expected change occurs in the rhyme scheme, it is never clearer than in sporadic rhyme, which may now be defined as rhyme for which there exists no a priori expectation whatsoever. Consider the example of Randall Jarrell's celebrated short dramatic monologue "The Death of the Ball Turret Gunner":

> From my mother's sleep I fell into the State,
> And I hunched in its belly till my wet fur <u>froze</u>.
> Six miles from earth, loosed from its dream of life,
> I woke to <u>black</u> <u>flak</u> and the nightmare fighters.
> When I died they washed me out of the turret with a <u>hose</u>. (Jarrell 144)

The poem's posthumous speaker served as a gunner on a bomber that had, as its "belly," a transparent turret with mounted machine guns that the gunner would occupy and shoot from in order to protect the aircraft. Resembling a fetus in the round turret, the speaker is describing the last flight on the aircraft, which resulted in his death. The moment of his death, or the moment preceding it, is rendered in the penultimate line, while the last line renders the extraction of his remains from the turret after his death.

Two highly significant rhymes are included in this five-line poem.[2] Both are sporadic, which is to say that neither of them has a progressive, forward pull. The first, *black* : *flak,* in the penultimate line, depicts the cause of the speaker's death, the enemy gunfire. The two rhyming words are maximally proximate, and thus there is very little time between them: no "forth," but not much "back," either. The markedness of the rhyme translates to a concentration of sound, an eruption of noise, which is iconically consonant with the shock or awakening that the speaker is depicting. The iconicity of sound is reinforced in this case by the phonetic quality of the (appropriately named) plosive sound [k], and the rhyme is augmented and enriched as the two words share the prevocalic /l/ and share the plosive sound with the word *woke.*

A longer interval exists for the second rhyme, *froze* : *hose,* which is only realized at the end of the poem. Nothing in the poem, and more specifically nothing in the second line, prepares us for the rhyming partner *hose.* Back in the second line, *froze* did not initiate any opening of expectations, but upon reaching *hose,* the reader is transported backwards: the word *hose* brings back the word *froze* and the two become a rhyme.

While also sporadic, the effect of this second pair is rather different from that of the first. The interval between the rhyming words, and the fact that the second rhyming partner is the last word of the poem, work to round off the poem's end. This rhyme evokes something of the traditional euphonious, soothing, and harmonious function of systematic rhyme. In the case of this poem, the pleasure and harmony in rhyme contributes to the speaker's tone of ironic complacency, the atrocity of death depicted in a seemingly calm, matter-of-fact mode: "When I died they washed me out of the turret with a hose." Unlike the couplets in the Marlowe example, however, the reader is awakened to the rhyme after the fact, which places more emphasis on it, creating a residual surprise, a mix of an easy feeling and a lingering suspicion or unease.

RHYME'S TIME

Sporadic rhyme does not partake of the expectation-fulfilling dynamic that systematic rhyme can observe. Pitted against systematic rhyme, sporadic rhyme can be seen as an alternative or rejection of the teleology in the anticipatory forward then backwards movement of the former. This rejection could very well be part of the motivation for the employment of sporadic rhyme on the part of some modern and contemporary poets, who, as we saw in chapter 1, objected to previous uses of rhyme for being overfamiliar (Ezra Pound) or excessive (T. S. Eliot). The unsympathetic views toward some forms of systematic rhyme and meter, and perhaps the reemergence of sporadic rhyme in modernism, also seem to broadly correlate with changing notions of temporality itself, namely the shift from an earlier view of objective and unchanging temporality, associated with the Newtonian tradition, to a post-Enlightenment experience of time as scattered, contingent, colliding, subjective, and momentary.[3] Sporadic rhyme is a much stronger candidate than systematic rhyme to embody the more scattered and contingent notions of time.

Conceptions of time as well as poetic norms have changed from Marlowe's sixteenth-century couplets to Jarrell's freer twentieth-century verse. And different uses of rhyme give rise to different ways of thinking about temporality, most notably the philosophical distinction between linear (progressive, continuous) time and cyclical time. It seems clear that rhyme in general is more on the side of the cyclical, because by definition rhyme is a return to or repetition of a similar sound. Yet the distinction between systematic and sporadic rhyme, and their respective senses of time, is pertinent. If rhyme is said to "mark time," it is because it typically returns at expected and regular intervals (as in the Marlowe example). In these instances of systematic rhyme, time is seen as rational and expected—returning, yes, but also objective and logically divisible. Systematic rhyme projects into the future; it marches forward. In the sporadic alternative, however, rhyme only harks back.

Whether teleologically forward oriented or circling back repetitiously, the temporality of rhyme is palpable enough to attach itself to realms that transcend poetics (and also transcend modernism). For example, Haun Saussy ("Materials of Poetry") puts forward the idea that rhyme appeals to Christian culture because the cyclical interchangeability and reversibility of the rhyming words echoes the Christian notion of *figura*, a type of interchangeability and reversibility of time and historical figures. Elsewhere ("Return of Orality" 313), Saussy suggests that rhyme emblematizes an ideology of return, not just to orality but generally to earlier times, a return that is the very opposite of secular liberal politics' preference for linearity and a looking to the future. And G. F. W. Hegel's illuminating discussion of rhyme brings its temporal dynamic to the realm of subjectivity. Hegel contrasts classical versification, based on longs and shorts and devoid of rhyme, with romantic poetry's versification of rhyme and accent (stress). He understands rhyme as a *necessary* component of romantic poetry's focus on subjective life, a poetry in which "our inner personality wishes to apprehend itself in the material medium of sound." Why is rhyme correspondent to subjectivity? Hegel writes that (the assonance in) rhyme "has the sole function of bringing us back to ourselves through the return of the same sounds" (1023–24).

Simon Jarvis extends Hegel's basic notion beyond accentually versified romantic poetry and identifies that, for Hegel, "the shape of versification in general, whether quantitative or accentual, answers to a need of the structure of human subjectivity as such." Jarvis shows that rhyme is crucial for an expression, experience, or creation of interiority because of its structure of excursion and return: "Only this excursion and return can convert the merely indifferent flow of time into the shaped and understood duration which makes subjectivity intelligible" ("Musical Thinking" 64).[4] Translated to our temporal terms, Hegel's "excursion" would be the progressive, future-oriented aspect of rhyme, while the "return" is the regressive backwards click.

PSYCHOANALYZING RHYME: *NACHTRÄGLICHKEIT*
In positing the role that rhyme plays in subjectivity, Hegel brings together rhyme, subjectivity, and temporality. After Hegel, the end of the nineteenth century and the beginning of the twentieth saw growing attention to the subjective experience of time, most notably by Henri Bergson and Edmund Husserl. In different ways, both of these philosophers showed the human subject to be "intimately immersed in the time of the experience" (Schleifer 52) and stressed the need to turn away from a scientific/objective account of time in favor of time's lived experience as duration (Bergson), or to devise a method to capture how our consciousness apprehends time or apprehends objects in time (Husserl).

Early versions of these phenomenologies of lived time developed in tandem with Freud's early discoveries of the unconscious and the gradual founding of psychoanalysis.[5] In the background, too, is philosopher Franz Brentano, with whom Freud studied at the University of Vienna.[6] But amid the new forms of philosophical attunement to temporality as subjective experience, it is psychoanalysis that offers the most exact and revealing theoretical terrain to help explain rhyme's captivating appeal, because psychoanalysis, more than other theoretical discourses, has centralized the specific structure of retrospectivity, through one of Freud's main theorizations of psychic temporality, *Nachträglichkeit* ("afterwardsness").[7]

Nachträglichkeit is not just a psychoanalytic concept among many. It is "a miniature of the modality of psychoanalytic knowledge at large," writes Perry Meisel, who traces it in Freud's various writings as well as in the very structure of his writing, as in his process of self-revision (*Literary Freud* 43).[8] Nachträglichkeit runs through the writing of Freud and of subsequent psychoanalytic theoreticians, in different forms, contexts, and guises. Probably the clearest instance is the case of Freud's patient Emma, a woman whose symptom is an acute fear of going into shops alone, which Freud details in part 2 of the early *Project for a Scientific Psychology* (1895). As the reason for her phobia, Emma cites an incident of having her clothes made fun of by two shop assistants at the age of twelve. After further work, an earlier memory is revealed, according to which a shopkeeper had "grabbed at her genitals through her clothes" at the age of eight. Freud explains that the situation at age twelve unconsciously brought about the memory of age eight, though now, following puberty, the memory of the former assault "aroused what it was certainly not able to at the time [before puberty], a sexual release, which was transformed into anxiety." This anxiety caused her to fear that the shop assistant would repeat the assault, and the phobia ensued (353–54).

Freud presents a formulation with which many have grappled. Jean Laplanche describes Freud's use of Nachträglichkeit in his seduction theory by an analogy to a time bomb: "the first memory is like a time-bomb which is triggered off by something outside it" ("Notes on Afterwardsness" 261). But this explanation does not capture the significance of the Emma case. As Laplanche himself says, there is no retroactivity in the time bomb analogy in the strict sense, since the arrow of time is not reversed.[9] André Green, another close reader of Freud, writes that in these situations we have "two epochs . . . the anticipatory event (*l'avant-coup*) and the retroactive attribution of new meaning (*l'apres-coup*)," whereby the "progression of meaning involves . . . a return backwards in time which adds, retroactively, to the content it had initially" (36). This is closer to what Freud describes in the Emma case. It acknowledges a backwards motion, with the operative word *add*: the return backwards in time *adds* to the content that was there initially.

In his Letter 52 to Wilhelm Fliess, Freud underscores how the psychic connection between present and past results in the blurring of the very notions of present and past: "The material present in the form of memory-traces" is "subjected from time to time to a *re-arrangement* in accordance with fresh circumstances—to a *re-transcription*" (233). The notion of retranscription assumes that our perception of the past changes in light of subsequent events. Underscoring this temporal bidirectionality is surely not limited to psychoanalysis; Søren Kierkegaard succinctly stated, "Philosophy is perfectly right in saying that life must be understood backwards. But then one forgets the other clause—that it must be lived forwards" (*Journals* 450). But while, for Kierkegaard, it is a question of living forward and interpreting the past, Freud teaches us that in the unconscious the past literally *changes*.[10] What we have is a situation, Freud says, in which a repressed memory *becomes* a trauma by deferred action (*Project* 356); Emma retrospectively experiences the events of age eight as traumatic. The past has affectively and effectively changed; something that was not there, is now/then there.

The backwards effect of the present on the past that the Emma case shows joins the complementary effect of the past on the present, crystallized in Freud's assertion that "neurotics are anchored somewhere in their past" ("Paths" 365). While subjects' being fixed to their past coheres with the popular understanding of psychoanalysis as itself a process of "going back" and digging up roots, or root causes, both effects are crucial and comprise the general problematizing of time and temporality in psychoanalysis. Indeed, the very term *Nachträglichkeit* is said by Laplanche to sometimes refer in Freud precisely to the deterministic impact of the past, which comes to affect the present belatedly.

But being true to Freud means recognizing the opposite as well, which is more radical than the much discussed notion of belatedness: the present determines the past. In Freud's essay on "screen memories," those seemingly innocent and unexplained recurring childhood memories, he further theorizes this backwards-looking effect and applies it not to trauma but to memory in general. Screen memories blur time in various directions, but the kind of blurring that Freud refers to as "retrogressive" occurs when an unconscious phantasy in the present is screened off by a childhood memory of something that occurred years earlier. The early childhood memory is brought about in order to serve a present-day purpose. Moreover, the two parts, the screen memory and the screened phantasy, blend into each other, so that it becomes "very possible that in the course of this process the childhood scene itself . . . undergoes changes" ("Screen Memories" 318). Freud closes the article with a characteristic extension from screen memories to all memories derived from childhood, claiming that childhood memories do not merely emerge but are *formed* in later periods, with motivations other than "historical accuracy" (322). The past is of doubtful ontological status, informed and formed by the present. Jacques Derrida articulates this notion of the past most succinctly when, in acknowledging an affinity between Freud's thinking and his own term *différance,* he characterizes Nachträglichkeit as demonstrating "a 'past' that has never been nor will ever be present" ("Differance" 152). And with the specific language of Freud in mind, along with the more recent insights of neurology, Arnold Modell is able, with biologist Gerald Edelman, to give a neurobiological backing to Freud's Nachträglichkeit and the constructed nature of memory, by understanding memory as "a dynamic reconstruction that is context-bound and established by means of categories" (60). In this model, memory is the "retranscription of categories," constantly in a state of potential alteration. Modell explains that, not unlike the time bomb analogy, affective experiences are stored as "affect categories" and "exist as a *potential* awaiting activation in current experience" (65). In short, a memory is not inscribed once and for all in the brain but is renewed and reinscribed in different contexts when it is evoked.[11]

Now, back to rhyme. A syllable becomes the rhyme partner of another syllable only *nachträglich* (afterward), through a kind of bending back on itself of the arrow of time; each bending back produces a rhyme "structure." Correcting the time bomb analogy, we can now say that the second event turns the first into a time bomb retrospectively, and in a like manner, the second rhyming word makes the first into its rhyming partner and *turns them both into a rhyme.*

Considered from a psychoanalytic angle, the structure of rhyme is akin to a structure of time in the unconscious. This kinship should be seen in the context of the relation between forms of language and forms of the unconscious, a parallelism for which Freud searches again and again in his work. So, in *The Psychopathology of Everyday Life* (1901), puns are shown to actualize repressed and conflicted wishes, and—most clearly—in "The Antithetical Meaning of Primal Words" (1910), the illogical tendency of dreams (and hence of the unconscious) to disregard contraries, or even to turn contraries into a unity and to represent them as one, finds a precise correlate in the way that, in some languages, the same word can have two opposite meanings.[12]

The inter-echoing of language and the unconscious was crystalized with Jacques Lacan's (1964) famous and ever-enigmatic proclamation that "the unconscious is structured like a language" (see, for instance, *Fundamental Concepts* 149).[13] Lacan exemplifies the isomorphism between language and the unconscious by linking two elements that Freud identified in the dream work and in what he calls "primary psychical process," condensation and displacement, with metaphor and metonymy, respectively (Écrits 122).[14] Incidentally, for this particular and pivotal link, Lacan needed the mediation of Roman Jakobson, who, in turn, was building on Ferdinand de Saussure.[15] Going back in time, Saussure identifies "two forms of mental activity, both indispensable to the life of language," namely the syntagmatic (signs appearing in succession and determining each other) and the associative (signs that share certain traits and are stored together in memory) (123–26). Jakobson then elaborates on each of these two designations, assigns to them the modes of combination and selection, and maps onto them the tropes of metonymy and metaphor. Metaphor and metonymy thus become, in Jakobson's formulation, not just local tropes but representations in miniature of entire operations or relations in language; the two poles of the very "bipolar structure of language" ("Two Aspects of Language" 111). With this, the tropes carry such weight that the relation that Lacan finds between them and Freud's unconscious operations becomes a relation not just with specific tropes but also with the very operation of language itself.

Rhyme carries its own weight and, I would like to suggest, could be added as another instance of this relation between the unconscious and language: metaphor and condensation, metonymy and displacement, opposite-meaning words and disregard for contraries—and rhyme and Nachträglichkeit. Rhyme also suggests the bidirectionality of the language/unconscious twinning: not only is the unconscious structured like language but also one form of language, rhyme, is structured like the unconscious. Rhyme thus comes to be regarded as a concrete realization in miniature of a specific temporal operation of the unconscious, an operation that an encounter with rhyme plays out every time. Could this view help account for part of rhyme's pervasiveness and its enduring fascination to poets and readers of so many different traditions, languages, and eras?

WHAT'S SO SPECIAL ABOUT RHYME?

Hegel takes a small prosodic element like rhyme and sees in it the much larger structure of subjectivity. Others also have found a world of subjectivity in a grain of prosody, though rhythm has been more instrumental in this than rhyme, its etymological twin (both come from the classical Latin *rhythmus*). Daniel Laferriere, for example, claims that the meaningless repetition of a poem's meter gives the reader an outlet for his repetition compulsion and provides the writer a defense by way of a distraction "away from any ego-distonic semantic elements that may be lurking below the threshold of consciousness" (434, 439).

Closer still to my approach is psychoanalyst and phenomenological prosodist Nicolas Abraham, who, in the context of quantitative metrics, argues that meter produces effects through which "I contemplate modes of recurrence as corresponding within me to essential structures of temporality" (77). As readers, then, can experience rhythm as "coessential" with their very structure of "temporal being," rhythm can represent, or rather realize, different temporal structures (78, 90). *Realize,* rather than *represent,* is the key. In the case of rhythm, *realize* is appropriate because of rhythm's special claim to embodiment (one thinks of the crude cliché that the heart beats iambically). Indeed, rhythm "rarely gets described without some claim that it can be heard, felt, and shared because it has physical effects on bodies or tympanums" (Glaser 6). In comparison to "the *bodily* pleasure experienced in the regular, musical rhythm of meter" (Aviram 3, emphasis mine), rhyme is perhaps less obviously felt "bodily," but it still can be palpable, perhaps in some sense even more so than the endlessly vague and expansive rhythm,[16] because rhyme is fairly self-contained, well-delineated, and often marked. In the special case of rhyme, then, I suggest that it is a palpable enactment of an abstract temporal structure, namely retrospectivity, with all its psychological significance and resonance.

On the horizon is perhaps a new definition of rhyme, one that significantly raises the stakes of what is involved. Rhyme is no mere ornamental or conventional device. Rhyme is not yet another example of the principle of equivalence, poetic repetition, or parallelism. Rather, I am proposing that we consider rhyme as a *concretization* of a structure of temporality, a linguistic-symbolic arena to experience and explore this temporality. Both writer and reader engage, through rhyme, in this creation and recreation of a strange, familiar temporality, a backwards-directed antichronology that, in Green's words, "explodes classical temporal models" of unidirectional movement from past to future (8). The writer and reader attentive to rhyme are attuning to their own temporality.

Every rhyme entails retrospectivity, which is also to say that it is, on some level, a surprise. The specific kind of rhyme that I am calling sporadic exhibits pure retrospectivity and entails a particularly acute surprise, not just in terms of which word will be chosen as the second rhyming partner but also in the fact that such a word is supplied at all. Still, rhyme is certainly not the only surprise in literary texts; indeed, retrospectivity and surprises are to be found everywhere, both within and outside of literature.

Naturally, a reader's encounters with surprises in a literary text are intimately tied in with the temporality of the reading process., and alertness to the temporality of the reading process is implicit in any theory that highlights the reader. Thus, one finds a discussion of surprises and retrospectivity in nearly every major reader response or reader aware theorist. The effect and uniqueness of rhyme, entangled with the temporality of reading, can therefore be best appreciated against other, somewhat similar phenomena in literature and language. One salient context to consider first, apropos of the retrospectivity and surprise of rhyme, is narrative.

In Wolfgang Iser's description of the reading process, Husserl looms large in the background:

> The reader's position in the text is at the point of intersection between retention and protension. Each individual sentence correlate prefigures a particular horizon, but this is immediately transformed into the background

for the next correlate and must therefore necessarily be modified. . . . Each
new correlate, then, will answer expectations (either positively or negatively)
and, at the same time, will arouse new expectations. . . . In most literary texts
. . . the sequence of sentences is so structured that the correlates serve to
modify and even frustrate the expectations they have aroused. *In so doing,*
they automatically have a retroactive effect on what has already been read, which
now appears quite different. Furthermore, what has been read shrinks in the
memory to a foreshortened background, but it is being constantly evoked in a
new context and so modified by new correlates that instigate a restructuring
of past syntheses. (Iser, *Act of Reading* 111, emphasis mine).

In Iser's account of reading a narrative—as in Kierkegaard's account of
reading life, as in my foregoing account of encountering rhyme—there
is a prominent element of Nachträglichkeit. For Iser, in the context of
narrative, this continuous process of rethinking past information and
adapting to new information is essentially, as he says a few pages later,
"a process of consistency-building" (*Act* 123), or an attempt "to optimize"
the structure of the text, "to build up the syntheses" (118), to achieve and
maintain coherence in the text. Iser is careful to qualify this process, to
speak of the subjective elements involved in forming this gestalt of the
text, to refer to other possibilities or readings that "cast their shadow"
on our formed gestalt (118, 126). Nonetheless, the basic aim, born out of
narrativity itself, is, as Iser says elsewhere, "to fit everything together in a
consistent pattern" ("Reading Process" 219).

As with Iser's constant adjusting of past information in light of new information coming in, so too with Meir Sternberg's understanding of narrative surprise. In a rigorous theory of narrative, Sternberg sees surprise,
beyond Aristotle's more limited use of the term, as "a universal narrative
force in its own right," which, together with curiosity and suspense, forms
the three "universals of narrative" (520). For Sternberg, surprises—born
out of the gap between the two temporal sequences, the events happening
(the world) and their telling (the discourse)—occur when the text covertly
"manipulates sequence for the purpose of withholding and distorting antecedents in the telling": "There is no shock of discovery without a *hidden*
gap in plot continuity for the reader to discover behind time, no reversal

of narrative expectation without a more or less imperceptible reversal of chronology in the narrative: late before early, effect before cause, deed before doer's (real) motive, world-stuff before world-picture, always secretly distributed to give a first and false impression—persuasive yet at best partial—before full and true knowledge is attained, if only knowledge of the trick played by art on our ignorance, credulity, stock responses, habits of reading and thinking" (Sternberg 519).

We see how, because of the logic of narrativity, surprise is a "shock of discovery" and entails a backwards glance and a readjustment of what the readers thought they knew. Sternberg refers to surprise as "a dynamics of recognition" that "subsumes and brings together all of the elements that make for *retrospective enlightenment*—for some hidden deformation of time and understanding, with a view to their belated reformation under the pressure of unforeseen (dis)closures" (519, 523, emphasis mine).[17]

Given the significance of retrospectivity in human psychology and memory, it is not surprising to find it exploited in the encounter with narrative structures. What, then, is unique in rhyme? One thing to keep in mind is that rhyme is simply a very small, palpable, material instance of these other retrospective instances in life, narrative, or poetry, and this smallness gives it much force.[18] Yet there is also a more fundamental difference between rhyme and narrative with regard to retrospectivity. Retrospectivity, for Iser and for Sternberg, is always in the service of narrative, of preserving some unity of the chain of narrative, whether one is adjusting expectations for the sake of "consistency building" (Iser) or integrating surprise after the fact in order to correct a gap created by the sequence of narration (Sternberg). But sporadic rhyme does not allow for this kind of after-the-fact integration of the surprise. As a sonic, nonnarrative element, it does not partake in the process of sense-making or gestalt-building; there is no "sense" to try to preserve with rhyme.[19]

Crucially, *sporadic* rhyme is the kind of rhyme that resists integration even into the fabric of the poem's sound and rhythm. By definition, it is not part of the rhyme scheme or the poem's prosody, which would be the equivalent of narrative plot on the level of the text's texture.[20] Think back to the two rhymes in Jarrell's poem. If, instead of a single stanza with two sporadic rhymes, the poem were made up of, say, five stanzas with the same rhyming pattern, the reader might come to expect the rhyming, and the retrospectivity would be curbed by an integration into the poem's form. But in sporadic rhyme this fails to occur. It is precisely the resistance to the integration, the appearance of rhyme out of the blue and its remaining out of the blue, that is its hallmark and the basis for its disorganizing potential, which we saw in chapter 3. As a surprising element on the level of the language, sporadic rhyme brings no "retrospective enlightenment," no "recognition," save for the fact of rhyme itself. It alone does not close any gaps in the text, nor does it reform anything that was previously deformed; it is the deformation itself.[21]

Even in narrative, surprises do not necessarily bring about closure and full or true knowledge. Sternberg talks of this possibility, too, whereby the narrative presents "surprise for the purpose of forcing an earlier stability or continuity into permanent ambiguity" (521). This kind of "negative" discovery is closer to rhyme because it shares with rhyme a resistance to smooth integration and resolution. But here, too, there is an important difference, in that rhyme—though it does not close anything on the larger level of the organizing principles of the text—does in fact create stability and closure on the local linguistic level, because rhyme is a well-defined and tightly knit entity of language. This is the other side of rhyme's disruptiveness and lack of integration: its harmonious asemantic "click." When the second word in a rhyme is reached, whatever rhyme that is, rhyme does in fact close, the second word integrating back with the first.

This is also one point that distinguishes rhyme from other linguistic structures working across the temporality of the reading process and entailing surprise and readjustments of the past. Enjambment is unique to poetry because it relies on lineation. Stanley Fish, always alert to readers as they encounter (or rather, create) the text, notes the retrospectivity of enjambment, demonstrating that if we attune to enjambment in the process of reading a sonnet by John Milton, a new line reverses the sense we made of a previous line (292–95).[22] One could see the opportunity for a similar operation in any given sentence—given, as it inevitably is, in time. With each new word of the sentence, readers are constantly reevaluating the information that was given at the beginning, the potential for the meaning to change remaining open until the sentence reaches its end.

Languages vary in the flexibility of their prescribed word order (Latin, with its relatively free word order, would seem to allow for expectations to hang in the air for longer than English), though the principle itself results from the temporal nature of language itself and is not limited to a specific language. Indeed, any trope or linguistic game that has as its basis the overturning of a previous word or statement entails retrospectivity. Consider the following silly witty ditty:

Mary had a little lamb,
the midwife died of shock.

There is surprise in these lines, and, just like rhyme, this construction is made up of two parts, whereby the second part (the second line) causes a retrospective change in the first, inasmuch as we now reinterpret the verb *had* from meaning "possessed" to "gave birth to." So how is this different from rhyme, from rhyme's Nachträglichkeit?

Again, rhyme is not just a miniature manifestation of the retrospective logic but a concrete enactment of it, because rhyme is defined not by *sense* but by *sound*. This affords rhyme special significance among these manifestations of retrospectivity. Since it does not rely on sense, rhyme concretizes and radicalizes the structure of retrospectivity, taking it from an epistemological to an ontological level. Whereas in this example *had* already included both potential meanings from the beginning, with the second line pushing us in the direction of realizing the least likely one, in rhyme, the second word actually turns the first into its rhyming partner to form a rhyme. Neither word alone can be a rhyme. And—this is always the second part of rhyme's dynamic—in rhyme, the two words lock together to create sonic harmony (its euphonious or musical function). Sporadic rhyme is thus uniquely a surprise that sticks out of the text as well as a well-fitting sound, a surprise of a different order.

RHYME AND TRAUMA

So far we have established that all rhyme realizes or literalizes Nachträglichkeit, with sporadic rhyme maximizing its realization, since there is no progressive movement from past to present, only a retrogressive one from present to past. And unlike some other examples of retrospectivity and surprise in language and in narrative, sporadic rhyme ontologically realizes this structure and proceeds to prop it up by emphatically *not* integrating into the fabric of the text, making rhyme particularly marked, laden with poetic potential.

But what are we to make of the fact that Freud founded the concept of Nachträglichkeit on a case of trauma (the Emma case) and theorized its operation as an operation of trauma? Is there some special connection between the temporal logic of Nachträglichkeit and the concept of trauma, and if so, what could the implications for rhyme be? What would it mean to say that rhyme enacts a kind of trauma-associated logic or, to put it differently, what could be gained for our understanding of rhyme by pursuing its possible ties with trauma?

First, how does Freud understand trauma? Standard accounts of psychic trauma often assume that, like physical trauma, it can be pinpointed, located in a specific event in time.[23] But heeding Freud's early formulation of trauma means thinking of the traumatic event as double and split and therefore not entirely locatable. Recall that Freud constructs Emma's situation as one in which "a memory is repressed which has only become a trauma by deferred action" (*Project* 356). In other words, Emma retrospectively experiences the events of age eight as traumatic; a trauma that was not there *becomes* there. Laplanche, writing on the Emma case, makes this point clearly: "The trauma is situated entirely in the play of 'deceit' producing a kind of seesaw effect between the two events. Neither of the two events in itself is traumatic" (*Life and Death* 41).

While Freud's conceptualization may not be intuitively synonymous with commonly held views of trauma, it is entirely consistent with psychoanalytic logic, according to which displacement is the rule and causality in the unconscious is anything but linear. In this spirit, and as distinct from a too-easy definition of trauma as attached to a single difficult event as assumed by the psychiatric category of posttraumatic stress disorder, Cathy Caruth, a pioneer in trauma studies, writes, "The pathology [of post-traumatic stress disorder] cannot be defined . . . by the event itself—which may or may not be catastrophic, and may not traumatize everyone equally." The pathology consists, rather, "solely in the *structure* of its experience or reception: the event is not assimilated or experienced fully at the time, but only *belatedly,* in its *repeated* possession of the one who experiences it. To be traumatized is precisely to be possessed by an image or event" (introduction to *Trauma* 4–5, emphasis mine).

Caruth highlights that trauma inheres not in an a priori event or inci- dent (such as being injured in a car accident, witnessing an act of violence, and so forth) but rather in a structure. And, through her inclusion of belatedness and repetition, she recognizes that time and temporality are problematized in the trauma, although she stops short of seeing trauma as never locatable in principle, or of echoing the fundamental reversal of the arrow of time that is an important part of Freud's early account. Rebecca Comay finds many of the same characteristics in her linking of Proustian involuntary memory to Freudian trauma. In Marcel Proust, the subsequent events themselves do not have to be overtly or blatantly catastrophic—Comay cites such events in the novel as the jolt of paving stones, the clink of a spoon, the swipe of a napkin, and the shriek of a water pipe (104, note 10). Following Freud's own reasoning in the Emma case leads to the understanding that trauma is not an exception but the rule, that, in Richard Boothby's words, "Every human being is subject to the effects of traumatic *Nachträglichkeit*" (203).

In truth, Freud himself is inconsistent in his use of the term *trauma.* In "Beyond the Pleasure Principle," a later work in which he deals with trauma, Freud does not insist on the radical two-event characteristic but rather places much importance on the issue of lack of preparedness, or surprise, which is another important tie between trauma, Nachträglich- keit, and rhyme. As the first characteristic of "ordinary traumatic neuro- ses," Freud states that "the chief weight in their causation seems to rest upon the factor of surprise, of fright." Freud goes on to specify that by "fright" he means "a state a person gets into when he has run into danger without being prepared for it," as opposed to anxiety, which describes "a particular state of expecting danger or preparing for it, even though it may be an unknown one" (12).

Caruth, in her readings of both "Beyond the Pleasure Principle" and *Moses and Monotheism,* insightfully claims that "the recurring image of the accident in Freud . . . becomes the exemplary scene of trauma *par excellence,* not only because it depicts what we can know about traumatizing events, but also, and more profoundly, because it tells of what it is, in traumatic events, that is *not* precisely grasped" (*Unclaimed Experience* 6). This too, then, seems a crucial component of trauma: the accident, or surprise, corresponds to an experience of such magnitude or strangeness that it cannot be grasped, comprehended, integrated, related to, or fully experienced; it is "the relation with the nonrelational" (Comay 88). Informed by work in neurobiology, using different language but evoking the same idea, Bessel van der Kolk and Onno van der Hart write, "Traumatic memories are the unassimilated scraps of overwhelming experiences, which need to be integrated with existing mental schemes, and be transformed into narrative language" (176).[24]

This double difficulty inherent in trauma, then, of locating and of assimilating, finds a striking parallel in sporadic rhyming. Rhyme belongs to the logic of the a posteriori and exhibits the warped temporality covered under the heading of "Nachträglichkeit," but in addition, rhyme, like trauma, is caught between the two rhyming words, neither in this word nor in that. Like the two events that together make up trauma, the two rhyming words come to bleed into each other, to literally fuse together and reverberate (with) each other in our memory in an unresolved acoustic confusion. And as the comparison with narrative surprises helped to articulate, sporadic rhyme is a surprise that is not assimilated into the fabric of the text. The lack of full integration, the way in which sporadic rhyme stands out and sticks out of the rhyme scheme or of any other prosodic configuration or systematization in the poem, as we have seen, then translates poetically to rhyme being semantically overwhelming (chapter 4) and organizationally disruptive (chapter 3).

Since not every surprise is devastating (one can imagine happy surprises and fortuitous accidents), it is best to remember, once again, that when we speak of trauma we are dealing more with a logic and a structure than with a single predetermined empirical effect or affect. Still, trauma is hardly semantically neutral, and neither are the words we have been using to list some of sporadic rhyme's poetic effects, such as "overwhelming" and "disruptive." Indeed, the affinity with trauma that we are exploring invites us to highlight the more disturbing or even sinister aspects of rhyme's operation. For one, whether two given words sound alike is not something the poet typically gets to choose; it is an accident that confirms the arbitrariness of language, at whose mercy poets operate.

As we saw in some of the earlier points made by poets writing about rhyme, systematic rhyme often evokes in the poet anxiety connected to being controlled by the rhyme, and by extension, by language.[25] In Susan Stewart's account, rhyme, even if systematic, is eerie and unmasterable: "Even as it is often an effect of conscious will, or, as we say, a 'scheme,' rhyme seems to come to us from somewhere else, from some outside that may be deeply inside, in the sense that it is unconscious or, perhaps, simply compulsive" ("Rhyme and Freedom" 41). Stewart's account takes the point of view of the writer, but when it comes to sporadic rhyme, the same anxiety is transferred to the reader and is potentially much intensi-fied. No longer is it a question of the extent to which the poet chose this specific word in order to meet the requirements of the rhyme scheme, since by definition there are no such requirements. Instead, the anxiety now takes the form of a more basic question: To what extent is the very rhyme encountered in the poem a result of contingency? The larger issue evoked is that of the submission to randomness and accidents in language, which is itself not divorced from trauma's essential link to the accidental.

A related dimension of the uneasy hold that rhyme may have on us is the fact that rhyme—any rhyme—has a transgressive nature. Po-etry in general, Roman Jakobson says, is "a province where the internal nexus between sound and meaning changes from latent into patent and manifests itself most palpably and intensely" ("Linguistics and Poetics" 87–88). Sporadic rhyme, maximally marked against the background of nonrhyming language, is the strongest instance of such discomforting, de-automatizing questioning of that which usually is not questioned. Donald Wesling uses the word *transgression* when he writes on rhyme: "That two words with separate meanings should be similar in sound is a transgression of our deepest language habits" (*Chances of Rhyme* ix). Although polysemy, puns, and rhyming are rampant in language and prove that difference in meaning does not always mean difference in sound, these phenomena still are perceived as strange, exceptional, and transgressive. It would seem that when two rhyming words carry highly disparate meanings (*tall* : *small, death* : *breath*), the discomfort would be maximized, but in a sense it is even more enigmatic and eerie when, as is usually the case, there is no apparent semantic connection whatsoever between the rhyming words.

For the early Roland Barthes, in *Elements of Semiology,* rhyme appears under the heading of "transgressions" because it is a perversion of the "normal relations" between the two planes or axes of language (Saussure's associative and syntagmatic planes, and Jakobson's paradigmatic and syntagmatic, which Barthes terms "systematic" and "syntagmatic"), "a fragment of the system extended into a syntagm" (86–87). These are the terms by which Jakobson defined the poetic function, in his assertion that it "projects the principle of equivalence from the axis of selection into the axis of combination" ("Linguistics and Poetics" 71). Jakobson's formulation situates rhyme, as a palpable form of equivalence, at the very heart of poetry. Barthes's formulation further situates rhyme at the very heart of (linguistic) transgression. Sporadic rhyme is even more scandalous than systematic rhyme, in that it flaunts its transgression in a nonsystematic, (seemingly) accidental mode of employment; any rhyme can appear anywhere and anytime.

RHYME, TRAUMA, AND PERFORMATIVITY

Rhyme and trauma? Rhyme like trauma? Rhyme as trauma? A connection between poetic conventions and trauma has been suggested before, most notably and brilliantly by Mutlu Konuk Blasing in a book on lyric poetry, but rhyme and trauma is an especially uncanny coupling.[26] The coupling may seem counterintuitive, first, because there is an unbridgeable chasm between the vast meaning that culture and personal experience have rightly bestowed upon the term *trauma* and something as seemingly small as rhyme. Second, the soothing, pleasurable, and harmonious associations that rhyme carries, the feel of something elegant, witty, and well-organized, is the exact opposite of traumatic.

Keeping this second objection at bay for the time being, and stepping back to consider the first, at core we are entertaining the idea—prior to any specific fit between rhyme and trauma—that a text can even host or replicate something like trauma. The difficulty is compounded because the suggestion that a text can do this flies in the face of many accounts of trauma. In the discourse of trauma, it is commonplace to find the proposition that trauma escapes both language and understanding, that it is so overwhelming that it cannot be adequately understood, let alone narrativized or verbalized—indeed, that putting trauma into words will itself constitute an act of lessening.[27]

However, sporadic rhyme is not a simple "putting into words," and it emphatically is *not* narrating past traumatic events as a way to assign them meaning and move past them. Rather, a shadow or echo of trauma (the strange logic, the form, the temporality, the incomprehensibility, the transgression, the surprise, the accident, the chill) can be found or created in language, not by describing an event but by reproducing something on the level of structure. That poetry *shows* rather than *tells* is in keeping with its traditional role, as revealed by the very etymology of the word *poet*: "to make," "to create," "to do."[28] If anything, then, rhyme would be an instance not of "writing about trauma" but of "writing trauma."[29]

One context for the literary text's ability to do, transmit, and perform rather than state, narrativize, or represent is speech act theory, in spite of J. L. Austin's own explicit exclusion of poetry from felicitous or "serious" speech acts.[30] But it is Shoshana Felman, in her essay "Education and Crisis, or the Vicissitudes of Teaching," who is most responsible for bringing together, and to an extent equating, testimony, poetics, and performativity. Felman starts by defining testimony in contradistinction to "a completed statement, a totalizable account" (5). She defines testimony as "a performative speech act" and "a discursive *practice,* as opposed to a pure *theory*": "In the testimony, language is in process and in trial, it does not possess itself as a conclusion" (Felman 5). In keeping with Adorno's near reversal of his earlier statement disparaging writing poetry after Auschwitz, when he comes to write, "It is now virtually in art alone that suffering can still find its own voice" (quoted in Felman 34), Felman offers the example of poet Paul Celan's later "disrupted and disruptively elliptical verse":

Your question—your answer.
Your song, what does it know?

Deepinsnow,
        Eepinnow,
                Ee—i—o. (Felman 35)[31]

Mallarmé refers to his report on the introduction of free verse into
French poetry as a "testimony of an accident," and Felman connects that
to Celan's poetry, and writes:

> In exploding . . . its own poetic medium, in dislocating its own language and
> in breaking down its own verse, the poetry of Paul Celan gives testimony, in
> effect, no longer simply to what Mallarmé refers to as an undefined, generic
> "accident," but to a more specific, more particularly crushing and more re-
> cent, cultural and historical breakdown, to the individual and the communal,
> massive trauma of a catastrophic loss and a disastrous fate in which nothing
> any more can be construed as *accident* except, perhaps, *for the poet's own
> survival. . . . The breakage of the verse enacts the breakage of the world.* (Felman
> 25, emphasis in the original)

Celan's disrupted verse thus testifies to the disruption of the world by
enacting it in his language, according to Felman, not unlike the way Mallarmé's disruption of the expected rhythm of the traditional alexandrine
"becomes itself a symptom and an emblem of the historical breaking of
political and cultural grounds" (20). Felman thus makes the point that
unlike "a completed statement, a totalizable account," which would be,
say, a narrative that treats language as transparent, testimony is achieved
as an enactment of breakage on the level of the text's own language.
    Celan offers a most appealing example of the idea that the broken
language of the poem is isomorphic with the brokenness of the world,
in part because the biography of the poet is impossible to ignore. But
there is a danger of overgeneralizing the case here, because so much of
poetry is full of breakings and surprises, from the rhetorical level to the

material-linguistic one, as in enjambment and disruptions of meter. If more nuanced discriminations within the general performativity of poetry are not allowed, each surprise or shattering of expectations, every neologism, broken word, enjambed line, ungrammaticality, or spondaic foot amid iambs becomes equally "traumatic."

Unlike instances of language or meter breaking down, sporadic rhyme is an instance of Nachträglichkeit. Rather than merely breaking, this specificity of structure, with all of its reverberations, affords sporadic rhyme distinction because it is a crucial, definitional component of trauma, as well as of time in the unconscious. As with Celan's breaking down of words or Mallarmé's breaking down of meter, there is an element of breakdown or surrender of control on the level of language, but in rhyme this breakdown goes together with a specific structure, coherent and tight, that comes to be realized upon reaching the second word.[32] This is the sonorous click of the rhyme, the drop of the second shoe, precisely because we only hear the drop of the first shoe in retrospect.

Sporadic rhyme is, then, as much an erecting of a structure as it is a breaking down of one. Unlike a textual breakdown, rhyme is rigid and pleasurable. In this way, even the most sporadic of sporadic rhymes erupts with no sense and evokes the elements of harmony and shattered "perfect language," detailed in the discussion of its dynamic as accidental and motivated. It is in this strict sense—a senseless, surprising, accidental glimpse of perfection, order, and harmony; a transgression of regular linguistic habit; a split linguistic event created after the fact—that rhyme performs.

PLEASURE REVISITED

If a psychoanalytically informed understanding of rhyme views it as a palpable symbolic manifestation of the temporality of Nachträglichkeit, with the added thrust of being a manifestation in miniature of the very structure of trauma, how does this square with the pleasure in rhyme? Do the soothing, at times humorous and witty associations of rhyme not stand opposed to this view? In what way does rhyme demonstrate that poetry's "pleasure is in the return to the site of pain" (Blasing 47)?[33]

To address these questions, I should note first that the soothing effects that are attributed to rhyme, and which are so foreign to the understanding of accidents or trauma, are mostly attributable to the recurrence of systematic rhyme and are themselves highly duplicitous and tentative, as the discussion of the rigidity of rhyme schemes in chapter 2 made clear. The pleasure in succumbing to the rigidity of rhyme, and the pleasure in resisting it, are activated most in systematic rhyme. Also, the euphonious function of rhyme, the musicality it imports into the poem, as in lullabies, comes into full play when rhyme is systematized, when it ends every line in the poem.

But what about sporadic rhyme and pleasure? Sporadic rhyme does not share in the misleadingly soothing regularity that is so characteristic of systematic rhyme. If systematic monotonous rhyme can lull the listener to sleep, sporadic rhyme awakens.

Though it replicates the structure of trauma, sporadic rhyme certainly is not limited to poems whose subject matter is explicitly traumatic. The accident/surprise of every rhyme, which sporadic rhyme maximizes and which I have connected to the structure of trauma and the transgressive element of rhyme, powerfully underlines rhyme's force and can be experienced as humorous or witty, not just as something troubling or painful. The wit can be attributed to the surprising discovery of an odd fit between two words, to the structural surprise of sporadicity, to the repetition of the same sound, to the sonorous quality of rhyme itself.

But if there is a special grain of pleasure that comes out more emphatically in disruptive sporadic rhyme, in opposition to soothingly regular systematic rhyme, this may be best understood by introducing a complication to the concept of pleasure, which Lacan makes and which Roland Barthes, in *The Pleasure of the Text*, applies more specifically to literary texts. This is the distinction between pleasure (understood as enjoyment and connected to Freud's pleasure principle) and the infamous *jouissance* (translated by Barthes's translator as "bliss" and understood—sexual connotations resonating—as beyond the pleasure principle, as an acute excitation that enmeshes pleasure and pain). Though the attribution to a text of one or the other type of pleasure is contingent upon historically changing standards, and though Barthes himself insists more than once that the distinction is hardly absolute, he nonetheless characterizes "a text of pleasure" and "a text of bliss": "Text of pleasure: the text that contents, fills, grants euphoria; the text that comes from culture and does not break with it, is linked to a *comfortable* practice of reading. Text of bliss: the text that imposes a state of loss, the text that discomforts (perhaps to the point of a certain boredom), unsettles the reader's historical, cultural, psychological assumptions, the consistency of his tastes, values, memories, brings to a crisis his relation with language" (Barthes, *Pleasure* 14).

Evidently, the text of bliss is defined in contradistinction to anything euphoric or euphonious. Beyond being generally discomforting or unsettling, the text of bliss is aligned by Barthes with some crisis on the level of language. Interestingly and perhaps not surprisingly, the text of pleasure is aligned not with language but with narrativity. Earlier, Barthes associates the pleasure in narrativity with the rhetorical trope of tmesis, with the reader's ability to cut through the narrative, with "the abrasions I impose upon the fine surface: I read on, I skip, I look up, I dip in again." But this, Barthes says, "has nothing to do with the deep laceration the text of bliss inflicts upon language itself" (11–12). The text of pleasure thus has to do with a fairly mild violent act the reader performs on the text, while the text of bliss has to do with a profound violence performed by the text on language itself. Once again bliss is associated with a crisis on the level of language.

To an extent, this distinction between language and narrativity, bliss and pleasure, mirrors the distinction between sporadic and systematic rhyme. Systematic rhyme can be aligned with the text of pleasure insofar as it offers the possibility of conventionalized and soothing regularity, comfortable and comforting, though confining. Sporadic rhyme represents a situation in which the harmony and pleasure in the chiming of the two words is thrown upon the reader out of the blue, a forceful encounter with randomness in language. Therefore, it is akin to the text of bliss inasmuch as sporadic rhyme entails a grain of pleasure, but one that is more disruptive than soothing, more surprising than expected, more disorganizing than organizing, more representing a loss of control over language than a control of it.

By definition, sporadic rhyme escapes conventionalization, and so while in systematic rhyme there is pleasure in *predictability,* in sporadic rhyme there is *jouissance* in *unpredictability.* And since sporadic rhyme is not just accidental/surprising but also, in fitting the two words together, signals something structured, ordered, harmonious in retrospect, this paradoxical duplicity can explain the witty effect that often is associated with rhyme. Taken together, rhyme offers rapture in rupture followed by a sense of order out of nowhere.

With this complex in mind, we can return to systematic rhyme, as in Marlowe's couplets, which can be understood retrospectively as the systematic repetition of sporadic rhyme, itself a form of repetition. Systematic rhyme entails a soothing effect that is a result of taming the shrew, schematizing the traumatic dynamic of sporadic rhyme in a rhyme scheme that is not just repetitious to a second degree (meta-repetition) but also contains a sense of plot, direction, teleology. Systematic rhyme thus comes to be seen as a result of a chronologically and logically late action upon sporadic rhyme, while sporadic rhyme, the fundamental form, may perhaps simply be called *rhyme*.

Conclusion

A Defense of Rhyme

As literature and its study continuously come under attack, attempts to offer justifications rise. But offering a defense of "poetry as poetry" is a tall order nowadays, given the suspicion that poetry as poetry harbors an abundance of dry and antiquated formalism. In fact, the very people who wish to defend literature sometimes find themselves, in doing so, attacking poetry. To take one, celebrated example, Martha Nussbaum comes close to ascribing "literary ethics" to the category of narrative, stressing prose fiction's engendering of compassion, empathy, or identification with literary characters, and sets this up against a kind of "extreme formalist" and "morally detached" view, which is associated with certain brands of poetry or poetry criticism, such as New Criticism, that is resistant to political agendas and detached from social dimensions (104–6).

To counter this privileging of prose fiction, I argue that one unique contribution of poetry is that it rewards close listening, which engenders its own brand of knowledge, empathy, and compassion. Unlike figurative uses of the notion of listening, in which an individual bemoans not being *heard,* a publisher seeks out emerging new *voices,* or a frustrated parent wants the child to finally *listen,* the concept of listening is best taken literally in poetry. The experience of engaging significantly with poetry often is an experience of hearing things that could easily go unheard.

If our senses and sensual responses are diminished, poetry rewards their reawakening, and no sense is more directly awakened by poetry than hearing. A good place to start this reawakening or relistening is rhyme, situated at the border between hearing and listening. It may be easier nowadays to hear the rhymes outside of what is traditionally perceived as poetry, in adjacent genres like rap, song lyrics, and nursery rhymes, and further out, in jingles and ads. But what of rhyme in poetry, even contemporary poetry? Henri Meschonnic writes, "Poetry is not poetry unless it invents or discovers new rhymes" (95). Throughout this study, I have asked what those new rhymes are and have found the answer under the umbrella term "sporadic rhyme" (along with the realization that these are not new in any strict historical sense).

It so happens that sporadic rhyme is in particular need of a sympa-thetic ear, because it is in particular danger of not being heard. John Creaser has recently introduced a subtle distinction between *manifest* rhyming, when readers' attention is directed to the rhyming and to spe-cific rhymes, and *latent* rhyming, when the "presence of rhyme colours all, yet individual rhymes do not seize the attention" (443). Like most commentators on rhyme, Creaser has in mind systematic rhyme (Alexan-der Pope's *Pastorals* are his prime example of latent rhyming). However, sporadic rhyme is curiously both the most manifest *and* the most latent. It is manifest because, not competing with a chain of other, similar rhymes, it enjoys a sonic advantage. But it is latent because, situated outside of a supporting framework of expectation or convention, it runs the risk of being literally unheard, ignored. And when it is unheard, our appreciation of the work it does in the poem is obviously jeopardized.

What exactly is put in jeopardy by ignoring rhyme? Throughout this book, we have seen how rhyme performs work that is essential to the poem at hand, to the poet's work, to poetry's work. But this is nowhere more crucial than in the engagement with temporality that rhyme man-ifests. Attention to the temporality of the reading process has shown the underacknowledged phenomenological fact that rhyme evokes a backwards movement; a reader encounters a word that performs on that reader a reaching back to an earlier word. From the reader's vantage point, rhyme exhibits a reversal of linear time and causality, in that what comes later changes the status of what came before. This dynamic and the confusedness of past, present, and future in the temporality of rhyme brings to mind Eliot's articulation of temporality as the folding together, or mixing, of times, in the famous opening of *Four Quartets*: "Time present and time past / Are both perhaps present in time future, / And time future contained in time past" (*Collected Poems* 175).

It also resonates with Augustine's wariness of a clear division among past, present, and future. For Augustine, neither past nor future times exist; the past is no longer and the future is not yet. Instead of past, present, and future, then, he suggests it is more proper to speak of "the present of things past, the present of things present, and the present of things future" (11.26, 293). Though Augustine also complicates the presence of the present in a Derridean (or Zenonian paradoxical) way,[1] this privileging of the present perspective with regards to the past and the future is very much in keeping with a reader response account of the reading process, which we have seen with Meir Sternberg and Wolfgang Iser. What rhyme brings to bear is both the way the present torques the past and the way we are pulled to, or anchored in, that past.

Something of rhyme's temporal dynamic is captured in Henri Meschonnic's enigmatic discussion of rhyme as "cheating": "Rhyme cheats the way destiny would cheat if it played cards. Because it would know ahead of time. Rhyme knows ahead of time. It is this relation in the words that knows of them and before them not what you want them to say but what they say about you. What they show about you" (96). Like destiny, rhyme knows "ahead of time," because whether words rhyme is a linguistic given in which readers find themselves implicated. But once it is encountered, rhyme has the eerie quality of being seen not just as if it were always there but also as if it *had* to be there. *Yes*, we may think, *of course these words rhyme.* This is a retrospective construction, an afterthought, rigidity in reverse. The fact that rhyme is a harmonious repetition of sound, structured sonic markedness rather than random noise, turns it from a mere accident to an instance of what we may term, paradoxically, "retrospective inevitability."

As we have seen, psychoanalytic accounts of temporality underscore the significance of the temporal play that rhyme imposes. With the con-

cept of Nachträglichkeit, psychoanalytic theory, focused on the unconscious, problematizes the unidirectionality of past to present as well as
the distinction between past and present. If rhyme is a particularly bare
material realization of this problematizing, one dimension of its appeal is
revealed: each rhyme becomes an encounter with the temporal logic that
operates in the unconscious; each rhyme operates the subject according
to the logic of the unconscious.

The isomorphism with Sigmund Freud's understanding of trauma,
and the distinction between rhyme and other modes of retrospectivity,
such as narrative, helps us to think of rhyme as a kind of textual trauma.
Thinking in the Freudian terms of trauma brings to the fore aspects of
rhyme that pertain to it being a split event, an accident, a transgression,
and a form that resists integration or synthesis. The set of antithetical
pairings, namely rhyme's disorganizing and organizing potential, its enigmatic evocation of sense and nonsense, and its brand of pleasure and rigidity, now can be thought of as iterations of rhyme's traumatic structure.
Whether it is experienced subjectively by an empirical reader as shocking
and disturbing or simply as witty and amusing, whether it appears in a
text whose subject matter is explicitly traumatic or not at all (though what
text is not at all about trauma?), something of the structure of trauma is
preserved in rhyme. Sporadic rhyme, which has been the focus of most of
the examples analyzed here, maximizes rhyme's markedness and therefore
lays bare its links with both Nachträglichkeit and trauma.

RHYME FUNCTIONS
John Hollander lists the four functions that traditionally are ascribed to
rhyme: the mnemonic, the schematic, the euphonious, and the semantic
(*Vision and Resonance* 121). These functions are primarily derived from
the world of systematic rhyme. Excepting the mnemonic, the present
investigation into sporadic rhyme has included, and mostly complicated,
these functions. And, in chapter 5, sporadic rhyme helped to bring into
relief another function, a psychic one, having to do with the way that
rhyme "tickles" the unconscious by actualizing the reverse temporality
of trauma. Here are some of the functions we have seen rhyme perform,
divided by chapters:

Chapter 2: Rigid/Pleasurable
- Hijack the reader's expectations for a specific rhyming word
- Signal a surrendering of control to language
- Exhibit linguistic dexterity and creativity by signaling control over language
- Evoke pleasure that results from sonic harmony, humor, and meeting or subverting expectations

Chapter 3: Organizing/Disrupting
- Organize the poetic material, as in grouping lines into stanzas
- Undercut other organizational means such as lineation and phrasing
- Facilitate a temporal dynamic of tension/resolution
- Create a sonic bridge between sections or semantic domains in the poem
- Signal various degrees of closure, including relatively open closure

Chapter 4: Accidental/Motivated
- Confer semantic excess on words, perplexing the reader with regards to their semantic relationship
- Allude to conspicuously rhymed poetry or its metonyms without emulating it
- Signal language that is other to prose, fully motivated or else completely arbitrary
- Invite interpretations that resist the surface level of proposition and reflect on the nature of rhyme itself

Chapter 5: Regressive/Progressive
- Lock the reader into a temporal game of forth and back
- Create a concrete manifestation of Nachträglichkeit and of the constant fluidity of the past
- Perform trauma on a textual level
- Offer an arena to explore the pleasures and risks that result from (linguistic) accidents, surprises, and transgressions

In spite of, or owing to, its material smallness, rhyme is able to perform a great deal. That smallness also stands opposed to the central place it has held in discussions of English poetry, as rhyme has been the topic of controversy for hundreds of years. Debates on rhyme have been some of the liveliest in the history of discussion on verbal art. These include Samuel Daniel's and Thomas Campion's treatises for and against rhyme at the beginning of the seventeenth century, John Milton's attack on rhyme as explanation for not rhyming *Paradise Lost* in 1674, Samuel Johnson's attack on Milton's attack in his *Lives of the English Poets* a century after Milton, John Dryden and Robert Howard's exchanges about the suitability of rhyme for the stage, critiques of Elizabeth Barrett Browning and Emily Dickinson centering on the legitimacy of their kinds of rhyming in the middle of the nineteenth century, all the way to a kind of love/ hate relationship with rhyme by modernist poets and the accusations of using rhyme as echoing an un-American attitude.[2] Though focused on rhyme, these heated debates are almost always extended to larger issues: the nature of the English language, what is fit for stage and life, pleasure in language, authorial control, freedom, and the politics of form.

Discussing rhyme is never just discussing rhyme, and rhyme often becomes a palpable echo of these larger concerns. Likewise, hearing rhyme is never merely hearing rhyme. And a focus on sporadic rhyme has the advantage of exposing some of the issues that systematic rhyme occludes, in particular the disruptive underpinning of the organizational function of rhyme (chapter 3), randomness and the contingencies of language (chapter 4), and the backwards effect and special brand of surprise in rhyme (chapter 5).

The attention to rhyme within a given poem is rewarding, but its significance, as I have been suggesting, reaches beyond a heuristic or hermeneutic tool for the analysis of individual poems; it is a window into the enduring capacity of a poetic device, or a test case for the relationship between reader and language that poetry materializes. If the materiality of language, which is prized in poetry, translates to a more palpable and dense manifestation of sound, a return to an interest in sound is the sine qua non of a return to poetry. It is, in fact, a return to poetry-as-poetry.

When Henri Meschonnic writes that "poetry is not poetry unless it invents or discovers new rhymes," he is recognizing an essential link between poetry and rhyme. The nature of this essential link has been my topic.

notes

1. What constitutes rhyme is subject to pragmatic and historical considerations as much as to linguistic ones, and different critics exercise varying degrees of border control in admitting or rejecting a pair of words into the category. Under the title of "rhyme," Donald Wesling pragmatically admits "alliteration and assonance, repeated 'figures of sound' . . . repeated words and phrases, and *homoeoteleuton*" (*Chances* 5). In its "rhyme" entry, the *Princeton Encyclopedia of Poetry and Poetics* describes the "paradigmatic case for English" as "the linkage in poetry of two syllables at line end . . . that have identical stressed vowels and subsequent phonemes but differ in initial consonant(s) if any are present." The writers proceed to make the crucial point that "the definition of what counts as rhyme is conventional and cultural: it expands and contracts from one national poetry, age, verse tradition, and genre to another" (Brogan and Cushman 1184–85). The definition also changes according to the function one prescribes to rhyme. In the case of this book, I am dealing more with the position of the rhyme within the poem than with the degree of the sound match, and more with rhyme in twentieth-century English-language poetry than any other age or verse tradition.

2. Alliteration is certainly prevalent in cultural sites outside of poetry. In the English context, see, for example, research on the use of alliteration in English place names (Jeremy Harte) and in presidential inaugural addresses (Helena Halmari). On alliteration's possible "lowish" status, see Roper (especially 12–15).

3. For a poetic form that began in the fourteenth century and uses alliteration in rhymed stanzas (such as the romance *Awntyrs off Arthure*), see Weiskott (103–6), who explains why these poems should not be grouped with (nonrhyming) alliterative poems.

Weiskott, whose recent study seeks to establish a claim for the continuity of the allit-erative tradition from Old English to Middle English, generally excludes end-rhyming poems from that tradition, arguing for a "perceptible metrical distinction" based on the way end rhyme "invites a deductive scansion because it performs a phonological identity at perceptually regular intervals," unlike (inductive) alliterative meter, which juxtaposes perceptually dissimilar metrical units, like the half line (105, 5).

4. "The vast majority of the world's literary cultures do not use and have never used structural rhyme at all" (Whitehall 23).

5. As Harold Whitehall explains, the breakdown of Old English inflections, together with the borrowing of French words with stress on the final or penultimate syllable, facil-itated end rhyme (25). The gradual change included a time of overlap, which Wesling calls "a moment of paradigm crisis and uncertainty": "A poetic device fostered by the church in its hymns, and brought from France, is gaining influence over a strictly indigenous related device. For a time the two overlap, until the insurgent device takes over" (*Chances* 45). The indigenous device is Anglo-Saxon alliteration, and the insurgent is of course rhyme. Again, we have in these descriptions a situation of rhyme existing sporadically, a device outside, or on the threshold, of the prosodic system. Weiskott also notes the appearance of internal rhyme in alliterative verse around 1100 (13).

6. In a more recent example, Andrew Osborn has written about Paul Muldoon's "fuzzy rhyme," or rhymes that rely on consonant sequences with certain variation and not at all on similarity of vowel sounds (335-40). This kind of rhyming "affords Muldoon much associative freedom" compared to the more rigid perfect rhyme (348).

7. For a detailed account of this entire cycle of influence, including Whitman's ambiva-lent attitude toward French and Eliot's ambivalent attitude toward Whitman, see Ferreira.

8. Pound, too, around the same time, shows a similar potential tolerance for a different kind of rhyme: "A rhyme must have in it some slight element of surprise if it is to give pleasure; it need not be bizarre or curious, but it must be well used if used at all" (*Literary Essays* 7). I discuss the issue of surprise in chapter 5.

9. The anthologies were Allen's *The New American Poetry: 1945-1960* (1960), Brinnin and Read's *The Modern Poets* (1963), and Halpern's *The American Poetry Anthology* (1975).

10. Stephanie Burt's division of rhymes into *foreground* rhyme and *background* rhyme is thus close to my designation of sporadic and systematic rhyme, respectively, except that the term *sporadic* underlines the dissemination of the rhyme within the text of the poem and does not require that the rhyme stand out in perception. Foreground rhyme, Burt explains, is rhyme that "pops out," rhyme that is no longer part of the "metrical contract" between poem and reader (61).

11. Sporadic rhyme thus subsumes the categories of sectional rhyme, interlaced rhyme, and cross rhyme (see Turco 50-51), if and when they do *not* occur systematically through-out the poem, and includes many other unnamed permutations.

12. Things get even trickier when these same two words are then used as the end rhymes in the third quatrain.

13. On this issue I am indebted to Tsur (*What Makes Sound Patterns Expressive?* 1–35). Tsur discusses speech sounds in terms of their "different expressive potentialities," so that the same sound can express, in different poetic contexts, vastly different qualities (for instance, /s/ can be either hushing or noisy). But, crucially, this is not to say that any sound can express any emotional quality, and Tsur goes on to show how the anatomy of the sound or its articulation constrains its expressive potential.

14. Jahan Ramazani discusses the subordinate place of poetry within postcolonial criticism in an essay that—by paying close attention to the poetry of Derek Walcott's *Omeros*, and in particular to its sound—proves precisely the utility of poetry to postcolonial literary studies. "Poetry," Ramazani writes, "at least in Walcott's hands, is less respectful than prose fiction of racial, regional, national, and gender loyalties" (414). This is, Ramazani argues, both the reason for poetry's marginalization and its promise.

15. On "visualism" (the preference for vision over sound) and the equating of sight with knowledge from Greek philosophy onward, see Ihde, especially 6–13. On the problem of trying to offer transhistorical accounts of the nature of sound, which, as he shows for Ong, "tend to carry with them the unacknowledged weight of a two-thousand-year-old Christian theology of listening," see Sterne, *Audible Past*, especially 13–18.

16. By *rhyme*, I do not mean only or necessarily the acoustic sound that would result from sounding out the text but also sound as subvocalized. So one does not need to insist on the primacy of language as sonic/spoken over language as graphic/written in order to be able to point to certain sonic features. See also Garrett Stewart, who speaks of the "'phonophobia' generated in the wake of the Derridean attack on the Logos," and insists that "deconstruction and poststructuralist stylistics are inherently compatible," since the former, "in retrieving literary language from phenomenology, gives it over entirely to the regimen of a textual analysis" (3, 103).

17. On American Sign Language poetry and the ways it can challenge the "ocularcentric" tendency of modern poetics (e.g., Imagism) as well as poetry's appeal to voice or the spoken, see Davidson (especially 104–11). In his close analysis of an American Sign Language poem by Clayton Valli, Davidson identifies something akin to rhyme: "The use of repeated handshapes in various positions assists in creating rhythm, much as rhyme or alliteration links elements in traditional English verse" (111).

18. See Sterne, *Sound Studies Reader* for a thorough sampling of work in the field. Editor Jonathan Sterne suggests expanding Eliot's notion of "auditory imagination" from the realm of poetry, syllables, and rhythms to "all manners of sounding things" (5), and one essay, by Douglas Kahn, discusses sound poetry, though the overwhelming majority of essays are silent on poetry. In John Mowitt's *Sounds: The Ambient Humanities,* at once a contribution to sound studies and a reflection on it, literature looms large, though less in the form of poetry. See, in particular, chapter 1, devoted to the concept of echoing and Michael Ondaatje's *Coming through Slaughter,* the syntax of which is said to be "structured like an echo" (26).

19. *Def Poetry Jam* was preceded, in the 1990s, by MTV's "Spoken Word" episodes of the *Unplugged* series and PBS's series *The United States of Poetry.*

20. I refer in particular to the free and ever-growing archive of *PennSound,* directed by Charles Bernstein and Al Filreis. See also the Library of Congress's *Archive of Recorded Poetry and Literature,* which is constantly digitizing and making available online its recorded readings and interviews, and UbuWeb's Sound wing, edited by Kenneth Goldsmith.

21. The tremendously valuable podcast *PoemTalk* (http://jacket2.org/content/poem -talk), with nearly 150 episodes as of this writing, is a collaboration among the Kelly Writers House, *PennSound* (from Penn's Center for Programs in Contemporary Writing), and the Poetry Foundation, and is produced and hosted by Al Filreis. The Poetry Foundation also produces *Poem of the Day* and *Poetry Now,* a weekly podcast featuring poets reading their own work.

22. Northrop Frye famously identifies *babble* as the basis of *melos* and *doodle* as the basis of *opsis,* both looming large in his account of lyrical poetry (*Anatomy of Criticism* 275). In a later essay, Frye foregrounds the element of the magical spell, high in sound-rich devices like refrain, rhyme, alliteration, and assonance, as the manifestation of *melos* (*Spiritus Mundi* 126). Andrew Welsh finds a wide range of poetries from different cultures that evidence the ways "poetry will often retain that archaic sense of casting a spell, of magical compulsion, that comes to it from charm" (148). Jonathan Culler's recent theorization and defense of the lyric devotes an entire chapter to rhythm and sound. After surveying nine canonical poems by writers ranging from Sappho to John Ashbery, Culler articulates four parameters of the tradition of the Western lyric, the third of which pertains to the "ritualistic dimension," and it is here that sound, together with rhythm, repetition, and stanzaic forms, comes in. Of course, linguistic patterning, like rhyme and meter, is found in other kinds of poetry, not just lyrical, as Culler himself is quick to point out, but in the lyric the effects born out of it seem to control more of our attention; they are "experienced as particularly central" (*Theory of the Lyric* 137). On the poetic mode of speech perception, see Tsur, *What Makes Sound Patterns* (5–18).

CHAPTER TWO

1. John Dryden, in "To the Memory of Mr. Oldham," writes, "maturing time / But mellows what we write to the dull sweets of rhyme" (*Poetical Works* 175), and in the "Essay of Dramatic Poesy" he has Neander compare the viewer's forgetting the "care and labour" that went into producing the rhyme because of its sweetness to the way "bees are sometimes buried in their honey" (75).

2. Within this orientation, other critics, such as William Harmon, have devoted much energy to elaborating a nomenclature and a taxonomy of the various kinds and subkinds of rhyme, from redundant heteromerous rhyme (such as *minute : my newt*) to deficient augmented rhyme (such as *signing : raining*).

3. Different versions exist. I take this from Links 2 Love, http://www.links2love.com /lyrics_sweet_violets.htm. Dinah Shore recorded the song in the early 1950s.

4. Using implied rhyme in more nuanced ways is certainly an option open to poets. For example, Geoffrey Hartman hears the subvocal word *tears* in Wordsworth's "A Slumber

Did My Spirit Seal" and explains that *tears* rhymes with *fears* and *years* to echo the poet's lament (149–50). Wordsworth does not fall into the trap Pope warns against because his rhyme is implied rather than supplied, and because it is a less obvious one.

5. The irony created by the fact that this declaration about abandoning rhyme is written in perfect rhyming couplets, whereas the declarations favoring rhyme are rendered in prose, hardly needs mentioning. Ben Jonson's poem quoted here employs the same irony. I read both as testimony to rhyme's power over the poet, the discrepancy between content and form informing the premise that rhyme is powerful, a premise shared by all of the poets discussed.

6. For a nuanced reading of Milton's "Note" vis-à-vis Dryden, and for a thorough review of eighteenth-century prosodic discussions, see Richard Bradford, who makes the point that Milton's resistance is not simply to rhyme but to closed heroic couplets (19). My foregrounding of the rhyme-as-tyrant metaphor is not meant to disregard other important elements in the rejection of rhyme. For example, Raymond Mackenzie has read Milton's rejection of rhyme as stemming not only from political and aesthetic reasons but also from his shifting views on the idea of sameness and difference, self and other. Gerard Cohen-Vrignaud highlights the political and religious overtones, reading Milton's attack as aimed at "the high-church sanctification of royalty" (990–91). Resistance to rhyme can also be expressed on the grounds of it being too "artificial" or too ornamental, a claim made later by some modernists. I will return to some of these arguments in subsequent chapters.

7. For the accusation and the explanation for it, see Doerr. While Whitman's advocacy of freedom and democracy could be linked to the relative dearth of traditional rhyming in his poetry, he presents a complex view on rhyme in the Preface to *Leaves of Grass* (1855). On the one hand, the "poetic quality," Whitman writes, "is not marshalled in rhyme or uniformity," but a few lines down he opens the door to rhyme when he says that "the rhyme and uniformity of perfect poems show the free growth of metrical laws and bud from them as unerringly and loosely as lilacs and roses on a bush" (v). Whitman seems to envision a place for rhyme that would, in the spirit of Coleridge's "organic form," emerge from the material itself. The category of sporadic rhyme may very well be an example of this kind of organic rhyme.

8. This is not the case for all verse forms. For example, there are forms that rely on repetition of words (sestina) or lines (villanelle), rather than on rhyming sounds. They have the element of rigidity and expectation, but those are not fulfilled via rhyme. The fact that most poetic forms in English do rely on rhyme attests to its extraordinary capacity to realize rigidity.

9. The rhyme scheme for the entire poem is reminiscent of the ottava rima (*abababcc*) in its introduction of a couplet at the end, but it differs from ottava rima significantly in what precedes that couplet. Wordsworth's rhyme scheme in "The Solitary Reaper" (*ababccdd*) is close but not identical.

10. Thomas Campion's contemporary Samuel Daniel answers this claim directly, saying that the prosodic system advocated by Campion is no less restrictive. If we were to accept

Campion's proposition, Daniel writes, "we shall but as it were change prison, and put off these fetters to receiue others" (12). He thus seems to accept the premise of a prosodic system, rhyme within it, as enslaving.

11. Rachel Mayer Brownstein's remark that, in *Don Juan*, "the reader is set to wondering whether the poet is forcing his stanza or the stanza its poet" (Brownstein 180) is spot on.

12. In spite of Lawrence McCauley's brilliant demonstration of how "in a variety of ways—most subtle, some less so—*Paradise Lost* does indeed rhyme" (242), the work still remains an emblem of resisting rhyme, certainly systematic rhyme.

13. Limericks too often employ outrageous rhyming on names of people and places. G. Legman, in a thorough introduction to his anthology of limericks, claims that this "obviously satiric use of proper names" entered the early limericks during the seventeenth century, though he makes the additional cautionary point that not every rhyme on a name at the time was intended to be burlesque, as it would seem today. An example is Herrick's rhyme *John : Revelation* in "To God," which Legman dubs "very serious" (xxix-xxx). Peter Dale echoes the difficulty of rhyming on proper names when he asks, "May one ever rhyme on these without leaving the suspicion of monikers chosen for the rhymer's convenience?" (82).

14. Nigel Fabb quotes another experiment that shows that unexpected fluency is more likely to produce these effects than expected fluency, and then applies this insight to rhyme: "This should mean that an unexpected rhyme should produce a greater effect than an expected one" (190). This point is very promising for an investigation of sporadic (unexpected) rhyme, and throughout many of the chapters of this book I am essentially claiming that sporadic rhyme indeed has greater effects. On the issue of the pleasure of sporadic rhyme, see also chapter 5.

15. Brennan O'Donnell finds in Wordsworth "ambivalence about the power of meter" (41). Arguing against a "simple dichotomy between organic and mechanic," O'Donnell writes that Wordsworth "places maximum emphasis on the importance of *both* artful arrangement and spontaneous expression" (42, emphasis mine). This caveat is important to keep in mind, since Wordsworth's notion of "language really used by men" should not be understood as ever having intended to be detached from more conventional habits of artistic production.

16. D. W. Winnicott brings up the classic "Rock-a-bye Baby" lullaby as an example of how the mother expresses some of the resentment, anger, and hate she feels towards the newborn baby, who "enjoys but fortunately does not understand" what she is singing (202). For more on a psychoanalytic understanding of nursery rhymes as outlets for various kinds of aggression, see Lucy Rollin, *Cradle and All,* especially chapter 4.

17. For another defense of rhyme on the basis of its relation to music and delight, see Sir Philip Sidney, "Defence of Poesy," especially 73.

18. Judy Jo Small, in a book dedicated to Dickinson's rhymes, claims that "readers of her poetry have found it difficult to come to terms with her rhymes" and provides Higginson's correcting of her rhymes as proof (Small 5–6). Partial rhyme is, of course, not simply a bad version of perfect rhyme; it has its own kind of aesthetic, which poets have been at pains

to establish. Small asserts that "the affective power of partial rhyme . . . is attributable to the fact that, as a deviation from normative full rhyme, it obscures the reader's 'feeling of tonal center' [a term Small borrows from Leonard Meyer's discussion of minor mode in music], creates ambiguity of expectation, disrupts a secure sense of acoustic progression, and thus arouses suspense and tension" (73–74).

19. In China, rhyme dictionaries or "rhyme tables" (such as *Qieyun,* the oldest remaining rhyme dictionary, from the year 601) were devised precisely as aids to correct and standardize pronunciation, and have also been instrumental in later efforts by linguists to construct the pronunciation of the medieval Chinese period (Ramsey 116–34).

20. For more on the connection between rap music and larger political issues (such as the support given by rappers to the Million Man March), see Kitwana 206–10. For an excellent treatment of the very category of the "political" vis-à-vis hip-hop culture, see Deis.

21. Cheryl Keyes traces the roots of rap music from the African bardic tradition to the rural South and urban North, and mentions some of the antecedents to the use of rhyme, such as the storytelling tradition of the toast (narrative poem in rhymed couplets) and the dozens (a verbal duel in rhyme) (23–24). To this, Keyes adds the use of rhyme in other African American expressive contexts, including the blues, the black traditional church, and the dance-song called the hambone (25–26). The purpose of my comments is to position this historical use of rhyme within rhyme's structural potentialities.

22. That nonstandard language usage involves questions of power relations and dominance reaches a clear articulation in the 1996 case of the Oakland School Board decision to make Ebonics (or African American Vernacular English) a language of instruction for African American students. Robin Lakoff shows how the tremendous amount of attention, and resistance, to that decision evinces the majority community's anxiety around its ability to "maintain its right to control language," determining "what form of language is 'good' English" (249).

23. This is not true only in rap. Christopher Ricks shows how Bob Dylan's singing can make rhyme something that "on the page" is not strictly a rhyme according to most standard pronunciations, as in *hers* and *yours* (*Dylan's Visions* 36). For Hip Hop Nation members' emphasis on "stretching the limits of language," see Alim, "Bring It to the Cypher."

24. Adam Bradley calls this "transformative rhyme" and gives the example of Tupac making *fire* rhyme with *denial* by pronouncing it like *file,* in "My life is in denial, and when I die / Baptized in eternal fire" (71).

25. The privileging of the oral over the orthographic in hip-hop makes finding an authoritative and agreed-upon written version of lyrics difficult and even beside the point. Both lineation and spelling are to a certain extent arbitrary; the indispensable component of DJing marks time and rhythm in the performance more than lineation can represent, and the shifts in pronunciation in the service of rhyme render any stable spelling obsolete. The lineation here represents some rhythmic regularity manifested in the beats and aided by the rhyming, and the division into stanzas or sections, which I term "rhyme stretches," is based on the rhyme sounds, as I will explain.

26. Thomas Eekman lists five factors that affect rhyming difficulty across languages, concluding that English is more constraining for poets than are Russian, Polish, or French (47, 61–64).

27. Surely there are many exceptions, where poets use more rhyming than usual. For example, Dante Rossetti's "The Woodspurge" is made up of four quatrains, each rhyming with a single rhyming sound (aaaa), and Robert Frost's "The Lost Follower" includes nine such monorhyming quatrains. Peter McDonald mentions Edward Thomas's densely rhymed late poetry (like the /aaaaa/-rhymed "Out in the Dark") and connects the rhyming there with the theme of submission to the will (McDonald, "Rhyme and Determination" 241). John Skelton is an early master of using a single rhyming sound for a large and unexpected number of times, as I will show. Of the more systematic forms, the "Burns stanza" (also used before Robert Burns) requires four A-rhymes, the rhyme scheme Chaucer used for "The Monk's Tale" needs four B-rhymes, and to write a Spenserian stanza, one likewise needs four B-rhymes. More than four is much rarer, but it exists. Swinburne's Roundels require five A-rhymes and five Bs, and anyone using the French rondeau in English will need eight(!) words for the A-rhyme across the form's three stanzas.

28. In the preface to *Lyrical Ballads*, Wordsworth connects "the pleasure which the mind derives from the perception of similitude in dissimilitude"—a principal he recognizes as "the great spring of the activity of our minds"—to the pleasure that meter affords (460).

29. Emily Dickinson ends "Forget! The lady with the Amulet" with five monorhyming lines comprising *rill : hill : fill : mill : will*. For a discussion, see Small (127). Sylvia Plath's famous poem "Daddy," in which "the compulsion to rhyme becomes obsession" (Nims 144), would be another interesting variation of sporadic monorhyming. Fifteen of the poem's sixteen five-line stanzas contain at least one line rhyming in the basic A-rhyme that runs throughout the entire poem, to include words like *do : you : shoe : achoo : blue : Jew : through*. At times, the end rhyme is accompanied by sporadic internal rhyme, which adds even more emphasis to the recurring rhyming sound, an ever growing cluster of words focused semantically around the *you* who is the speaker's addressee, and the *do* of the marital speech act she is evoking, reversing, and negating in the poem's rhyming first line: "You do not do, you do not do" (Plath 73).

CHAPTER THREE

1. For a brief discussion of the differences between the two figures and their application to English, see Richard Lanham's entry for *homoeoteleuton* in his *Handlist of Rhetorical Terms* (83–85). For a classic study of ancient rhetorical prose, including the issue of rhyme and other like endings, see Norden.

2. In Julia Kristeva's terms, "In 'artistic' practices the semiotic—the precondition of the symbolic—is revealed as that which also destroys the symbolic" (50).

3. Combining both experiments in line length and rhyme schemes, George Herbert is said by Albert McHarg Hayes, in a fascinating study of the interdependence between Herbert's rhyme schemes and line lengths, to have used 111 different stanza patterns in the 127 stanzaic

poems of *The Temple* (283). Alicia Ostriker contextualizes Herbert's experimentation and notes particularly the influence of Elizabethan song on his work. John Donne is infamous for the trouble he has caused prosodists, a fact echoed in the opening sentence of a 1950 article by Michael Moloney: "Of commentaries upon Donne's prosody there would seem to be no end and of final agreement upon the details of his metrics there would seem to be no hope" (171).

4. There are other possibilities that stand between sporadic and systematic. For one of them, see Lazar Fleishman's account of Lev Gomolitsky's acromonogram, or diagonal rhymes, in which the end of a line rhymes with either the first or second foot of the next line. In those instances, we can count on the occurrence of rhyme (systematic), though we don't know exactly where in the beginning of the line it will come (sporadic).

5. See Frank M. Chambers, who estimates that "of the over 2,500 troubadour lyrics now extant, at least some 1,500 are unique in their precise combinations of meters and rhyme-schemes" (106). For rhyme schemes and verse forms as partial defense against performers' shifting of the sequence of stanzas of the "original" version, and a discussion of the notion of a fixed or closed text in the context of the troubadours, see Van Vleck, particularly chapter 5.

6. John Heath-Stubbs writes that "the Italian canzone, with its complex stanza shape and its alternation of long and short rhyming lines, forms the actual source of much English composition in the ode form—far more in fact than the practice of Pindar or of Horace" (13). Ants Oras makes the point that Milton's careful employment of irregular rhyme in "Lycidas" derives from his studies of Italian versecraft in the Renaissance (13–15). Mary Ellen Rickey attributes much of Crashaw's rhymecraft to Italian poetry, especially Giambattista Marino, whom he also translated. Edmund Spenser's "Epithalamion," notwithstanding debates about its structure, is considered an adaptation of the canzone (Greene 162–63).

7. Abraham Cowley mistakenly took Pindar's odes to be completely irregular, and his *Pindarick Odes* became a source of controversy around the legitimacy of its irregularity and his own understanding of Pindar. In *Discourse on the Pindaric Ode*, William Congreve tries to set the record straight and argue that, contrary to the belief and habit of the time, "there is nothing more regular than the Odes of Pindar" (quoted in Heath-Stubbs 49). Though more sympathetic to Cowley's irregularity than to others' ("The Beauty of his Verses, are an Atonement for the Irregularity of his Stanzas"), Congreve explains that according to true Pindaric habit, one should choose the form of the strophe, repeat it in the antistrophe, choose another for the epode, then repeat the same throughout the same ode, so that "every Epode in the same Ode is eternally the same in Measure and Quantity, in respect to itself; as is also every Strophé and Antistrophé, in respect to each other" (Heath-Stubbs 50). Some famous Pindaric Odes, like Thomas Gray's "The Progress of Poesy," are written in this way, or close to it.

8. Because we are dealing with end rhyme that does not fully cohere into a rhyme scheme, a major dynamic at play is the approximation to a more recognizable rhyme scheme. When John Milton ends the irregularly rhyming "Lycidas" with an ottava rima, the poem signals a return to order. At the other extreme, T. S. Eliot ends the "Preludes" with a nonrhyming three-line coda, thus achieving a strong differentiation in sound and tone be-

tween it and previous lines. Ants Oras writes that "Lycidas" shows that Milton's "so-called irregularity is essentially calculated complexity" (21). William Keach writes that Percy Bysshe Shelley's "rhyme in 'Mont Blanc' is not . . . as 'wildly irregular' as it has been thought to be" (349). And Enid Welsford writes that "Spenser's free variant of the canzone stanza is exquisitely fitted to express that mingling of joy and solemnity, of personal feeling, social revelry, and stately ceremonial that is one of the great beauties of *Epithalamion*" (70). Eliot critics have also relished finding patterns. Frank Burch Brown, for example, has found "an elaborate (though covert) rhyme scheme" in the lyric that opens section 2 of "East Coker" in *Four Quartets* (421-22). John Bugge has found uncharacteristic but methodical rhyme scheme in the sestina-like portion of section 2 of "The Dry Salvages" and says that it is meant to "echo certain prominent sounds made at regular intervals by the surf breaking against the beach" (313-14). These instances of finding parallelism between content and form, or trying to find method in the madness, attest to the highly intriguing nature of this rhyming.

9. For additional comments on the rhyming in "The Love Song of J. Alfred Prufrock," see Ann Brady (13) and John Chalker (87). On the way the poem changes the conventions of the ode, and "enacts a crisis in rhyme" by rhyming a word with itself, see Chris Beyers, who also traces the "loose verse tradition" from Abraham Cowley in the seventeenth century all the way to this poem (61-99). For a reading of Lafogue's "Solo de lune," and in particular its rhyming free verse stanza, which is remarkably similar to Eliot's here, see Scott, chapter 6.

10. If not, rhyme will be only "for the eye" and may not be experienced sonically while the reader is reading. The number of lines the reader needs to endure before the arrival of the rhyme is stretched to extremes in some liminal cases. Eliot's "Gerontion" has nearly seventy lines between *gates* and *straits*. Robert Lowell's "Man and Wife" is a twenty-eight-line poem in which the very last word finds its rhyming partner at the very beginning of the poem. These cases are surely beyond the capacity of working memory, though they can be contemplated by an attentive reader or an overzealous critic. Nigel Fabb makes a valuable distinction between the location of the rhyme (typically at the end of the line) and the rhyme pattern. While the location is relative to a unit of the text that is small enough to fit into working memory, the pattern can far exceed working memory's limited capacity. He then suggests the possibility that the processing of patterns that do not fit into working memory "involves an interplay between working and long-term memory" (19).

11. For a remarkable reading of rhyme and repetition as emblematic of the concerns of "Ode," see McDonald, *Sound Intentions* 102-14.

12. A rhyme can also come even sooner, before the end of the next line, but that kind of rhyme falls outside the category of irregular end rhyming and will be explored separately.

13. B. J. Pendlebury gives Philip Larkin's celebrated "Church Going" as an example (80). But, in its seven nine-line stanzas, Larkin usually positions the thorn line in the same place, so it might be thought of as a "systematic thorn line" or systematic nonrhyming.

14. See also Christopher Ricks's comparison of Bob Dylan and Thomas Hardy both leaving the word *love* unrhymed, in Dylan's "Lay, Lady, Lay" and in Hardy's "Shut Out That Moon" (*Dylan's Visions of Sin* 160-63).

15. The other sound elements in the stanzas, like the /c/ consonance in the first half of the first stanza (*convict, clothes, course, doctor*), buttress, rather than diminish, the perception of the rhyme, which is always fuller and more harmonious than any of them. In the case of that stanza, the sporadic rhyme also has sonic distinction because its long vowel sound, which it shares with the systematic rhyming (*clothes, gloats, notes, pose, blows*), contrasts with the plosive /c/ sound in these very lines.

16. Since I understand the meter to be more accentual than accentual-syllabic, I have marked rhythmic beats with bold font on the syllable on which that beat is realized. For a systematic account of beats in English prosody, see Attridge, *Rhythms of English Poetry*.

17. I have underlined the rhyming, both sporadic and systematic. There is yet another rhyming sound in this stanza, consisting of the words *my* : *I* : *my* : *my* : *cry* : *I* : *I*, but it does not pertain to the internal rhyming I am concerned with here, namely one that interacts in some way with the rhyme scheme.

18. Another designation would be English dolnik. For a recent explanation of the form, including the distinction between its duple and triple varieties and a demonstration with another of William Blake's *Songs*, see Attridge, "Rhythms of the English Dolnik."

19. On the relation between systematic rhyme and meter, see Nikitina and Maslov, who find, at least in the Onegin stanza, that "stricter adherence to the metrical template . . . counterpoise[s] a looser rhyme, and vice versa" (453), which is to say that lines in which the requirements of rhyme are more rigid will tend to be looser in terms of their adherence to meter. The reason for this, as they explain, is that both rhyme and meter impose formal constraints and so there is a compensatory relation between them. No such reasoning applies to sporadic rhyme.

20. There is much to say about the connection between rhyme and Gerard Manley Hopkins's sprung rhythm. Helen Vendler (*Breaking of Style* 10-12) underscores sprung rhythm's twoness on various levels, including prosodic ("stressed march beats versus rapid, tripping, almost liquid footfalls") and formal (four lines of narrative followed by four lines of meditation in "The Wreck of the Deutschland"). Though Vendler does not discuss the rhyming in this context, it is easy to see why it would be a corollary for this realization of doubleness. Merriman draws an interesting connection between Hopkins's theological views and his understanding of rhyme. For example, she writes that, for Hopkins, the relationship between "the exigency of rhyme . . . and the poet's ability to use rhymes 'to the finest and most natural effect' . . . [is] a matter emblematic of religious doctrine on salvation and the relationship between human free will and divine power" (92). Though Merriman deals with end as well as internal rhyming, her understanding of Hopkins's use of rhyme does not distinguish between these two options. For the best treatment of rhyme in Hopkins's poetry, as "metaphor for, as well as manifestation of, its abiding problems and concerns," especially with regards to Hopkins's theology and poetics pertaining to chance and will, see McDonald's chapter devoted to Hopkins in *Sound Intentions* (268).

21. Each of these two stanzas has its own internal sporadic rhyming, which I have not underlined because my focus is on *tits* : *sits,* the interstanzaic rhyme.

22. For example, a poem in the Chinese *Book of Odes* (*Shi jing*) about dynastic continuity across generations appropriately uses rhymes across stanzas as an "auditory analogue" to the way "the past generations recede while leaving behind traces of their presence" (Saussy, "Repetition" 537).

23. Robert Browning's "My Last Duchess," where the rhyming of the couplets is drowned by the consistent enjambment, is a famous poetic example.

24. See, for instance, Charles Hartman's statement that "verse is language in lines" (11), in the context of an entire study that highlights how counterpointing the line and phrasing (that is, levels of enjambment) is at the heart of William Carlos Williams's free verse.

25. Lineation is notoriously tricky with Emily Dickinson, and confusion or disagreements often occur when the manuscript is put into print form (see Freeman, "Body in the Word"). For this stanza, I have verified that the printing represents her actual lineation, which is preserved in the manuscript that can be viewed in the Emily Dickinson Archive (https://www.edickinson.org).

26. Richard Cureton has been propounding a componential approach to rhythm that realizes the relative contribution of rhythmic phrasing, consisting of grouping and prolongation. The former, "our rhythmic response to points of structural culmination within delimited structural spans," is the rhythmic component that "'chunks' a rhythmic medium into parts" (136). Cureton writes that we "prefer a group that contains similar linguistic forms" and that at middle and low levels of the text's material, "poets often use continuities and discontinuities in syntactic and phonetic texture to reinforce or blur our impressions of textual divisioning" (258–59). I argue that the high markedness of sporadic internal rhyme can do more than reinforce textual divisioning; it becomes a strong divisioning agent in and of itself. Put differently, internal rhyme can compete with lineation for the determination of grouping.

27. Frederic Ness, in his investigation of Shakespeare's use of rhyming in his plays, finds many organizational functions, like using rhyme at the end of a blank verse speech to lend special emphasis, conclude the speech, or afford it "dramatic intensity," or using rhyme to mark a change in tone (28–44). Similarly, Ness finds rhyming couplets that come at the end of a scene or an act "to indicate the completion of the action," and extended uses of rhyming that "differentiate certain groups of characters" (such as the rhyming and nonrhyming characters or sections in *A Midsummer Night's Dream*) (70–83).

28. I am indebted to Jon Rosenblatt's reading of this poem and its ending, though he is silent on the issue of rhyming.

29. Another notable use of this rhyming pair at the end of a poem is Eliot's "Rhapsody on a Windy Night": "'Put your shoes at the door, sleep, prepare for *life*.' // The last twist of the *knife*." (*Collected Poems* 18). In all three of these cases, the acute semantic incongruity between the two words is striking.

30. Compare this to a technique that Thomas Shaw identifies in Alexander Pushkin's nonrhyming dramas (for instance, in scene 10 of *Boris Godunov*), where Pushkin will introduce rhyming lines just before a key moment and will then return to the nonrhyming

norm for that key moment (such as the revelation that a character is dead). Shaw describes, in effect, how sporadic rhyme serves, in his words, as a "preclimax," whereas the climax is nonrhyming (*Pushkin's Poetics* 227–28).

CHAPTER FOUR

1. The term *markedness* speaks to the asymmetricality of binaries, with the unmarked alternative being the default or usual case and the marked being the narrower or more special case. On the concept of markedness from its inception in the 1930s in the field of phonology, with the work of Nikolai Trubetzkoy and Roman Jakobson, see Linda Waugh, "Marked and Unmarked." Interestingly, though rhyme is the marked alternative, it is generally *not* considered hierarchically lower, unlike what often happens with binary oppositions (as when *man* is taken to be the unmarked "norm" and therefore the hierarchically higher alternative to the marked *woman*). Markedness relies on context. Within a prose context (which is itself the unmarked context) rhyme is the marked option because prose usually eschews rhyme. Within many poetic forms, systematic end rhyme is the *unmarked* option because these forms require end rhyming. But internal rhyme in those poems, as well as rhyme in free verse, is, once again, marked.

2. See Rugg for the initial research. For more recent studies, see Grossi et al. and Wagensveld et al., "Neural Correlates."

3. For a review of research across different languages that shows that "forms of nonarbitrariness are more widespread than previously assumed," see Dingemanse et al. (603). For Saussure in the *Course in General Linguistics,* "the bond between the sound and the idea is radically arbitrary," and the arbitrary nature of the sign is the first of its two "primordial characteristics" (113, 67). Saussure says that onomatopoeic formations "are of secondary importance" and questions their status as truly motivated (69–70).

4. "Poetic iconicity is the means whereby the poet manipulates the semiotic iconic features inherent in language to capture the essence of an experience," writes Margaret Freeman, and she notes the "exponential" increase in the very use of the terms *icon* and *iconic* in the second half of the twentieth century ("Aesthetics of Human Experience" 729). "It is striking," writes Linda Waugh, "that much of literary theory takes as its point of departure the principle of arbitrariness but studies texts that contain so much iconicity" ("Against Arbitrariness" 80). Iconicity operates in poetry on many levels beyond sound. Michael Golston, for example, identifies in postmodern American poetry an "allegorical impulse," which operates not on the level of theme or narrative but rather on the work's overall form or linguistic features (6). Allegory and iconicity are closely related, both manifestations of Jakobson's poetic principle. More broadly, Golston highlights a transition from form as arbitrary and conventional (symbolic, in Charles Sanders Peirce's terms) to more motivated (indexical and iconic) (18–27).

5. John Wilkins (1614–1672) sought to combat the arbitrary nature of language and suggested a universal language that would be simple, would cover in a systematic way all possible objects and ideas, and would show a direct link between the name and the nature

of the thing. See also the humorous account of Wilkins given by Jorge Luis Borges in "John Wilkins' Analytical Language." In that work, Borges shows that any attempt at a systematic and nonarbitrary classification will inevitably be arbitrary because "we do not know what the universe is" (231). For other criticisms of Wilkins, and for a discussion of the issue of his system's openness to new words, see Eco (*Search for the Perfect Language* 248–58).

6. There are other ways besides rhyme to mark a collection of words as particularly congruous, motivated, or even coming "from beyond the world." For example, alphabetical acrostics in the Hebrew Bible (most notably in *Psalms* and in the *Book of Lamentations*), where each verse starts with a subsequent letter of the Hebrew alphabet, have been sometimes said to exhibit particular wholeness (because all the Hebrew letters are represented), if not holiness (because the alphabet derives from God). See Melitz.

7. For example, Haun Saussy shows how subgenres in the Chinese *Book of Odes* are characterized by certain "typical rhymes" or "rhyme families," sets of rhyming words that are both sonically and thematically linked and that not only come to be expected in poems of their respective subgenres but also gain "independent power and meaning" and are used together, or evoke each other, even outside of verse ("Repetition" 538–42).

8. While not everyone has viewed rhyme this way, this view is salient not just historically but also structurally, which is to say that it results from rhyme's inherent characteristics. Others have likewise pointed to the otherworldly aspect of rhyme. From an object-relations psychoanalytic orientation, M. D. Faber has claimed that rhyme "gratifies us or reassures us at the deepest level of response—the unconscious level—by engaging our delight in separation at the same time that it engages our delight in oneness and union," a dynamic of separation/union of mother and child that is echoed in rhyme's dual attributes of unity (words sound alike) and difference (words mean different things, or have different consonants before the similar vowel) (377).

9. Petra Filkuková and Sven Hroar Klempe (2013) extended the results to advertising slogans and Norwegian and found the same effect.

10. See, for example, Frank Rich's piece titled "Will the Democrats Betray Us?," published days after the ad ran.

11. For an alternative to attempts to offer one essentialist definition of the literary, see Harshav, "Literariness Revisited."

12. In contrast to studies of English rhyme, scholarship on rhyme in Russian verse is much more interested in the segments to the left of the rhyme proper, how many such segments one finds, when such enrichment turned from embellishment to a norm, how it works to create subdivisions with a rhyming set, and how it informs the works of individual poets. For a sampling of work on enrichment in this tradition, see Worth's "On Eighteenth-Century Russian Rhyme," Shaw's "Horizontal Enrichment" and Lilly.

13. Helen Vendler does make this argument with regard to the shadow of the traditional alternate rhyming, which she uses to account for the three last rhymes in the poem. I have tried to motivate the rhymes in terms of their semantic functioning as well as their *not* being systematic.

14. Annie Finch has made a similar point with regard to meter, namely that a poet's use of meter in a rhythmically diverse poem "encodes" that poet's attitude toward the tradition of that meter, with all its literary and cultural associations. For example, Emily Dickinson's use of iambic pentameter is connected to her attitudes toward patriarchy (Finch 13–30). Any use of rhyme is also a nod to the tradition of using rhyme in English poetry.

15. Jacques Derrida brings up rhyme toward the end of the second part of "The Double Session" (277). See also Garrett Stewart's discussion of Derrida's remarks on rhyme (71–72).

16. That this elegy is a poem first and foremost, and should be read as such, is given partial reinforcement by Theodore Roethke's own short discussion of the piece, which focuses on nothing but its "technical effects" (*On the Poet and His Craft* 81–83).

17. I borrow the dye analogy and the term *ecological* from Neil Postman's discussion of the effect technological change has had on society and culture.

CHAPTER FIVE

1. Rhyme can be realized textually without being consciously realized by the listener/reader. Such is the case when the interval between the two rhyming partners is so wide that we do not consciously register them as rhyming, or when readers simply do not "hear" the rhyme, regardless of the distance between its members. Whether or not the effects that I am describing apply to these instances remains, for me, an open question.

2. Strictly speaking, there is also the rhyme *my* : *I*, which I do not address, and—as is almost always the case—an entire host of other sound relations among words in the poem.

3. Ronald Schleifer tells this story of early twentieth-century post-Enlightenment's understanding of temporality with particular clarity, with recourse to the fields of economics, science, philosophy, and literature. Walter Benjamin features prominently as a representative of post-Enlightenment modernism, which Schleifer understands as a "collision of two modes of conceptualizing and apprehending temporality" (109). He associates the newer of these modes with the wide-ranging concept of "abundance."

4. For a particularly helpful account of these issues in Hegel (and Jarvis), see Isobel Armstrong, who underscores Hegel's contrasting of classical meter and romantic rhyme.

5. Perry Meisel recognizes Henri Bergson's 1889 *Essai sur les données immédiates de la conscience* as a "deeply buried influence" on Sigmund Freud's 1895 *Project for a Scientific Psychology* (Meisel, *Literary Freud* 47–56). In Meisel's account, Freud adds neurology/physiology/science to Bergson's philosophical psychology and plays one influence (Bergson) against the other (science). For a positioning of Freud within the philosophical ideas flourishing in the 1890s, with particular attention to Bergson, William James, Friedrich Nietzsche, and then later Gestalt psychology and phenomenology, see Boothby (especially chapter 1).

6. On the way in which Franz Brentano's epistemology was instrumental for Freud's notion of temporality in the *Project* (though with no reference to *Nachträglichkeit*), see Pearl (77–103).

7. Freud never gave a systematic account of the term, which is mainly translated in the *Standard Edition* as "deferred action." Other suggested translations of the term have been

"afterwardsness," "retrospective attribution," and, in French, "après-coup" (see Faimberg 1). "Deferred action" is a problematic translation in that it implies a temporal movement from past to present, which, as I will show, covers only part of the meaning of the term as actually elaborated by Freud. For an overview of the term in Freud, as well as a rebuttal of the idea that Freud's discoveries subsequent to the Emma case invalidate his conclusions from it, see the entry "Deferred Action," by Laplanche and Pontalis, in *The Language of Psycho-Analysis* (111–14).

8. Elsewhere, Perry Meisel brings the logic of deferred action to bear on Bob Dylan's work, understanding "temporal movement or deferred action" as "Dylan's active principle both poetically and musically, the very nature of his labor" ("Dylan and the Critics" 116). Deferred action manifests the passage of time, Dylan's "central theme," and becomes apparent, Meisel writes, in the different performances of the same song throughout the years, and in the constant reinventions of the self with which Dylan is concerned.

9. Jean Laplanche finds that "Freud's concept of afterwardsness contains both great richness and a certain ambiguity, combining a retrogressive and a progressive direction," and insists that the use that actually reverses time, and goes in the opposite direction from Freud's determinism of past dictating the present, is "relatively rare" ("Notes on Afterwardsness" 265, 261). I argue that these instances, which are more common than is usually thought, represent the true significance of the concept.

10. In a longer text on the past, Søren Kierkegaard bemoans the "mental illusion" involved in the way people come to view the past, namely that they mistakenly see historical events as necessary after a long time has passed, "just as the person who at a distance sees something square as round" ("Is the Past" 79). Psychoanalysis, rather than treating our constructions of the past as illusory, takes them as literal truth. This is both its strength (theoretically, affectively) and weakness (scientifically, empirically).

11. More recently, the fact that one's construction of the past shifts in light of subsequent events has received new confirmation from neuroscience, bringing empirical validation to Freud's early beginnings in neurology. In an experiment on rats published in *Nature* in 2015, scientists were able to show that the neural circuits involved in the retrieval of a fear memory change over time (Do-Monte, Quiñones-Laracuente, and Quirk). The pathways for retrieving a fresh memory, they found, were different from those used after a few days had elapsed, and new parts of the brain are recruited for this retrieval. These shifts can help explain belated effects of fear.

12. For instance, in a dream, the very same branch may come to represent both sexual innocence and its opposite, as Freud shows in *The Interpretation of Dreams* (*Standard Edition* 4:318). For the linguistic corollary, Freud quotes German philologist Karl Abel, particularly Abel's work on ancient Egyptian. Emile Benveniste disputes the factual correctness of Abel's findings and his methodology, pointing out the errors in example after example that appear in Freud's essay (68–71). But Benveniste's criticism, while quite possibly scientifically sound, misses what, to my mind, is the main thrust of Freud's overall position, namely that—empirical findings notwithstanding—the unconscious structures language

and vice versa. The issue is later recuperated with Derrida's discussion of Plato's *pharmakon*, which is said to mean both "medicine/remedy" and "poison" ("Plato's Pharmacy").

13. For Jacques Lacan's use of the term(s) *language* (*langue, langage,* and *lalangue*), see Evans (99–101). Lacan's pairing of language and the unconscious is entirely tied to Ferdinand de Saussure and (as I show later) Roman Jakobson. Saussure's *langue* (in opposition to *parole*) is that which "exists in the form of a sum of impressions deposited in the brain of each member of a community, almost like a dictionary of which identical copies have been distributed to each individual" (19). Some of the ways in which Lacan characterizes the unconscious seem especially reminiscent of this description of *langue*, like the idea that the unconscious is not interior but exterior and trans-individual (Evans 220). Further confirmation for the *langue*/unconscious pairing is the issue of sensitivity to change. For Saussure, language is on the side of the immutable and conservative; it is a social institution used by everyone all the time, and so it is "least amenable to initiative" (74). In like manner, in Freud's thinking, the processes of the unconscious system "have no reference to time at all" ("Unconscious" 187). For an alternative view, see Lydia Liu, who argues that Lacan's notion of the unconscious (and of language) is based less on Saussure and French structural linguistics and more on Claude Elwood Shannon and American cybernetics and game theory.

14. For these in Freud, see "Unconscious" (186).

15. Lacan acknowledges Roman Jakobson twice in the notes to the essay "The Agency of the Letter." For a critique of Jakobson's use of the term *metaphor* and a consideration of Lacan's use following Jakobson, see Grigg (chapter 11, "Lacan and Jakobson").

16. On the current and historical expansiveness of *rhythm*, a term both intermedial and cross-disciplinary, corporeal and metaphysical, see Nowell Smith ("What Is Called Rhythm").

17. The narrative universal that Meir Sternberg dubs *curiosity* is, for him, the main one associated with "the dynamic of retrospection," where "rather than diverting attention from a missing antecedent, the narrative signals or even focuses its absence and the resultant loss in coherence." In *surprise,* we therefore have "belated recognition of disorder," whereas *curiosity* entails "early retrospection on disorder" (Sternberg 524–25). I have focused on surprise rather than curiosity because it is, to my mind, the closest to rhyme and therefore the most revealing of the difference from rhyme. For an account of surprise as affect in stories, within a larger framework that explores the fundamental relation between emotions and storytelling, see Wesling, *Joys and Sorrows of Imaginary Persons.* Wesling makes the compelling assertion that "surprise is the quintessential emotion of storytelling because it keeps me-the-reader attached to a process that's about the past, as the past is re-performed in the present" (87).

18. Small, but not the smallest. A smaller-level operation of retrospectivity in language, dubbed "regressive action," is pointed to by Jakobson in the example of the change to /r/ of the first /l/ of *colonel* in the service of "regressive dissimilation" with the soon-to-come second /l/ ("Language in Operation" 54). The difference with rhyme is that the phonetic harmony created by this change, on a level lower than the word, is significantly

less pronounced; clearly this kind of regressive operation, unlike rhyme, has not become an institutionalized poetic device in English.

19. "Nonsense may be the condition . . . to which devices of sound in themselves aspire" (Justice, "Meters and Memory" 150).

20. Sound and rhythm are asemantic elements in verse that entail surprises, and these surprises, unlike sporadic rhyme, can be integrated into the poem's sound and rhythm strata. Nicolas Abraham talks of "retrospective synthesis" as a "fundamental course of action" in his "rhythmizing consciousness," a way in which "the unforeseen emergence is incorporated into what preceded it," which results in the creation of a new unit that we now expect to recur (83; see also 77–81). This is a way of incorporating ("synthesizing") the surprise into the system of future expectation and therefore regularizing it, creating a new expectation based on it, and it is akin to Wolfgang Iser's account of the phenomenology of reading, save for the fact that Abraham's phenomenology is focused on rhythm rather than sense units. Reuven Tsur similarly shows how rhyme schemes themselves, as groupings, are formed "after the event" (*Toward a Theory of Cognitive Poetics* 118). In systematic rhyme situations, when a surprise occurs, as in a change in the rhyme scheme or a disruption of it, the reader is forced to look back and readjust, as long as a certain level of disruptiveness is not reached that makes readjustment impossible. The difference between these accounts of systematic rhyme and metrical variation, on the one hand, and sporadic rhyme, on the other, is that sporadic rhyme, though retrospective, does not partake in "retrospective synthesis."

21. It is because sporadic rhyme does not integrate on the level of sound that it attains a high degree of markedness, which in turn affords it the poetic potential to impact the reading or interpretation of the text, as chapter 4 demonstrated.

22. Stanley Fish, like Tsur, Abraham, Iser, and Sternberg, is acutely aware of the temporality of the reading process. Another notable theorist who highlights the temporal dimension, in conjunction with a psychoanalytic perspective of a different orientation, is Norman Holland. In tracing the reading process of actual (rather than imagined) readers, Holland describes their "re-making" of the poem as an act in time: "The reader tries, *as he proceeds through the work*, to compose from it a literary experience in his particular lifestyle. In particular, *line by line and episode by episode*, he responds positively to those elements that, at any given point in the work, he perceives as acting out what he would characteristically expect from another being in such circumstances" (*Poems* 77, my emphasis). Though I am highlighting one general aspect shared by these reader-aware theorists, I do not mean to imply that my account of rhyme or reading agrees with their basic assumptions. In fact, while I speak of rhyme as a structure manifested in time, Fish and Holland would probably question the very existence of a structure "out there" that is independent of the hypotheses we propose to reality (Holland) or of our conventionalized ways of reading (Fish). For some of these differences within reader response theory, see Holland, *The Critical I* (52–57, 184–86).

23. See, for example, the definition and criteria for posttraumatic stress disorder found in the *Diagnostic and Statistical Manual of Mental Disorders*, whose first diagnostic criterion

is "Exposure to actual or threatened death, serious injury, or sexual violence," and whose diagnostic features go as far as listing potential traumatic events (being kidnapped, being taken hostage, severe motor vehicle accidents, and so on). The assumption here is that there is a specific, locatable traumatic event, as such.

24. I read the problematic rhetoric of the imperative voice, namely that these memories need to be integrated and "transformed into narrative language," as attesting to the incongruity between trauma as experience and the very notions of narrative, language, and integration. This incongruity is something that trauma shares with sporadic rhyme.

25. Peter McDonald phrases the general issue, and its application to the poetry of Gerard Manley Hopkins and Edward Thomas, in terms of mastery over rhyme, submission to rhyme, and ultimately "mastery in the art of submission" (McDonald, "Rhyme and Determination" 244). See also McDonald, *Sound Intentions.*

26. Mutlu Konuk Blasing writes that poetic conventions "carry a history of communal acknowledgement of a shared trauma of individuation/socialization," a trauma that she associates with language acquisition, the process of which involves "the transformation of random muscular and sonic phenomena into recognizable elements of a sign system" (62, 46). Like Freud and Cathy Caruth, Blasing understands trauma as an event that exhibits belatedness and that cannot enter consciousness or be recovered and assimilated, an understanding that is very close to my account, save for the double-event aspect that the Emma case brings forth.

27. The term *overwhelming* is used extensively. For example, Caruth gives a "general definition" according to which "trauma is described as the response to an unexpected or overwhelming violent event or events that are not fully grasped as they occur, but return later in repeated flashbacks, nightmares, and other repetitive phenomena" (*Unclaimed Experience* 91). Judith Lewis Herman writes, "Traumatic events are extraordinary, not because they occur rarely, but rather because they overwhelm the ordinary human adaptations to life" (33).

28. *The Oxford Dictionary of Word Histories* lists the Greek *poiein* ("to create") as the base for *poet* (Chantrell 385). See also the etymology in the *Oxford English Dictionary*'s entry for "poet."

29. This distinction is made by Dominick LaCapra: "Writing about trauma," within historiography, is "related to the project of reconstructing the past as objectively as possible," whereas "writing trauma" has to do with "acting (or playing) it out in performative discourse or artistic practice" (186–87). Rhyme would thus be an instance of something close to "writing trauma," performing trauma on the level of the text. I find this basic distinction tremendously helpful, though I part ways with LaCapra when he associates "writing trauma" not just with acting out but also with "processes of coming to terms with traumatic 'experiences'" (186).

30. J. L. Austin's speech-act theory is elaborated in *How to Do Things with Words,* with the first stage entailing a (later qualified) distinction between the constative (a true-or-false statement or a description) and the performative (an utterance that performs an action rather than reports on one, such as "I declare war"). Austin famously excludes poetry from

the set of circumstances needed for the performative not to be void: "Surely the words must be spoken 'seriously' and so as to be taken 'seriously'? . . . I must not be joking, for example, nor writing a poem" (9). In addition to Derrida's attack on Austin in "Signature Event Context," where he argues that the infelicities Austin excludes are the very condition for any performative to be successful (17), discussions and applications of speech-act theory to poetry are found in Barbara Johnson, J. Hillis Miller, and Maximilian De Gaynesford. As elements of the performative, Miller highlights things like alliteration, assonance, and rhyme, devices that "make words into things and things that have power to do other things in their turn" (183–84). Both Miller and De Gaynesford give examples of iconicity, where the words of the poem act out what they are saying (De Gaynesford 645–46; Miller 186, 188). Jonathan Culler likewise prefers to restrict the notion of the performative to cases in which the lyric is "bringing about what it describes" (*Theory of the Lyric* 131).

31. For the German original and Michael Hamburger's English translation, see Celan, *Poems*, 216–17.

32. It is curious that the very lines that Shoshana Felman quotes twice from Paul Celan possess rhyme—not only *know* : *deepinsnow*, which is not there in the German original, but also the gradually diminishing consonants of *deepinsnow*, a gesture that creates nothing but rhyme, in both the original and the translation: *deepinsnow* : *eepinow* : *ee-i-o*. Felman makes no mention of this fact, nor does Walter Benn Michaels, who highlights the meaningless noise in his reading of Felman's reading. While rhyme is noise, it is a specific kind of noise, and hardly meaningless. One context in which to consider Celan's diminishing words is the tradition of "echo verse" (see Hollander, *Figure of Echo* 26–31 and elsewhere), except that in that case, the echo, repeating the ending of a previous word, often reveals hidden meanings (for instance, *light* echoes *delight*), while in Celan the direction is away from meaning.

33. Blasing identifies the mother tongue, and the socializing process of entry into language (a process that produces the human subject), as the site of pain. Poetic language, with the special status it affords sound, "remembers the history of the process of language acquisition," and "resounds the transition from somatic to representational language and recalls individual relationships to sound images" (47). I likewise see a mix of pleasure and pain in the material elements of poetry, namely rhyme, but on different grounds.

CONCLUSION

1. The present "has no space," Augustine explains, because it can always be chunked into smaller units, like a day, an hour, or a minute (11.19, 289).

2. For an explicit articulation of rhyme supposedly echoing an un-American attitude, see Diane Wakoski's equation of denunciations of free verse with "growing conservatism" in the United States.

works cited

Abernathy, Robert. "Rhymes, Non-Rhymes, and Antirhyme." In *To Honor Roman Jakobson: Essays on the Occasion of His Seventieth Birthday,* 1:1–14. The Hague: Mouton, 1967.

Abraham, Nicolas. *Rhythms.* Trans. Benjamin Thigpen and Nicholas T. Rand. Stanford, CA: Stanford UP, 1995.

Alim, H. Samy. "'Bring It to the Cypher': Hip Hop Nation Language." In *That's the Joint!: The Hip-Hop Studies Reader,* 2nd ed., ed. Murray Forman and Mark Anthony Neal, 531–63. New York: Routledge, 2012.

———. "On Some Serious Next Millennium Rap Ishhh: Pharoahe Monch, Hip Hop Poetics, and the Internal Rhymes of Internal Affairs." *Journal of English Linguistics* 31, no. 1 (2003): 60–84.

American Psychiatric Association. *Diagnostic and Statistical Manual of Mental Disorders,* 5th ed. (*DSM-5*). Washington, DC: American Psychiatric Association Publishing, 2013.

Anderson, Karrin Vasby. "'Rhymes with Rich': 'Bitch' as a Tool of Containment in Contemporary American Politics." *Rhetoric and Public Affairs* 2 (1999): 599–623.

Armstrong, Isobel. "Hegel: The Time of Rhythm, the Time of Rhyme." *Thinking Verse* 1 (2011): 124–36.

Arnold, Matthew. *The Poetical Works of Matthew Arnold,* ed. C. B. Tinker and H. F. Lowry. London: Oxford UP, 1961.

Attridge, Derek. *Moving Words: Forms of English Poetry.* Oxford: Oxford UP, 2013.

———. "The Rhythms of the English Dolnik." In *Critical Rhythm: The Poetics of a Literary Life Form,* ed. Ben Glaser and Jonathan Culler, 153–73. New York: Fordham UP, 2019.

———. *The Rhythms of English Poetry.* London: Longman, 1982.

Augustine. *The Confessions of St. Augustine.* Trans. John K. Ryan. New York: Image Books, 1960.

Austin, J. L. *How to Do Things with Words.* 2nd ed. Cambridge, MA: Harvard UP, 1975.

Aviram, Amittai F. *Telling Rhythm: Body and Meaning in Poetry.* Ann Arbor: U of Michigan P, 1994.

Baddeley, A. D. "Short-Term Memory for Word Sequences as a Function of Acoustic, Semantic, and Formal Similarity." *Quarterly Journal of Experimental Psychology* 18, no. 4 (1966): 362–65.

Barthes, Roland. *Elements of Semiology.* 1968. Trans. Annette Lavers and Colin Smith. New York: Noonday Press, 1988.

———. *The Pleasure of the Text.* Trans. Richard Miller. New York: Hill and Wang, 1975.

Bécam, Susan E. *Rhyme in Gace Brulé's Lyric.* New York: Peter Lang, 1998.

Benn Michaels, Walter. "'You Who Never Was There': Slavery and the New Historicism—Deconstruction and the Holocaust." In *The Americanization of the Holocaust,* ed. Hilene Flanzbaum, 181–97. Baltimore: Johns Hopkins UP, 1999.

Benveniste, Emile. "Remarks on the Function of Language in Freudian Theory." In *Problems in General Linguistics,* trans. Mary Elizabeth Meek, 65–75. Coral Gables, FL: U of Miami P, 1971.

Bernstein, Charles, ed. *Close Listening: Poetry and the Performed Word.* New York: Oxford UP, 1998.

———. "The Expanded Field of L=A=N=G=U=A=G=E." In *Pitch of Poetry,* 60–77. Chicago: U of Chicago P, 2016.

Beyers, Chris. *A History of Free Verse.* Fayetteville: U of Arkansas P, 2001.

Blake, William. *The Complete Poetry and Prose of William Blake,* rev. ed., ed. David V. Erdman. Berkeley: U of California P, 1982.

Blasing, Mutlu Konuk. *Lyric Poetry: The Pain and Pleasure of Words.* Princeton, NJ: Princeton UP, 2007.

Boothby, Richard. *Freud as Philosopher: Metapsychology after Lacan.* New York: Routledge, 2001.

Borges, Jorge Luis. "John Wilkins' Analytical Language," trans. Eliot Weinberger. In *Selected Non-Fictions,* ed. Eliot Weinberger, 229–32. New York: Penguin, 1999.

Bradford, Richard. *Augustan Measures: Restoration and Eighteenth-Century Writings on Prosody and Metre.* Aldershot: Ashgate, 2002.

Bradley, Adam. *Book of Rhymes: The Poetics of Hip Hop.* New York: Basic Civitas Books, 2009.

Brady, Ann P. *Lyricism in the Poetry of T. S. Eliot.* Port Washington, NY: Kennikat Press, 1978.

Brogan, T. V. F. "Sound." In *The New Princeton Encyclopedia of Poetry and Poetics,* ed. Alex Preminger and T. V. F. Brogan, 1172–80. Princeton: Princeton UP, 1993.

Brogan, T. V. F., and Stephen Cushman. "Rhyme." In *The Princeton Encyclopedia of Poetry and Poetics,* 4th ed., ed. Roland Greene and Stephen Cushman, 1182–92. Princeton, NJ: Princeton UP, 2012.

Brown, Frank Burch. "Covert Rhyme in the Scheme of Eliot's 'East Coker.'" *Papers on Language and Literature* 18, no. 4 (1982): 421–27.

Brownstein, Rachel Mayer. "Byron's *Don Juan*: Some Reasons for the Rhymes." *Modern Language Quarterly* 28 (1967): 177–91.

Bruns, Gerald L. *Modern Poetry and the Idea of Language.* New Haven, CT: Yale UP, 1974.

Bugge, John. "Rhyme as Onomatopoeia in 'The Dry Salvages.'" *Papers on Language and Literature* 10, no. 3 (1974): 312–16.

Burt, Stephanie [published as Stephen]. "Cornucopia, or, Contemporary American Rhyme." In *The Monkey and the Wrench: Essays into Contemporary Poetics,* ed. John Gallaher and Mary Biddinger, 59–77. U of Akron P, 2011.

Byron, George Gordon. *Don Juan.* In *The Poetical Works of Lord Byron,* 635–857. London: Oxford UP, 1961.

Bysshe, Edward. *The Art of English Poetry.* 1708. The Augustan Reprint Society. Project Gutenberg. http://www.gutenberg.org/files/35094/35094-h/35094-h.htm.

Campion, Thomas. "Observations in the Art of English Poesie." In *The Works of Dr. Thomas Campion,* ed. A. H. Bullen, 231–62. London: Chiswick, 1889.

Caplan, David. *Questions of Possibility: Contemporary Poetry and Poetic Form.* Oxford: Oxford UP, 2005.

———. *Rhyme's Challenge: Hip Hop, Poetry, and Contemporary Rhyming Culture.* Oxford: Oxford UP, 2014.

Caplan, Harry, trans. *Rhetorica ad Herennium.* London: Heinemann, 1954.

Caruth, Cathy, ed. Introduction to *Trauma: Explorations in Memory,* 3–12. Baltimore: Johns Hopkins UP, 1995.

———. *Unclaimed Experience: Trauma, Narrative, and History.* Baltimore: Johns Hopkins UP, 1996.

Celan, Paul. *Poems of Paul Celan,* rev. and expanded ed., trans. Michael Hamburger. New York: Persea Books, 2002.

Chalker, John. "Aspects of Rhythm and Rhyme in Eliot's Early Poems." *English* 16, no. 93 (1966): 84–88.

Chambers, Frank M. "Versification." In *A Handbook of the Troubadours,* ed. F. R. P. Akenhurst and Judith M. Davis, 101–20. Berkeley: U of California P, 1995.

Chantrell, Glynnis, ed. *The Oxford Dictionary of Word Histories.* Oxford: Oxford UP, 2002.

Ciardi, John. *I Met a Man.* Boston: Houghton Mifflin, 1961.

Clark, Arthur Melville. *Studies in Literary Modes.* London: Oliver and Boyd, 1958.

Cohen-Vrignaud, Gerard. "Rhyme's Crimes." *ELH* 82, no. 3 (2015): 987–1012.

Comay, Rebecca. "Impressions: Proust, Photography, Trauma." *Discourse* 31, no. 1/2 (2009): 86–105.

Cooper, G. Burns. *Mysterious Music: Rhythm and Free Verse.* Stanford, CA: Stanford UP, 1998.

Creaser, John. "Rhymes, Rhyme, and Rhyming." *Essays in Criticism* 62, no. 4 (2012): 438–60.

Creeley, Robert. *The Collected Poems of Robert Creeley: 1945–1975.* Berkeley: U of California P, 1982.

Culler, Jonathan. "In Defence of Overinterpretation." In *Interpretation and Overinterpretation,* ed. Stefan Collini, 109–23. Cambridge: Cambridge UP, 1992.

———. *Theory of the Lyric.* Cambridge, MA: Harvard UP, 2015.

Cureton, Richard D. *Rhythmic Phrasing in English Verse.* London: Longman, 1992.

Dale, Peter. *An Introduction to Rhyme.* London: Agenda Editions and Bellew Publishing, 1998.

Daniel, Samuel. *A Defence of Ryme.* 1603. London: John Lane the Bodley Head, 1925.

Dante Alighieri. *De vulgari eloquentia,* ed. and trans. Steven Botterill. Cambridge: Cambridge UP, 1996.

Davidson, Michael. *Concerto for the Left Hand: Disability and the Defamiliar Body.* Ann Arbor: U of Michigan P, 2008.

De Gaynesford, Maximilian. "Speech Acts and Poetry." *Analysis* 70 (2010): 644–46.

Deis, Christopher. "Hip-Hop and Politics." In *The Cambridge Companion to Hip-Hop,* ed. Justin A. Williams, 192–205. Cambridge: Cambridge UP, 2015.

Derrida, Jacques. "Differance." In *Speech and Phenomena and Other Essays on Husserl's Theory of Signs,* trans. David B. Allison, 129–60. Evanston, IL: Northwestern UP, 1973.

———. "The Double Session." In *Dissemination,* trans. Barbara Johnson, 173–285. London: Athlone, 1981.

———. "Plato's Pharmacy." In *Dissemination,* trans. Barbara Johnson, 61–171. London: Athlone, 1981.

———. "Signature Event Context," trans. Samuel Weber and Jeffrey Mehlman. In *Limited Inc.,* 1–23. Evanston, IL: Northwestern UP, 1988.

Dickinson, Emily. *The Poems of Emily Dickinson: Variorum Edition,* vol. 1., ed. R. W. Franklin. Cambridge, MA: Belknap Press, 1998.

Dingemanse, Mark, Damián E. Blasi, Gary Lupyan, Morten H. Christiansen, and Padraic Monaghan. "Arbitrariness, Iconicity, and Systematicity in Language." *Trends in Cognitive Sciences* 19, no. 10 (2015): 603–15.

Do-Monte, Fabricio H., Kelvin Quiñones-Laracuente, and Gregory J. Quirk. "A Temporal Shift in the Circuits Mediating Retrieval of Fear Memory." *Nature* 519 (2015): 460–63.

Doerr, Joe Francis. "New Formalism." In *Encyclopedia of American Poetry: The Twentieth Century,* ed. Eric L. Haralson, 503–506. Chicago: Fitzroy Dearborn, 2001.

Drory, Rina. *Models and Contacts: Arabic Literature and Its Impact on Medieval Jewish Culture.* Leiden: Brill, 2000.

Dryden, John. Dedication of *The Rival Ladies.* 1664. In *Dryden and Howard: 1664–1668,* ed. D. D. Arundell, 1–4. Cambridge: Cambridge UP, 1929.

———. *Essay of Dramatic Poesy,* ed. Nichol Smith. London: Blackie, n.d.

———. *The Poetical Works of Dryden,* ed. George R. Noyes. Boston: Houghton Mifflin, 1950.

———. Prologue to *Aureng-Zebe.* 1675. In *Dryden and Howard: 1664–1668,* ed. D. D. Arundell, 120. Cambridge: Cambridge UP, 1929.

Eco, Umberto. *Interpretation and Overinterpretation,* ed. Stefan Collini. Cambridge: Cambridge UP, 1992.

———. *The Search for the Perfect Language.* Trans. James Fentress. Oxford: Blackwell, 1995.

Eekman, Thomas. *The Realm of Rime: A Study of Rime in the Poetry of the Slavs.* Amsterdam: Verlag Adolf M. Hakkert, 1974.

Eliot, T. S. *Collected Poems 1909–1962.* New York: Harcourt Brace, 1991.

———. "Reflections on Vers Libre." In *To Criticize the Critic and Other Writings,* 183–89. London: Faber, 1965.

———. "Tradition and the Individual Talent." In *Selected Essays,* 13–22. London: Faber, 1976.

Evans, Dylan. *An Introductory Dictionary of Lacanian Psychoanalysis.* London: Routledge, 1996.

Fabb, Nigel. *What Is Poetry?* Cambridge: Cambridge UP, 2015.

Faber, M. D. "The Pleasures of Rhyme: A Psychoanalytic Note." *International Review of Psycho-Analysis* 15 (1988): 375–80.

Faimberg, Haydée. "Après-Coup." *International Journal of Psychoanalysis* 86 (2005): 1–6.

Fay, Sarah. "Kay Ryan, The Art of Poetry No. 94." *Paris Review* 187 (Winter 2008). http://www.theparisreview.org/interviews/5889/the-art-of-poetry-no-94 -kay-ryan.

Felman, Shoshana. "Education and Crisis, or the Vicissitudes of Listening." In *Testimony: Crises of Witnessing in Literature, Psychoanalysis, and History,* ed. Shoshana Felman and Dori Laub, 1–56. New York: Routledge, 1992.

Ferreira, Carla Sofia. "Seeing through French Eyes: *Vers Libre* in Whitman, Laforgue, and Eliot." *Cambridge Quarterly* 45, no. 1 (2016): 20–41.

Figlerowicz, Marta. "Emotional Comedies: Lorine Niedecker's 'For Paul.'" In *Humor in Modern American Poetry,* ed. Rachel Trousdale, 59–75. New York: Bloomsbury, 2018.

Filkuková, Petra, and Sven Hroar Klempe. "Rhyme as Reason in Commercial and Social Advertising." *Scandinavian Journal of Psychology* 54 (2013): 423–31.

Finch, Annie. *The Ghost of Meter.* Ann Arbor: U of Michigan P, 2000.

Fish, Stanley. "Interpreting the *Variorum.*" In *Modern Criticism and Theory,* ed. David Lodge, 288–306. Harlow: Longman, 2000.

Fleishman, Lazar. "The Acromonogram Rhyme in Lev Gomolitsky." *Stanford Slavic Studies* 41 (2012): 161–69 [Venok: Studia slavica Stefano Garzonio sexagenario oblata].

Freeman, Margaret. "The Aesthetics of Human Experience: Minding, Metaphor, and Icon in Poetic Expression." *Poetics Today* 32, no. 4 (2011): 717–52.

———. "The Body in the Word: A Cognitive Approach to the Shape of a Poetic Text." In *Cognitive Stylistics: Language and Cognition in Text Analysis,* ed. Jonathan Culpeper and Elena Semino, 23–47. Amsterdam: John Benjamins, 2002.

Freud, Sigmund. "The Antithetical Meaning of Primal Words." In *Standard Edition,* 11:155–61.

———. "Beyond the Pleasure Principle." In *Standard Edition,* 18:7–64.

———. "Letter 52." In *Standard Edition,* 1:233–39.

———. "The Paths to the Formation of Symptoms" [lecture 23 of Introductory Lectures on Psychoanalysis]. In *Standard Edition,* 16:358–77.

———. *Project for a Scientific Psychology.* In *Standard Edition,* 1:281–397.

———. "Screen Memories." In *Standard Edition,* 3:303–22.

———. *The Standard Edition of the Complete Works of Sigmund Freud,* ed. James Strachey. 24 vols. London: Hogarth Press, 1950–1974.

———. "The Unconscious." In *Standard Edition,* 14:166–204.

Fried, Debra. "Rhyme Puns." In *On Puns: The Foundation of Letters*, ed. Jonathan Culler, 83–99. Oxford: Basil Blackwell, 1988.

Frost, Robert. *The Poetry of Robert Frost: The Collected Poems*, ed. Edward Connery Lathem. New York: Henry Holt, 1969.

Frye, Northrop. *Anatomy of Criticism*. Princeton, NJ: Princeton UP, 1957.

———. *Spiritus Mundi*. Bloomington: Indiana UP, 1976.

Fussell, Paul. *Poetic Meter and Poetic Form*. Rev. ed. New York: McGraw-Hill, 1979.

Gardner, W. H. *Gerard Manley Hopkins: A Study of Poetic Idiosyncrasy in Relation to Poetic Tradition*. Vol. 2. New Haven: Yale UP, 1949.

Gasparov, M. L. *A History of European Versification*. Trans. G. S. Smith and Marina Tarlinskaja. Oxford: Clarendon P, 1996.

Glaser, Ben. Introduction to *Critical Rhythm: The Poetics of a Literary Life Form*, ed. Ben Glaser and Jonathan Culler, 1–17. New York: Fordham UP, 2019.

Glück, Louise. *The First Five Books of Poems*. Manchester: Carcanet, 1997.

Golston, Michael. *Poetic Machinations: Allegory, Surrealism, and Postmodern Poetic Thought*. New York: Columbia UP, 2015.

Green, André. *Time in Psychoanalysis*. Trans. Andrew Weller. London: Free Association, 2002.

Greene, Thomas M. "Spenser and the Epithalamic Convention." In *The Prince of Poets: Essays on Edmund Spenser*, ed. John R. Elliott Jr., 152–69. New York UP, 1968.

Grigg, Russell. *Lacan, Language, and Philosophy*. Albany: State U of New York P, 2008.

Grossi, Giordana, Donna Coch, Sharon Coffey-Corina, Phillip J. Holcomb, and Helen J. Neville. "Phonological Processing in Visual Rhyming: A Developmental ERP Study." *Journal of Cognitive Neuroscience* 13, no. 5 (2001): 610–25.

Halmari, Helena. "Alliteration in Inaugural Addresses: From George Washington to Barack Obama." In *Alliteration in Culture*, ed. Jonathan Roper, 45–61. New York: Palgrave Macmillan, 2011.

Hardy, Thomas. *The Complete Poems of Thomas Hardy*, ed. James Gibson. London: Macmillan, 1976.

Harmon, William. "Rhyme in English Verse: History, Structure, Functions." *Studies in Philology* 84, no. 4 (1987): 365–93.

Harshav, Benjamin. "Literariness Revisited." In *Explorations in Poetics*, 161–73. Stanford, CA: Stanford UP, 2007.

———. "The Meaning of Sound Patterns in Poetry." In *Explorations in Poetics*, 140–60. Stanford, CA: Stanford UP, 2007.

Harte, Jeremy. "Love, Silver, and the Devil: Alliteration in English Place-Names." In *Alliteration in Culture*, ed. Jonathan Roper, 21–33. New York: Palgrave Macmillan, 2011.

Hartman, Charles O. *Free Verse: An Essay on Prosody.* 1980. Evanston, IL: Northwestern UP, 1996.

Hartman, Geoffrey H. "The Interpreter's Freud." In *Easy Pieces*, 137–54. New York: Columbia UP, 1985.

Hayes, Albert McHarg. "Counterpoint in Herbert." In *Essential Articles for the Study of George Herbert's Poetry*, ed. John H. Roberts, 283–97. Hamden: Archon, 1979.

Hayes, Rachel A., Alan Slater, and Elizabeth Brown. "Infants' Ability to Categorise on the Basis of Rhyme." *Cognitive Development* 15 (2000): 405–19.

Heath-Stubbs, John. *The Ode.* Oxford: Oxford UP, 1969.

Hegel, G. W. F. *Aesthetics: Lectures on Fine Art.* Vol. 2. Trans. T. M. Knox. Oxford: Clarendon, 1975.

Hejinian, Lyn. *The Cell.* Los Angeles: Sun and Moon, 1992.

———. "The Rejection of Closure." In *The Language of Inquiry*, 40–58. Berkeley: U of California P, 2000.

Herman, Judith Lewis. *Trauma and Recovery.* New York: Basic Books, 1992.

Holland, Norman N. *The Critical I.* New York: Columbia UP, 1992.

———. *Poems in Persons: An Introduction to the Psychoanalysis of Literature.* 1973. New York: Columbia UP, 1989.

Hollander, John. *The Figure of Echo.* Berkeley: U of California P, 1981.

———. *Vision and Resonance: Two Senses of Poetic Form.* New York: Oxford UP, 1975.

Hopkins, Gerard Manley. *The Poems of Gerard Manley Hopkins.* 3rd ed. London: Oxford UP, 1956.

Hrushovski (Harshav), Benjamin. "Main Methods of Hebrew Rhyming from the Piyoot to Our Day." *HaSifroot* B.4 (1971): 721–49.

Ignatow, David. *Poems 1934–1969.* Middletown, CT: Wesleyan UP, 1970.

Ihde, Don. *Listening and Voice: Phenomenologies of Sound.* Albany: State U of New York P, 2007.

Iser, Wolfgang. *The Act of Reading: A Theory of Aesthetic Response.* Baltimore: Johns Hopkins UP, 1980.

———. "The Reading Process: A Phenomenological Approach." In *Modern Criticism and Theory*, ed. David Lodge, 212–28. London: Longman, 1996.

Jakobson, Roman. "Language in Operation." In *Language in Literature*, ed. Krystyna Pomorska and Stephen Rudy, 50–61. Cambridge, MA: Belknap Press, 1987.

———. "Linguistics and Poetics." In *Language in Literature*, 62–94.

———. "Two Aspects of Language and Two Types of Aphasic Disturbances." In *Language in Literature*, 95–114.

Jakobson, Roman, and Linda Waugh. *The Sound Shape of Language*. Bloomington: Indiana UP, 1979.

Jarrell, Randall. *The Complete Poems*. New York: Farrar, Straus and Giroux, 1981.

Jarvis, Simon. "For a Poetics of Verse." *PMLA* 125 (2010): 931–35.

———. "Musical Thinking: Hegel and the Phenomenology of Prosody." *Paragraph* 28, no. 2 (2005): 57–71.

———. "Why Rhyme Pleases." *Thinking Verse* 1 (2011): 17–43.

Jay Z. "99 Problems." *The Black Album*. Roc-A-Fella Records, 2003.

———. "Run This Town." *The Blueprint 3*. Atlantic Records, 2009.

Johnson, Barbara. "Poetry and Performative Language." *Yale French Studies* 54 (1977): 140–58.

Johnson, Samuel. *Lives of the English Poets*. Vol. 1. London: Everyman's Library, 1964.

Jonson, Ben. *Ben Jonson: The Complete Poems*, ed. George Parfitt. Harmondsworth: Penguin Education, 1975.

Justice, Donald. *Collected Poems*. New York: Knopf, 2006.

———. "Meters and Memory." In *A Donald Justice Reader*, 149–55. Hanover, NH: Middlebury College P, 1991.

Kahn, Douglas. "Noises of the Avant-Garde." In *The Sound Studies Reader*, ed. Jonathan Sterne, 427–48. London: Routledge, 2012.

Keach, William. "Rhyme and the Arbitrariness of Language." In *Romantic Poetry: Recent Revisionary Criticism*, ed. Karl Kroeber and Gene W. Ruoff, 345–51. New Brunswick, NJ: Rutgers UP, 1993.

Kennedy, X. J. "Fenced-in Fields." In *Claims for Poetry*, ed. Donald Hall, 203–12. Ann Arbor: U of Michigan P, 1982.

Kenner, Hugh. "Pope's Reasonable Rhymes." *ELH* 41 (1974): 74–88.

Keyes, Cheryl L. *Rap Music and Street Consciousness*. Urbana: U of Illinois P, 2002.

Kierkegaard, Søren. "Is the Past More Necessary than the Future? Or: Has the Possible, by Having Become Actual, Become More Necessary than It Was?." In *Philosophical Fragments*, trans. Howard V. Hong and Edna H. Hong, 72–88. Princeton, NJ: Princeton UP, 1985.

———. *Journals and Papers*. Vol. 1. Trans. Howard V. Hong and Edna H. Hong. Bloomington: Indiana UP, 1967.

Kitwana, Bakari. *The Hip Hop Generation: Young Blacks and the Crisis in African American Culture*. New York: Basic Civitas, 2002.

Kristeva, Julia. *Revolution in Poetic Language*. Trans. Margaret Waller. New York: Columbia UP, 1984.

Lacan, Jacques. *Écrits: A Selection.* Trans. Alan Sheridan. London: Routledge, 2001.

———. *The Four Fundamental Concepts of Psycho-Analysis.* Trans. Alan Sheridan. London: Karnac, 2004.

LaCapra, Dominick. *Writing History, Writing Trauma.* Baltimore: Johns Hopkins UP, 2001.

Laferriere, Daniel. "The Teleology of Rhythm in Poetry." *Poetics and Theory of Literature* 4 (1980): 411–50.

Lakoff, Robin Tolmach. *The Language War.* Berkeley: U of California P, 2000.

Lange, E. B., and Oberauer, K. "Overwriting of Phonemic Features in Serial Recall." *Memory* 13, no. 3/4 (2005): 333–39.

Lanham, Richard A. *A Handlist of Rhetorical Terms.* 2nd ed. Berkeley: U of California P, 1991.

Lanz, Henry. *The Physical Basis of Rime.* New York: Greenwood, 1968.

Laplanche, Jean. *Life and Death in Psychoanalysis.* Trans. Jeffrey Mehlman. Baltimore: Johns Hopkins UP, 1976.

———. "Notes on Afterwardsness." In *Essays on Otherness,* 260–65. London: Routledge, 1999.

Laplanche, J., and J.-B. Pontalis. *The Language of Psycho-Analysis.* Trans. Donald Nicholson-Smith. New York: Norton, 1973.

Legman, G., ed. "Introduction to the Limerick." In *The Limerick.* New York: Bell, 1969.

Lillo, Antonio. "From Alsatian Dog to Wooden Shoe: Linguistic Xenophobia in Rhyming Slang." *English Studies* 4 (2001): 336–48.

———. "The Rhyming Slang of the Junkie." *English Today 66* 17, no. 2 (2001): 39–45.

Lilly, Ian K. "On the Rich Rhymes of M. N. Murav'ev." *International Journal of Slavic Linguistics and Poetics* 23 (1981): 147–61.

Liu, Lydia H. "The Cybernetic Unconscious: Rethinking Lacan, Poe, and French Theory." *Critical Inquiry* 36, no. 2 (2010): 288–320.

Logan, John. *The Collected Poems.* Brockport, NY: BOA Editions, 1989.

Lotman, Yury. *Analysis of the Poetic Text,* ed. and trans. D. Barton Johnson. Ann Arbor, MI: Ardis, 1976.

Mackenzie, Raymond N. "Rethinking Rhyme, Signifying Friendship: Milton's *Lycidas* and *Epitaphium Damonis.*" *Modern Philology* 106, no. 3 (2009): 530–54.

Marlowe, Christopher. *The Complete Works of Christopher Marlowe,* vol. 2, ed. Fredson Bowers. Cambridge: Cambridge UP, 1973.

McCauley, Lawrence H. "Milton's Missing Rhymes." *Style* 28 (1994): 242–59.

McDonald, Peter. "Rhyme and Determination in Hopkins and Edward Thomas." *Essays in Criticism* 43, no. 3 (1993): 228–46.

———. *Sound Intentions: The Workings of Rhyme in Nineteenth-Century Poetry.* Oxford: Oxford UP, 2012.

McGlone, Matthew S., and Jessica Tofighbakhsh. "Birds of a Feather Flock Conjointly (?): Rhyme as Reason in Aphorisms." *Psychological Science* 2 (2000): 424-28.

———. "The Keats Heuristic: Rhyme as Reason in Aphorism Interpretation." *Poetics* 26 (1999): 235-44.

McKie, Michael. "The Origins and Early Development of Rhyme in English Verse." *Modern Language Review* 93, no. 4 (1997): 817-31.

———. "Semantic Rhyme: A Reappraisal." *Essays in Criticism* 46, no. 4 (1996): 340-58.

Meisel, Perry. "Dylan and the Critics." *Raritan* 26, no. 3 (2007): 101-19.

———. *The Literary Freud.* New York: Routledge, 2007.

Melitz, Amram. "Biblical Acrostics." *Beit Mikra: Journal for the Study of the Bible and Its World* 36/C (1991): 250-62.

Merriman, Emily Taylor. "Corresponding Grace: Hopkins' Theory and Use of Rhyme." *Hopkins Quarterly* 32 (2005): 85-111.

Meschonnic, Henri. "Rhyme and Life," trans. Gabriella Bedetti. *Critical Inquiry* 15 (1988): 90-107.

Miller, J. Hillis. "Naming and Doing: Speech Acts in Hopkins's Poems." *Religion and Literature* 22 (1990): 173-91.

Milton, John. "The Verse" [note attached to the second edition of *Paradise Lost*]. In *The Poems of John Milton,* ed. John Carey and Alastair Fowler, 456-57. London: Longman, 1968.

Modell, Arnold H. *Other Times, Other Realities: Toward a Theory of Psychoanalytic Treatment.* Cambridge, MA: Harvard UP, 1990.

Moloney, Michael F. "Donne's Metrical Practice." In *Essential Articles for the Study of John Donne's Poetry,* ed. John R. Roberts, 171-77. Sussex: Harvester, 1975.

Morgan, Marcyliena. *Language, Discourse, and Power in African American Culture.* Cambridge: Cambridge UP, 2002.

Morlier, Margaret M. "*Sonnets from the Portuguese* and the Politics of Rhyme." *Victorian Literature and Culture* 27 (1999): 97-112.

Morris, Adalaide, ed. *Sound States: Innovative Poetics and Acoustical Technologies.* Chapel Hill: U of North Carolina P, 1997.

Mowitt, John. *Sounds: The Ambient Humanities.* Oakland: U of California P, 2015.

Mullen, Harryette. *The Cracks between What We Are and What We Are Supposed to Be: Essays and Interviews.* Tuscaloosa: U of Alabama P, 2012.

———. *Sleeping with the Dictionary.* Berkeley: U of California P, 2002.

Nänny, Max. "Iconic Uses of Rhyme." In *Outside In Inside Out: Iconicity in Language and Literature,* ed. Costantino Maeder, William J. Herlofsky, and Olga Fischer, 195–215. Amsterdam: Benjamins, 2005.

Nash, Ogden. *The Private Dining Room.* Boston: Little, Brown, 1953.

Nemerov, Howard. *Trying Conclusions.* Chicago: U of Chicago P, 1991.

Ness, Frederic W. *The Use of Rhyme in Shakespeare's Plays.* New Haven, CT: Yale UP, 1941.

Niedecker, Lorine. *Collected Works,* ed. Jenny Penberthy. Berkeley: U of California P, 2002.

Nikitina, Tatiana, and Boris Maslov. "Verse Structure and Literary Tradition: The Interaction between Rhyme and Stress in the Onegin Stanza." *Style* 49, no. 4 (2015): 439–69.

Nims, John Frederick. "The Poetry of Sylvia Plath: A Technical Analysis." In *The Art of Sylvia Plath: A Symposium,* ed. Charles Newman, 136–52. London: Faber, 1970.

Norden, Eduard. *Die antike Kunstprosa: Vom VI Jahrhundert v. Chr. bis in Die Zeit der Renaissance.* 2 vols. Darmstadt: Wissenschaftliche Buchgesellschaft, 1958.

Nowell Smith, David. *On Voice in Poetry: The Work of Animation.* London: Palgrave Macmillan, 2015.

———. "What Is Called Rhythm?" In *Critical Rhythm: The Poetics of a Literary Life Form,* ed. Ben Glaser and Jonathan Culler, 40–59. New York: Fordham UP, 2019.

Nussbaum, Martha C. *Cultivating Humanity: A Classical Defense of Reform in Liberal Education.* Cambridge, MA: Harvard UP, 1997.

O'Donnell, Brennan. *The Passion of Meter: A Study of Wordsworth's Metrical Art.* Kent, OH: Kent State UP, 1995.

Oras, Ants. "Milton's Early Rhyme Schemes and the Structure of *Lycidas.*" *Modern Philology* 52 (1954): 12–22.

Osborn, Andrew. "Skirmishes on the Border: The Evolution and Function of Paul Muldoon's Fuzzy Rhyme." *Contemporary Literature* 41, no. 2 (2000): 323–58.

Oster, Judith. "Frost's Poetry of Metaphor." In *The Cambridge Companion to Robert Frost,* ed. Robert Faggen, 155–77. Cambridge: Cambridge UP, 2001.

Ostriker, Alicia. "Song and Speech in the Metrics of George Herbert." In *Essential Articles for the Study of George Herbert's Poetry,* ed. John H. Roberts, 298–310. Hamden, CT: Archon Books, 1979.

Pearl, Joel. *A Question of Time: Freud in the Light of Heidegger's Temporality.* Amsterdam: Rodopi, 2013.

Pendlebury, B. J. *The Art of the Rhyme.* New York: Charles Scribner's Sons, 1971.

Perloff, Marjorie. "Packed in Ice and Salt: W. B. Yeats's Paragrams." *NO: A Journal of the Arts* 1, no. 2 (2003): 189–202.

———. *Rhyme and Meaning in the Poetry of Yeats.* The Hague: Mouton, 1970.

———. "The Sound of Poetry." *PMLA* 123, no. 3 (2008): 749–61.

———. *Wittgenstein's Ladder: Poetic Language and the Strangeness of the Ordinary.* Chicago: U of Chicago P, 1996.

Perloff, Marjorie, and Craig Dworkin, eds. *The Sound of Poetry/The Poetry of Sound.* Chicago: Chicago UP, 2009.

Plath, Sylvia. *Ariel: The Restored Edition.* London: Faber, 2004.

Pope, Alexander. "An Essay on Criticism." In *The Poems of Alexander Pope,* ed. John Butt, 144–68. New Haven, CT: Yale UP, 1963.

Postman, Neil. "Five Things We Need to Know about Technological Change." Talk delivered March 28, 1998, Denver, Colorado. https://web.cs.ucdavis.edu/~rogaway/classes/188/materials/postman.pdf.

Pound, Ezra. "Affirmations: As for Imagisme." In *Selected Prose 1909–1965,* ed. William Cookson, 344–47. London: Faber, 1973.

———. *The Literary Essays of Ezra Pound,* ed. T. S. Eliot. New York: New Directions, 1968.

Puttenham, George. *The Arte of English Poesie.* Cambridge: Cambridge UP, 1970.

Ramazani, Jahan. "The Wound of History: Walcott's *Omeros* and the Postcolonial Poetics of Affliction." *PMLA* 112, no. 3 (1997): 405–17.

Ramsey, S. Robert. *The Languages of China.* Princeton, NJ: Princeton UP, 1987.

Read, Kristen. "Clues Cue the Smooze: Rhyme, Pausing, and Prediction Help Children Learn New Words from Storybooks." *Frontiers in Psychology* 5 (2014): 1–10.

Rice, Jordan. *Constellarium.* Asheville, NC: Orison, 2016.

Rich, Frank. "Will the Democrats Betray Us?" *New York Times,* September 16, 2007. http://www.nytimes.com/2007/09/16/opinion/16rich.html.

Rickey, Mary Ellen. *Rhyme and Meaning in Richard Crashaw.* U of Kentucky P, 1961.

Ricks, Christopher. "Dryden's Triplets." In *The Cambridge Companion to John Dryden,* ed. Steven N. Zwicker, 92–110. Cambridge: Cambridge UP, 2004.

———. *Dylan's Visions of Sin.* New York: Ecco, 2005.

Roethke, Theodore. *The Collected Poems of Theodore Roethke.* London: Faber, 1966.

———. *On the Poet and His Craft: Selected Prose of Theodore Roethke,* ed. Ralph J. Mills Jr. Seattle: U of Washington P, 1965.

Rollin, Lucy. *Cradle and All: A Cultural and Psychoanalytic Reading of Nursery Rhymes.* Jackson: U of Mississippi P, 1992.

Roper, Jonathan. "Introduction: Key Topics in the Study of Alliteration." In *Alliteration in Culture*, ed. Jonathan Roper, 1–19. New York: Palgrave Macmillan, 2011.

Rosenblatt, Jon. *Sylvia Plath: The Poetry of Initiation*. Chapel Hill: U of North Carolina P, 1979.

Rubin, David C. *Memory in Oral Traditions*. Oxford: Oxford UP, 1995.

Rugg, Michael D. "Event-Related Potentials and the Phonological Processing of Words and Non-Words." *Neuropsychologia* 22, no. 4 (1984): 435–43.

Ryan, Kay. *The Best of It: New and Selected Poems*. New York: Grove, 2010.

Saintsbury, George. *A History of English Prosody*. 3 vols. New York: Russell, 1961.

Saussure, Ferdinand de. *Course in General Linguistics*. Trans. Wade Baskin, ed. Perry Meisel and Haun Saussy. New York: Columbia UP, 2011.

Saussy, Haun. "The Materials of Poetry." Workshop on "Materiality," Needham Research Institute, University of Cambridge, April 2008.

———. "Repetition, Rhyme, and Exchange in the *Book of Odes*." *Harvard Journal of Asiatic Studies* 57, no. 2 (1997): 519–42.

———. "The Return of Orality." *Comparative Literature* 67, no. 3 (2015): 312–18.

Schafer, R. Murray. "The Soundscape." In *The Sound Studies Reader*, ed. Jonathan Sterne, 95–103. London: Routledge, 2012.

Scherr, Barry P. *Russian Poetry: Meter, Rhythm, and Rhyme*. Berkeley: U of California P, 1986.

Schleifer, Ronald. *Modernism and Time: The Logic of Abundance in Literature, Science, and Culture, 1880–1930*. Cambridge: Cambridge UP, 2000.

Scott, Clive. *A Question of Syllables: Essays in Nineteenth-Century French Verse*. Cambridge: Cambridge UP, 1986.

Shakespeare, William. *The Poems and the Sonnets of William Shakespeare*. Hertfordshire: Wordsworth Editions, 1994.

Shaw, J. Thomas. "Horizontal Enrichment and Rhyme Theory for Studying the Poetry of Pushkin, Batjuskov, and Baratynskij." In *Russian Verse Theory: Proceedings of the 1987 Conference at UCLA*, ed. Barry P. Scherr and Dean S. Worth, 351–76. Columbus, OH: Slavica, 1989.

———. *Pushkin's Poetics of the Unexpected: The Nonrhymed Lines in the Rhymed Poetry and the Rhymed Lines in the Nonrhymed Poetry*. Columbus, OH: Slavica, 1993.

Shklovsky, Viktor. *Shklovsky: A Reader*. Ed. and trans. Alexandra Berlina. New York: Bloomsbury, 2017.

Shusterman, Richard. "Rap Aesthetics: Violence and the Art of Keeping It Real." *Hip Hop and Philosophy*, ed. Derrick Darby and Tommie Shelby, 54–64. Chicago: Open Court, 2005.

Sidney, Sir Philip. *A Defence of Poesy,* ed. J. A. Van Dorsten. Oxford: Oxford UP, 1966.

Skelton, John. *The Complete English Poems,* ed. John Scattergood. New Haven, CT: Yale UP, 1983.

Small, Judy Jo. *Positive as Sound: Emily Dickinson's Rhyme.* Athens: U of Georgia P, 1990.

Smith, Barbara Herrnstein. *Poetic Closure: A Study of How Poems End.* Chicago: U of Chicago P, 1968.

Soldo, John J. "T. S. Eliot and Jules LaForgue." *American Literature* 55, no. 2 (1983): 137–50.

Steele, Timothy. *All the Fun's in How You Say a Thing.* Athens: Ohio UP, 1999.

Stein, Gertrude. *Geography and Plays.* New York: Something Else Press, 1968.

Steiner, Peter. *Russian Formalism: A Metapoetics.* Ithaca, NY: Cornell UP, 1984.

Sternberg, Meir. "Telling in Time (II): Chronology, Teleology, Narrativity." *Poetics Today* 13 (1992): 463–541.

Sterne, Jonathan. *The Audible Past: Cultural Origins of Sound Reproduction.* Durham, NC: Duke UP, 2003.

———, ed. *The Sound Studies Reader.* London: Routledge, 2012.

Stevens, Wallace. *The Collected Poems.* New York: Vintage, 1990.

Stewart, Garrett. *Reading Voices: Literature and the Phonotext.* Berkeley: U of California P, 1990.

Stewart, Susan. *Poetry and the Fate of the Senses.* Chicago: U of Chicago P, 2002.

———. "Rhyme and Freedom." In *The Sound of Poetry/The Poetry of Sound,* ed. Marjorie Perloff and Craig Dworkin, 29–48. Chicago: U of Chicago P, 2009.

Stone, Ruth. *In the Next Galaxy.* Port Townsend, WA: Copper Canyon Press, 2002.

Swenson, May. *The Complete Love Poems of May Swenson.* Boston: Houghton Mifflin, 2003.

Tartakovsky, Roi. "Acoustic Confusion and Medleyed Sound: Stevens' Recurrent Pairings." *The Wallace Stevens Journal* 39, no. 2 (2015): 234–49.

Todorov, Tzvetan. "Three Conceptions of Poetic Language." In *Russian Formalism: A Retrospective Glance,* ed. Robert Louis Jackson and Stephen Rudy, 130–47. New Haven, CT: Yale Center for International and Area Studies, 1985.

Trediakovskij, Vasilij. "A New and Brief Method for Composing Russian Verse." 1735. In *Russian Versification,* ed. Rimvydas Silbajoris, 36–67. New York: Columbia UP, 1968.

Treiman, Rebecca, and Catalina Danis. "Short-Term Memory Errors for Spoken Syllables Are Affected by the Linguistic Structure of the Syllables." *Journal of Experimental Psychology* 14, no. 1 (1988): 145–52.

Trilling, Lionel. "The Immortality Ode." In *The Liberal Imagination,* 129–59. London: Secker and Warburg, 1951.

Tsur, Reuven. *Toward a Theory of Cognitive Poetics.* Amsterdam: North Holland, 1992.

———. *What Makes Sound Patterns Expressive? The Poetic Mode of Speech Perception.* Durham, NC: Duke UP, 1992.

Tucker, Nicholas. "Lullabies and Child Care: A Historical Perspective." In *Opening Texts: Psychoanalysis and the Culture of the Child,* ed. Joseph H. Smith and William Kerrigan, 17–27. Baltimore: Johns Hopkins UP, 1985.

Turco, Lewis. *The Book of Forms: A Handbook of Poetics.* 3rd ed. Lebanon, NH: UP of New England, 2000.

Tynianov, Yuri. *The Problem of Verse Language,* ed. and trans. Michael Sosa and Brent Harvey. Ann Arbor: Ardis, 1981.

Van der Kolk, Bessel A., and Onno van der Hart. "The Intrusive Past: The Flexibility of Memory and the Engraving of Trauma." In *Trauma: Explorations in Memory,* ed. Cathy Caruth, 158–82. Baltimore: Johns Hopkins UP, 1995.

Van Vleck, Amelia E. *Memory and Re-Creation in Troubadour Lyric.* Berkeley: U of California P, 1991.

Vendler, Helen. *The Breaking of Style.* Cambridge: Harvard UP, 1995.

———. *Wallace Stevens: Words Chosen Out of Desire.* Cambridge: Harvard UP, 1984.

Wagensveld, Barbara, Petra van Alphen, Eliane Segers, and Ludo Verhoeven. "The Nature of Rhyme Processing in Preliterate Children." *British Journal of Educational Psychology* 82 (2012): 672–89.

Wagensveld, Barbara, Petra van Alphen, Eliane Segers, Peter Hagoort, and Ludo Verhoeven. "The Neural Correlates of Rhyme Awareness in Preliterate and Literate Children." *Clinical Neurophysiology* 124 (2013): 1336–45.

Wakoski, Diane. "The New Conservatism in American Poetry." *American Book Review* 8 (May–June 1986): 3.

Walker, John. *The Rhyming Dictionary of the English Language,* rev. ed., ed. J. Longmuir. London: George Routledge and Sons. https://www.google.com/books/edition/The_Rhyming_Dictionary_of_the_English_La/Tck_AAAAcAAJ?hl=en&gbpv=1.

Waugh, Linda. "Against Arbitrariness: Imitation and Motivation Revived, with Consequences for Textual Meaning." *Diacritics* 23, no. 2 (1993): 71–87.

———. "Marked and Unmarked: A Choice Between Unequals in Semiotic Structure." *Semiotica* 38, no. 3–4 (1982): 299–318.

Weiskott, Eric. *English Alliterative Verse: Poetic Tradition and Literary History.* Cambridge: Cambridge UP, 2016.

Wellek, René, and Austin Warren. *Theory of Literature.* Harmondsworth: Penguin, 1963.

Welsford, Enid. *Spenser: Fowre Hymnes, Epithalamion—A Study of Edmund Spenser's Doctrine of Love.* Oxford: Basil Blackwell, 1967.

Welsh, Andrew. *Roots of the Lyric.* Princeton, NJ: Princeton UP, 1978.

Wesling, Donald. *The Chances of Rhyme: Device and Modernity.* Berkeley: U of California P, 1980.

———. *Joys and Sorrows of Imaginary Persons: On Literary Emotions.* Amsterdam: Brill Academic Publishers, 2008.

Whitehall, Harold. "Rhyme: Sources and Diffusion." *Ibadan* 25 (1968): 21-26.

Whitman, Walt. *Leaves of Grass.* 1855. In *The Walt Whitman Archive,* ed. Ed Folsom and Kenneth M. Price. http://www.whitmanarchive.org.

Wilde, Oscar. *Complete Poetry,* ed. Isobel Murray. Oxford: Oxford UP, 1998.

———. "The Critic as Artist, Part 1." In *The Writings of Oscar Wilde,* ed. Isobel Murray, 241-66. Oxford: Oxford UP, 1989.

Williams, William Carlos. *I Wanted to Write a Poem: The Autobiography of the Works of the Poet.* London: Jonathan Cape, 1967.

Wimsatt, William K., Jr. "One Relation of Rhyme to Reason." In *The Verbal Icon,* 153-66. Lexington: U of Kentucky P, 1967.

Winnicott, D. W. "Hate in the Countertransference." In *Collected Papers: Through Paediatrics to Psycho-Analysis,* 194-203. London: Tavistock, 1958.

Wordsworth, William. *The Poems,* ed. John O. Hayden. Vol. 1. New Haven: Yale UP, 1972.

———. "Preface to the Second Edition of *Lyrical Ballads.*" 1800. In *Selected Poems and Prefaces,* ed. Jack Stillinger, 445-64. Boston: Houghton Mifflin, 1965.

Worth, Dean S. "On Eighteenth-Century Russian Rhyme." *Russian Literature* 2, no. 1 (1972): 47-74.

———. "Roman Jakobson and the Study of Rhyme." In *Roman Jakobson: Echoes of His Scholarship,* ed. Daniel Armstrong and C. H. Van Schooneveld, 515-33. Lisse: Peter De Ridder, 1977.

Yeats, William Butler. *The Collected Poems of W. B. Yeats,* ed. Richard J. Finneran. New York: Scribner Paperback Poetry, 1996.

Yoon, Yeo Bom, and Bruce L. Derwing. "A Language without a Rhyme: Syllable Structure Experiments in Korean." *Canadian Journal of Linguistics* 46, no. 3/4 (2001): 187-237.

Zhirmunsky, Viktor. "Introduction to *Rhyme: Its History and Theory,*" trans. John Hoffmann. *Chicago Review* 57, no. 3/4 (2013): 121-28.

index

Printed in the USA
CPSIA information can be obtained
at www.ICGtesting.com
LVHW090934090324
774033LV00002B/9